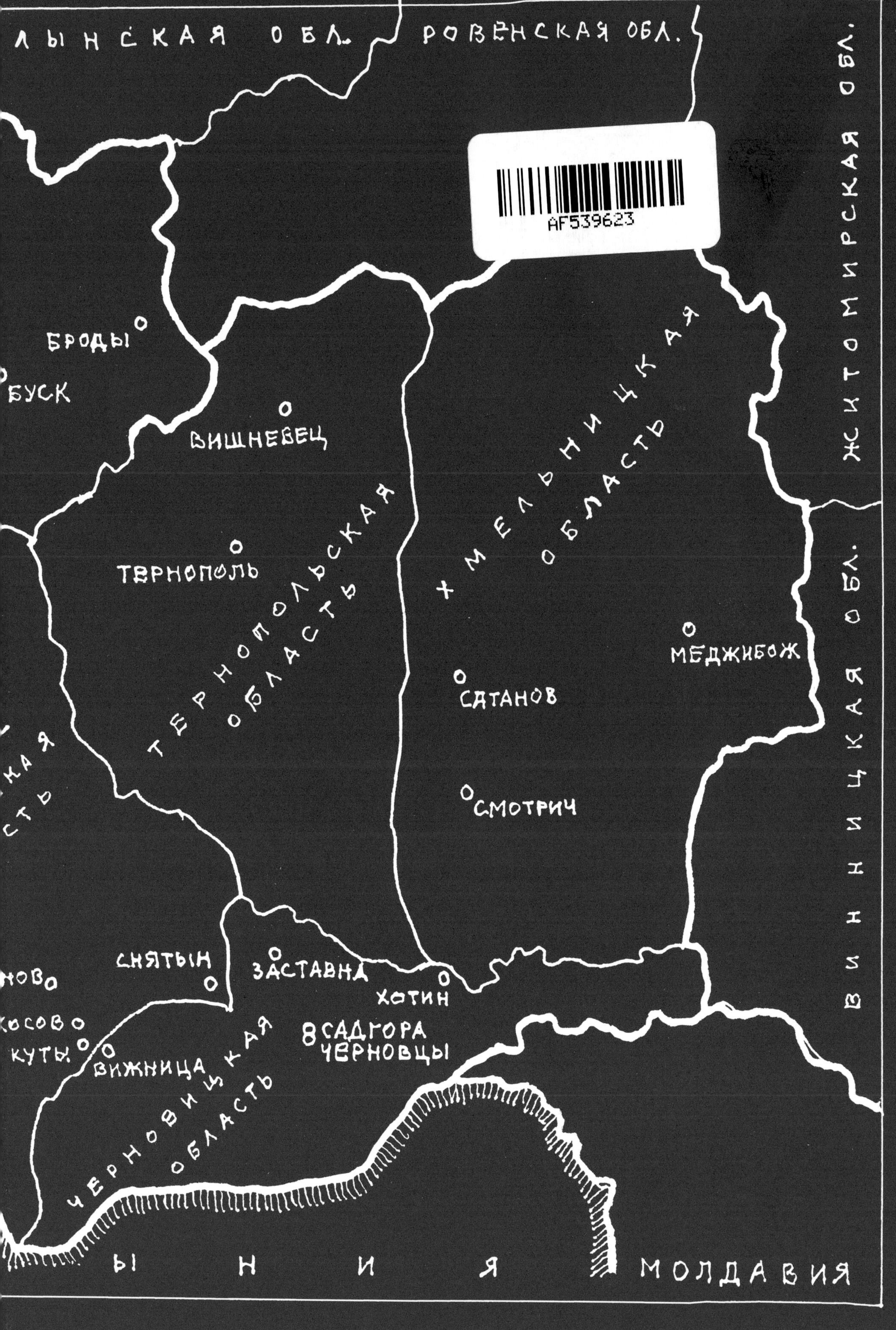
ЛЫНСКАЯ ОБЛ.
РОВЕНСКАЯ ОБЛ.
ЖИТОМИРСКАЯ ОБЛ.
БРОДЫ
БУСК
ВИШНЕВЕЦ
ТЕРНОПОЛЬ
ТЕРНОПОЛЬСКАЯ ОБЛАСТЬ
ХМЕЛЬНИЦКАЯ ОБЛАСТЬ
МЕДЖИБОЖ
САТАНОВ
СМОТРИЧ
ВИННИЦКАЯ ОБЛ.
КАЯ
СТЬ
СНЯТЫН
ЗАСТАВНА
ХОТИН
НОВО
ОСОВО
КУТЫ
ВИЖНИЦА
САДГОРА
ЧЕРНОВЦЫ
ЧЕРНОВИЦКАЯ ОБЛАСТЬ
Ы Н И Я
МОЛДАВИЯ

Carved Memories
Heritage in Stone from the Russian Jewish Pale

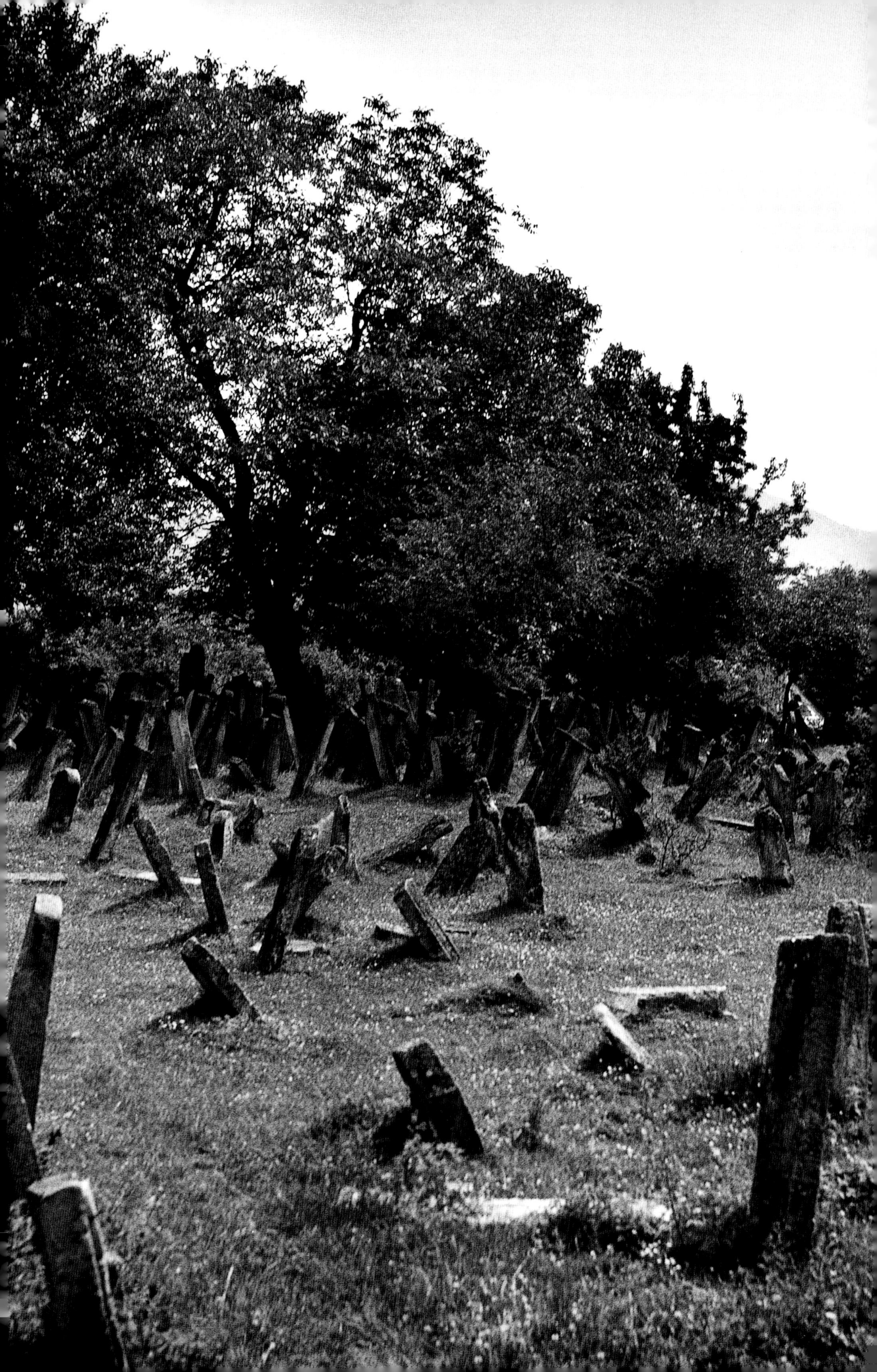

CARVED MEMORIES

Heritage in Stone from the Russian Jewish Pale

DAVID GOBERMAN

Introduction by
ROBERT PINSKY

Essay by
GERSHON HUNDERT

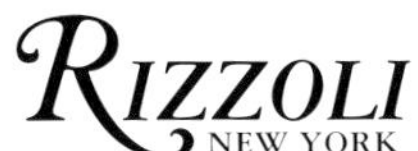

First published in the United States of America in 2000 by
Rizzoli International Publications, Inc.
300 Park Avenue South
New York, NY 10010

ISBN: 0-8478-2256-7
LC: 99-75835

Front Cover: Chernovtsy. Between 1850 and 1900.
The hand of God severing a flower, a reference to the Song of Songs: "God's hand went down and plucked a flower."
Frontispiece: Kuty Cemetery.

Project Development:
Anne Sommerfeld Halliwell
Kenneth A. Pushkin

Edited by Christopher Lyon
Designed by Kathleen Oginski
Maps by Sven M. Dolling
Printed in Italy

Contents

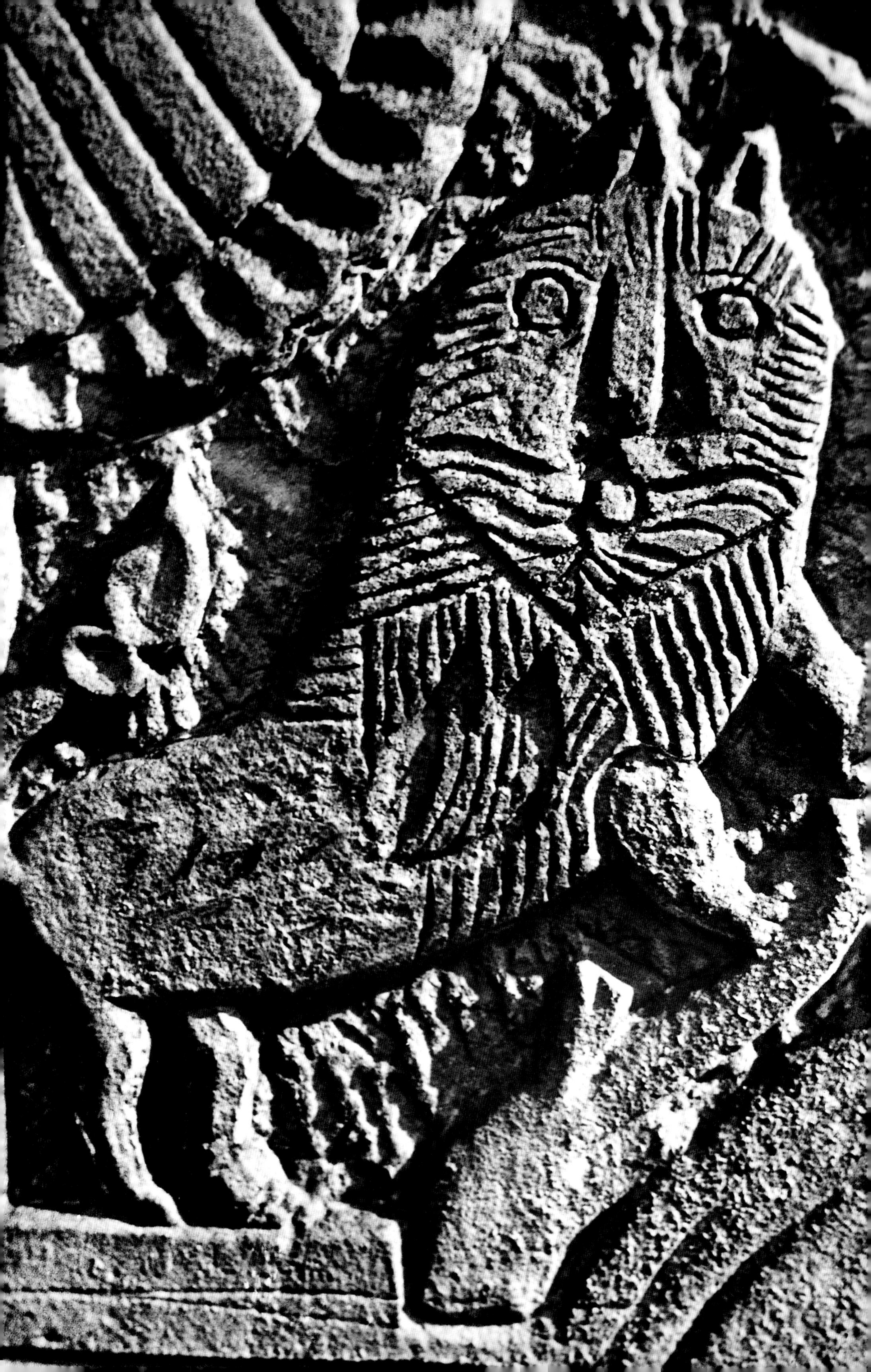

ROBERT PINSKY

Instruments of Memory

Two instruments of memory, photography and stone: each gesturing toward eternity, the gesture that always becomes elegiac. Our effort to preserve a moment of light or the momentum of tools incising character or image, to extend some particle or surface beyond the iron boundary between *is* and *was*, emphasizes in each medium the pathos of our desire for infinite memory.

In the stunning photographs of David Goberman, the silence of light on emulsion, the silence of rock, become the terrible, eternal silence of a murdered world.

It has been said that photography, shaving time into fractions of a second, with a quick slice of the shutter isolates the moment into its own funerary marker, the changing element of light unchanged, while what is depicted changes. And carved stone, with its wide gulp of time, records how its memorial marks and symbols are weathered or crumbled away by the elements—by air moving, by water dripping and freezing and melting and earth shifting.

But the light striking the grain of these stones reveals for us the historical as well as the elemental processes of loss. The silence of light and the silence of stone defer to the articulate imagination of the European Jews who designed and commissioned and carved and tended these stones, markers that now memorialize more than their original intention: the death of a world.

Revenant in Goberman's work, the world returns in images: flowers, tools, menorahs, geometrical shapes in relief like a cloth draped over the background stone; an elegant deer amid leaves and ferns, looking over its shoulder as if in calm retrospect at life in nature; a charmingly dynamic lion gazing at the viewer with insouciance, its forepaws on a branch, its tail breaking the enclosing frame, the cat afloat yet solid, an anticipation of Marc Chagall; hands; peacocks; and above all the flamelike Hebrew characters that are images and runes. This world so intensely populated in stone, then repopulated in light by the photographer, indicates the variety and infinite mystery of a mortal, violated abundance.

Beltsy. 1800s.
A catlike lion rampant, with forepaws against a branch.

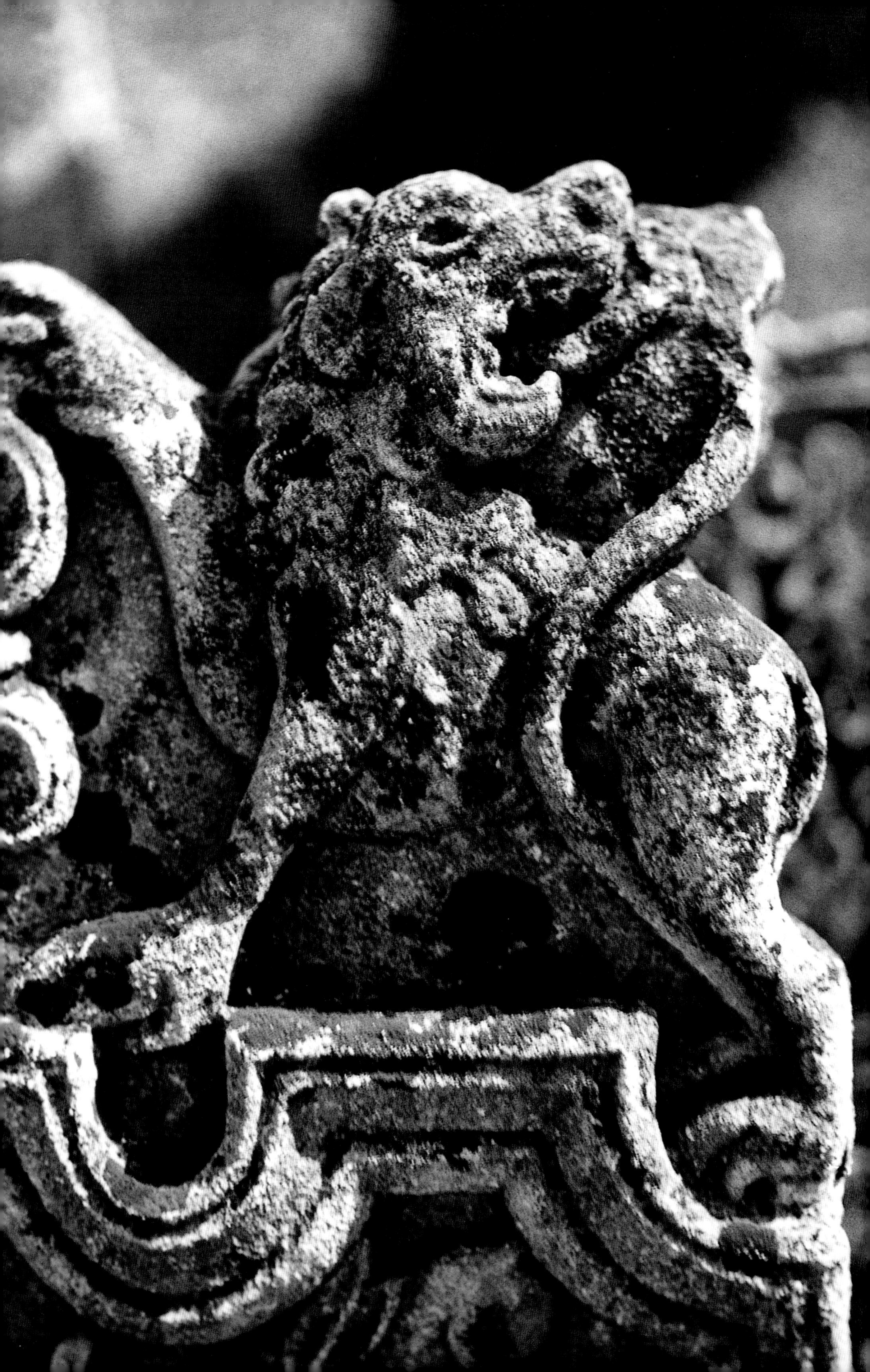

DAVID GOBERMAN

Jewish Tombstones

Carved tombstones are one of the most notable expressions of traditional Jewish art. This form of artistic creativity belongs to the past: examples are found throughout the Diaspora, and it attained a particularly high level of development in the Pale of Czarist Russia and in Galicia. The gravestones of Ukraine and Moldova, two regions formerly within the Pale and now independent countries, are especially noteworthy for their decorative quality and inventive figurative design. This book explores the art of carved stone in these regions.

In the places where Jews had lived longest in the Pale, there existed for centuries, on the borders of cities and towns, cemeteries in which tombstones were honored as though they were sacred relics. At the beginning of this century, some of them were three and four hundred years of age, or even older. Only a small number of the monuments have come down to us. During the Nazi occupation, as hundreds of synagogues perished, cemeteries that held the priceless creativity of the stone carvers were destroyed along with manuscripts and ancient books, and precious objects in carved wood, metal, and fabric. Even those cemeteries that survived were subject to methodical destruction by local administrations, sanctioned by the official atheism of the communist state and by a populace intolerant of religious feelings. As a result, in many places where stones covered with carving once crowded together over graves, there is today a wasteland. Only an occasional protruding remnant or a few broken and tilted slabs may remain. The destruction of graveyards that happen to be in areas of economic development continues. Old stones are disappearing under an onslaught of new burials; occasionally, ancient carving can be discovered amidst the most recent graves.

A visit to an old graveyard inevitably evokes feeling of a receding past. The impression is unforgettable. The stones stand in thinning rows, moss-covered, their bases coming out of the ground. Some remain erect, but more often they tilt, leaning toward the ground. Approached from a distance they seem mysterious and severe, but as one nears, they open up as the unexpected forms of carving come into view. When the oblique rays of the sun skip across a shallow relief, the intricate writing, designs, and ornamentation spring to life.

Sniatyn. Late 1800s. Roaring lion.

Scholarly interest in Jewish tombstones began in the second half of the nineteenth century. From the beginning it was very one-sided, and the constraints of historical research limited the scope of investigations. Various cemeteries were discussed in articles and monographs that included analyses of numerous tombstone texts, especially epitaphs of the *tsadikim*, or holy ones, and other famous individuals. Scholars were attracted to the content of the texts, uncovering biblical references and often finding intriguing abbreviations of Hebrew. However, they showed no evident interest in the carving. As works of art, reliefs on tombstones were not considered noteworthy, an indifference due to the bias against folk art or, as it was called then, "simple folk" art.

In the early twentieth century, a serious interest in tombstones as an expression of artistic creativity began to emerge. The major focus was on the stones of the Prague cemetery, already recognized as a part of the Czech people's historical and artistic legacy, and a subject featured in many photography books. The tombstones of Poland also were researched. Many well-known artists, impressed by the power of the imagery of these creations, contributed to the growing interest in Jewish tombstone sculptural relief. An aesthetic understanding of the carved stones is apparent in the work of S. B. Yudovin (1892–1954), who recorded the stones in many sketches and occasionally made expressive wood engravings on the themes depicted by the carved reliefs. In these engravings a fine decorative sensibility is employed in the symbolic interpretation of the reliefs. The subjects of the carved stones are reflected in the work of N. I. Altman (1889–1970) and images of the stones appear in the works of A. L. Kaplan (1903–1980).

From the late 1930s on in Belarus, and beginning just after the war in the cemeteries of Ukraine and Moldova, the author collected hundreds of photographs and drawings of stones. The result is a fixed record of objects that have significantly deteriorated since that time or may no longer exist. The core of the present work is specifically drawn from this collection, which preserves a record of the monuments of Sniatyn, Kosov, Sadgora, Sambor, Kishinev, Orgeyev, Beltsy, and other places. Many of the stones pictured are, or were, genuine masterpieces of carved stone art.

Ancient examples of carved Jewish burial stones are known. Thin slabs with the simplest of designs, from the first century of the Common Era, have been found

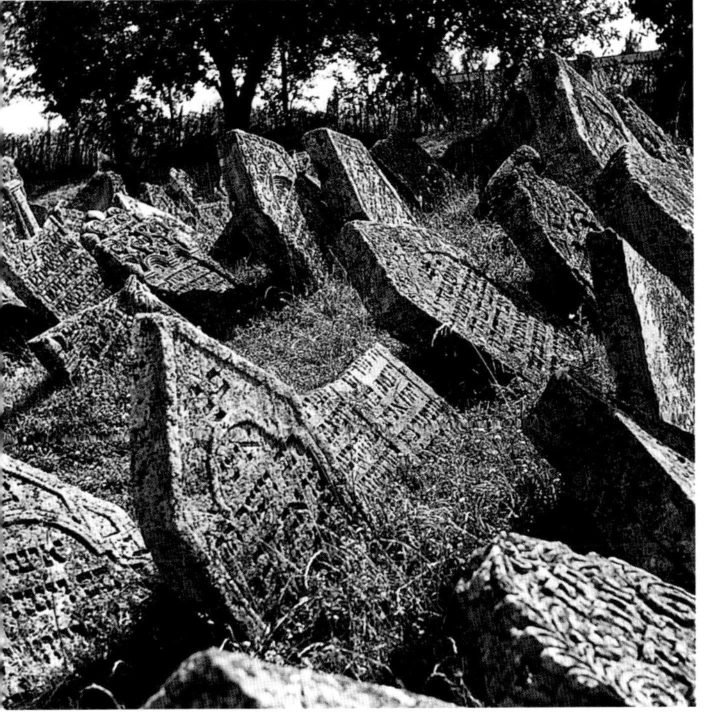

Sniatyn cemetery.

in Galilee; stones from Egypt with Greek inscriptions have been dated to the third decade of the first century. Markers of the same period from Jewish catacombs in Italy and Spain have been preserved. The chronology of the gravestones that have been studied reflects the migration of Jews in Europe. Thus, the oldest monuments in France date from the seventh century and were found in brickwork and the walls of medieval structures. The earliest stones in the Prague cemetery date from the tenth century and the oldest in Germany from the eleventh. The oldest in Ukraine were found in the no longer extant Lvov cemetery, which is first mentioned in documents dating from 1414. It is important to note that the ancient monuments of the Crimea may belong to the Jewish-Karaite culture, which followed its own path of development. In the sanctuary cemetery in Chufut-Kale, near Kerch, there are stones dating from the seventh century and possibly much earlier, though the dates are debatable, given the poor condition of the stones.

The vertical stone slab is the basic type of Jewish tombstone (*matsevah*) but we should note that there is considerable diversity. It is common to see a stone together with a sarcophagus, an aboveground box with a top that may be either flat or sloped, with two to three pitches. In places rich in limestone, a cheap and easily cut material, the sarcophagus and the tombstone will be carved from a single piece of stone. Over the graves of some distinguished rabbis and Hasidic leaders (rebbes), which were places of pilgrimage for the observant, tent-like structures (*ohel*) were built, either with a canopy on pillars or left open. Tombstones themselves had various configurations. The vertical slab might be a simple rectangle; the corners might be cut, or there might be decorative elements defining the form: circles, corners with two pitches, and other more complicated shapes. The face of the stone typically has an epitaph and a design in relief, which is rarely carried over onto the back of the stone. In general, stones face eastward, but their orientation was not especially significant, and if the terrain were not suitable, it wouldn't matter. In poor communities, the cemetery would be located on the land that was least suitable for cultivation or development, and therefore inexpensive.

In the Diaspora, the basic form of tombstones remained unchanged, with their original simplicity preserved over the centuries. In their stone inscriptions and simple cut patterns, the stones carried the spirit of the ancient East, which provided the artistic foundation of this art. For centuries the figurative design elements remained consistent, and the visual impact of the stones was severe and ascetic. Finally, however, the weakening of medieval prohibitions and the influence of the Renaissance opened the way toward a freer formal treatment and more elaborate decoration. Influenced by art of the countries in which Jews lived and by current religious and social trends, the stones acquired new features and became objects of artistic experimentation.

A type of stone developed that had a portal (*shaar*) with a slightly recessed niche for text and strips along the side that complete the design. Some associate the niche on the tombstone with the gates of Heaven, seeing in it a messianic symbol. At the same time, the portal reflects a universal architectural form, which gives each design a firm artistic foundation. In the sixteenth century many stones in the countries of the Jewish Diaspora featured an arched portal and other elements of Renaissance architecture. Later, Baroque influence enriched the cuttings with strong relief, which created a contrasting play of light and shadows. A great variety of little columns, volutes, and broken pediments appeared. In Eastern Europe, images appeared that were taken from the rituals of specific sects and from everyday life.

Social content can be read in every aspect of the stone monuments: their cutting, subject matter, methods of execution, and the degree of complexity. Naturally, the more complicated, labor-intensive works are monuments to people of substance. Such stones are larger than normal, and are more elaborately decorated. We should remember, however, that the number of these exceptional stones is proportionately small. Most stones have extraordinarily modest decoration and are artisan in nature.

Jewish tombstones are considered sacred. They manifest the eternal essence of the spirit of the deceased, and every activity related to the stones is ritualized. The tombstone would be erected a year after the death of an individual. In the course of that year, the elders of the family would keep alive the memory of the deceased. Visiting the cemetery, they would look at the existing tombstones and discuss ideas for the stone's design and text with the master cutter. In Moldova, there was a tradition that the epitaph be carved by the son. Sometimes this was the wish of the deceased, but in other cases it may simply have been that the family could not afford a professional stone carver. Such stones, sometimes decorated with designs, were done without skill, but were still valued by the family as the son's tribute to the memory of his parents. Tombstones weren't erected only to people. Sacred books or scrolls might be buried. There are tombstones that mark the resting-places of Torah scrolls buried after being desecrated in pogroms.

The oldest known tombstones in the Ukraine date from the sixteenth century. In the photo archives of the Lvov Museum of Ethnography and Crafts in Ukraine, there are records of stones from 1547 and 1575 in the Lvov and Ternopol cemeteries (neither of which now exist). Of the preserved tombstones from the sixteenth century, there are several from Satanov, the oldest of which dates from 1576, and a stone from 1556 in Medzhibozh. The stones from Orgeyev are among the earliest in Moldova. One of them, from 1640, is on display in the Kishinev National Museum of the Jews of Moldova. These very old, rather thick stones, with modest framing and the simplest straight or two-pitched tops, have a striking monumentality. They evoke a strong feeling of time and thoughts of the power and immortality of the human spirit.

The development of the art of carved tombstones can be seen as a movement from simple to more complex forms. Already in the stones of the sixteenth century, one can see attempts to introduce decoration, accenting the area above the text on the stone with the simplest ornamental themes and abbreviations of Hebrew script. The gravestones of the seventeenth century witness the rapidly growing interest of stonecutters in ornamentation and, more importantly, in designs that reflect the regional character of the art. The epitaph is more frequently accompanied by figurative imagery. In the first half of the century, symbols of religious castes are introduced: the praying hands of the Cohanim and the pitcher or bowls of the Levites, servants of the temple. Timeless symbols such as the tree of life, the menorah, a cluster of grapes, and animals and birds, which appear on ancient Jewish carved stone as demure sketches, now are done with fine artistic sensibility. Carved designs and subject matter continue to occupy more and more space on the stones, displacing the text, which in any case was always rather brief.

Artistry and thoughtfulness are the major characteristics of the stones of the nineteenth and early twentieth centuries. The restriction of Jews to the Western provinces of the Russian empire, the so-called "Pale of Settlement," created the largest concentration of Jews in Bessarabia, Galicia, and the Carpathians. In that region there emerged a unique culture of stone carving, not found outside the boundaries of the area. Traditional in its basics, it discovered new lines of creative development, tied to the life of the people. For ordinary people—needy, subjected to religious oppression, but brought up in the spirit of tolerance and hope for their religion—the gravestone was a binding link between the living and the dead, between the real world and the hereafter. Cemeteries became places of pilgrimage, where people would pray by the graves of relatives for protection and for a better life.

During this period, the designs of the gravestones became more individualized. Each had to be different from its neighbors and easily recognized among the many stones. This resulted in a drive for originality, a fear of repetition, reflected in the stones. In the design of the stones one increasingly sees the expression of the personal traits of the deceased, his or her family, religious orientation, sex, and age. Biblical subjects and images of animals associated with the name on the stone appear. Personal signs, indications of profession and spiritual worth, as well as allegories reflecting popular concepts of life and death can be found. Gravestones are covered with images of animals, birds, plants, objects of everyday life, craft objects, and art designs. And all the above appear in diverse variations.

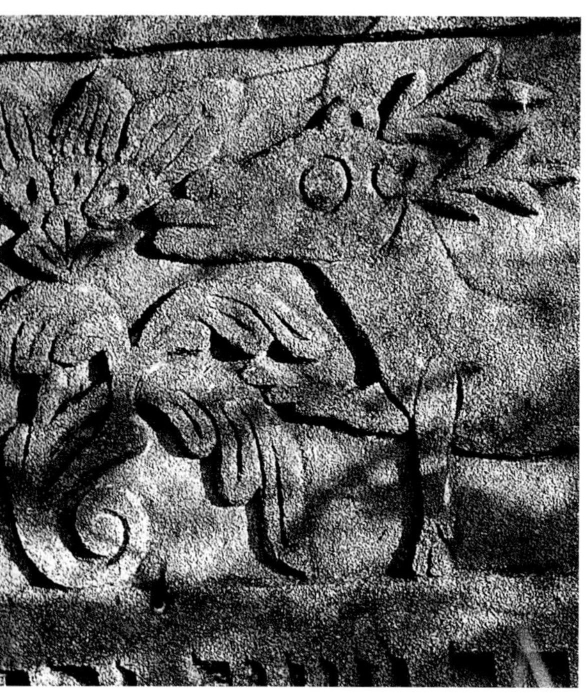

Carved stone is tied stylistically and by content to other forms of popular art, and the mutual influence of each cannot be doubted. The connection

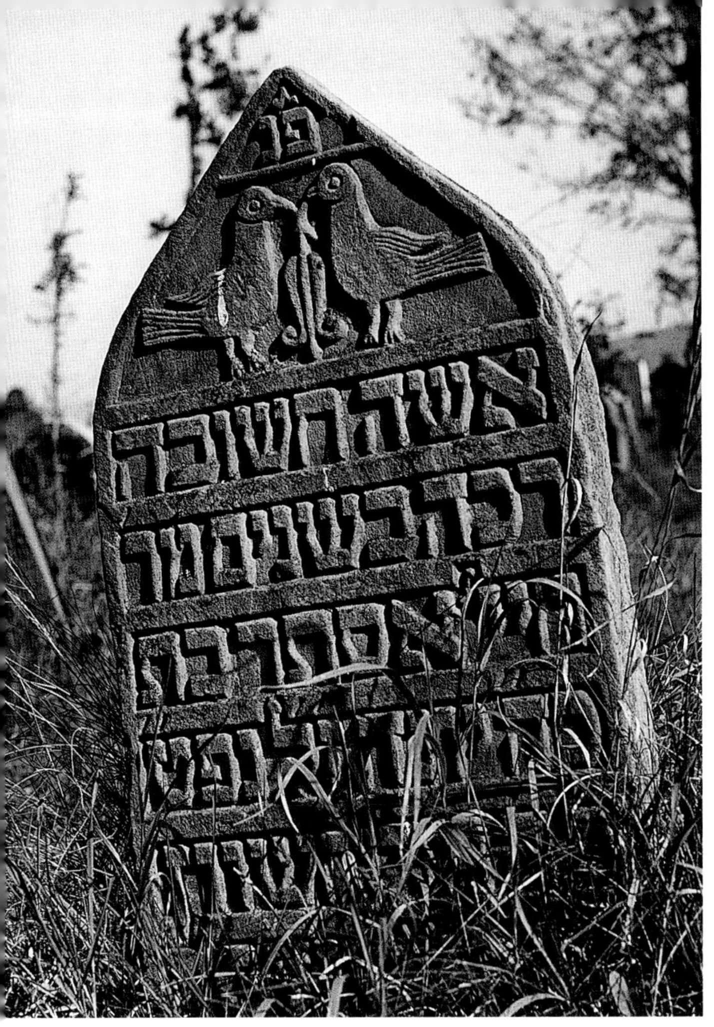

Uzhgorod. 1870s.
Two birds and a flower. The stone is representative of the inscribed epitaph, as opposed to the relief carving that is alternatively seen on stones. A Torah passage condemns inscriptions on monuments as a distraction from sacred writings, especially the Torah. Raised relief epitaphs were accepted, however, as being outside the prohibition.
A worthy woman Chaya Esther. Young [literally, "soft"] in years, a bitter life. In memory for a blessing.

Opposite:
Khotin. Between 1850 and 1900.
A stag tasting a leaf or fruit.
A pure and honest man. Elisha, son of Israel.

between art motifs of the stones and other traditional kinds of art is also evident. It is easy to see the similarity between certain carvings and Passover engravings in the Haggadah, decorative elements of illuminated marriage contracts (*ketubbot*), or cut paper wall decorations, known as *mizrah* or *shiviti*, which are hung on walls facing Jerusalem. The art of the synagogue has a lot in common with tombstone art: drawings on the walls and ceilings of the temple, the carved wooden doors of the *aron Kodesh*, golden embroidery of its curtains (*parochet*), the fine metal designs for chandeliers and for the plates, tops, and crown (*tass, rimonim, keter Torah*) of Torah scrolls, as well as the decorative art of domestic ritual objects—Hannukah light fixtures (*channukkia*), chests for incense (*besamim*), Passover items, and the like.

Carved stone was not isolated from other kinds of Jewish art, nor from the art of nations in which the stone carvers lived. There was mutual influence. The cross-fertilization of Jewish and Christian gravestone design is especially evident in Kishinev, Moldova, where stonecutters clearly had a strong awareness of their counterparts' work. We find the fruits of cross-cultural influence in Kosov, where well-known Ukrainian potters in the second half of the nineteenth century expressed their interest in local Jewish gravestones through designs on tiles and dishes. In the same period in Sadgora and other places, Jewish relief cutting gives rise to similar images in Ukrainian art and in Russian national art. This sort of borrowing enriched carved stone art and played a very evident role in the midst of a diverse set of sources. Everything that came from outside found its own graphic expression; it was transformed as it became part of a new expression in a new material. Elements of high art that were assimilated were simplified under the chisel, receiving a new folk-like quality.

Gravestones owe their diversity to an abundance of creative "schools." Stonecutting, as is well known, was a hereditary craft, passing from father to son. This helped strengthen family traditions and the cultivation of favorite forms, which gave each cemetery its own distinct image. At the same time, this process, which lasted for generations, was not stable, and grew with explosions of fresh creative talent. Innovations of one individual could define a whole group of gravestones or, in the case of a powerful creative style, shape an entire stream of creative design.

Almost every cemetery offers examples of one cutter who produces variations on a theme, each making more demands on the master's talent than the previous one. Thus in Sniatyn, at the end of the eighteenth and beginning of the nineteenth centuries, complex Baroque compositions often are completed with three-dimensional animal images. A group of Kuty stones from the 1870s, done by masters named Raizer, improvise on themes of reclining deer and lions surrounded by interwoven plants. In Chernovtsy, where the last representatives of the Tseller dynasty still worked in the pre–World War I years, the image of a bookcase with the books of the Bible under mighty lions appeared in many variations in the last quarter of the nineteenth century. Khotin monuments are distinguished by their asymmetry of design and the fine decorative work of the vegetation, as well as by interwoven animals and birds. The Mukachevo and Beregovo stones feature variations on the theme of a lion in his "eternal home." Some of the later stones of the Orgeyev cemetery are noteworthy for ornamental compositions created from simple geometric forms that are close to the script design, contributing to a unified artistic structure. Images from the deceased's profession are seen more frequently in the Kishinev cemetery than anywhere else. Kishinev also has an attractive set of 1860s stones with theater-like Baroque decorations of garlands and drapes.

By the turn of the twentieth century, Jewish carved stone art was, like other folk art of that era, in decline. The themes have less content, and the designs become dry and less expressive. The laconic tone in the images gives way to coarseness, traditionalism to a haphazard approach. Master stonecutters now have templates that bring a deadening monotony to the stones. Gravestones are replaced by monuments of various forms, including obelisks and pylons, in which the popular language is lost and stylistic chaos reigns. Great traditional art is forgotten.

The gravestone reliefs open up a rich complex of artistic imagery. Understanding these reliefs provides a unique and extraordinarily interesting perspective on popular artistic tradition. We need to remember that the development of Jewish art was constrained by the widespread acceptance of the famous Biblical prohibi-

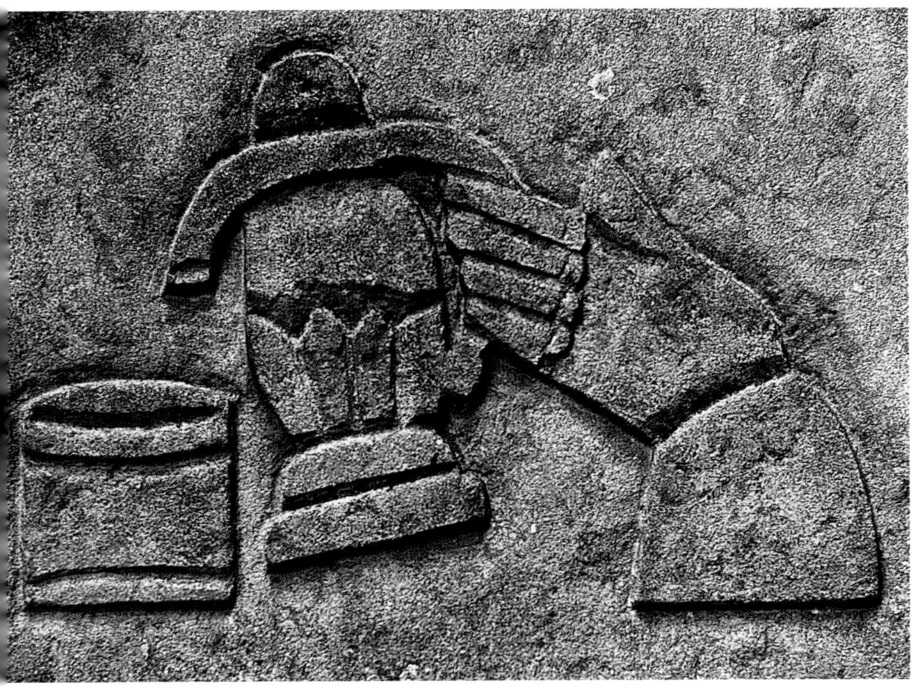

Chernovtsy. Late 1800s. A Levite with a pitcher and a bowl or basin.

tion against the depiction of the animal world, so that such images would not, like the golden calf, become an object of veneration. In reality, such imagery existed in Jewish art from ancient times. For example, in the mosaics of synagogues in Israel dating from the beginning of the Common Era, humans are portrayed along with animals. Later the same imagery appears in other kinds of creative work.

Human images are extremely rare on the gravestones. In those situations where a human being is represented, the artist will show, instead of the whole figure, only an arm, the part in place of the whole, or the carver will substitute an animal or a bird for a human image. Thus a jug (symbol of the Levites) is usually held by a hand, sometimes by a lion. There is a common composition of a lion cub bound on the sacrificial altar, a reference to the Biblical story of Isaac being offered up as a sacrifice by his father in a test of his faith in God. In these cases, the deceased's name is Isaac. The biblical tale of the scouts returning to the encampment in the desert with joyous news of the land of milk and honey they have found in Canaan is portrayed as two bears carrying the legendary cluster of grapes. Human virtues are represented by images of the animal world: the deceased could be portrayed as a bird reading a book, or giving a coin for charity, or feeding a baby bird. The emotional impact of these images is made more powerful by the poetic folk rendering.

Some themes are tied to religious symbolism. The most important theme is the menorah, or candelabra, which is usually depicted as having seven branches, though some have up to nine, and some fewer than seven. On the stones, the menorah is a symbol of female virtue, expressed in a complicated design that depicts the ritual of Sabbath candle lighting. On a young girl's grave one might see a single—sometimes broken—candlestick. The hands of a woman often accompany the menorah, the fingers locked in prayer.

Graves of Cohains or priests (*kohanim*), descendants of the priestly caste, are signified by the symbol of blessing hands with divided fingers. The symbol of a Levite is the jug, since it was the duty of Levites in the Temple to wash the hands of the priests. Crowns are used to convey various meanings: the crown of Study of Torah (*keter torah*); the crowns on the Torah scrolls signifying a scholar; or the crown of priesthood (*keter kehuna*) over the blessing hands of the priest. For a highly regarded individual, the epitaph may speak of the "crown of a good name" (*keter shem tov*).*

Animal images impart meaning as well. The famous Talmudic saying, "Be as courageous as a leopard, as light as an eagle, as fast as a deer, and as strong as a lion to do the will of your Father in Heaven" (Mishnah, Avot 5:23), was a rich source for the artist's imagination, with each image providing a means for expressing a quality of the deceased. These animals, together with the griffin, unicorn, and several others, become like genies guarding the sacred place. Sculpted in pairs, such figures may flank the menorah, the ark of the Torah, a bookshelf holding the five books of the Torah and the six books of the Mishnah, or a host of other symbols, underscoring their symbolic importance.

The image of a fallow deer is a reference to beauty and goodness. Praised in the Song of Songs, it symbolizes love and could decorate the grave of a girl or young woman. The image of the unicorn is also interesting, since it has several interpretations. One is that this mythical creature lives high in the mountains and is an embodiment of the loftiness of the human spirit. More difficult to interpret is the symbol of two unicorns, or a unicorn fighting with a lion (with its horn in the lion's throat). Such images may be associated with messianism and life after death. The dream of eternal bliss amid the incredible beauty of Paradise is captured in the image of a peacock. The coiled "king of the sea," the leviathan (*liviatan*), together with the wild ox (*shor habar*), both intended for the heavenly table, should remind the faithful of the blessings of the messianic future. Two fish symbolize the month of Adar, the month in which the Messiah is supposed to appear.

These designs, captured in stone, provided an opportunity for innumerable improvisations. Over the course of time, mystical themes give way to real, human ones. If one follows the development of artistic symbolism from the second half

* Mishnah, Avot 4:17: "There are three crowns: the crown of Torah, the crown of priesthood, and the crown of royalty, but the crown of a good name excels them all."

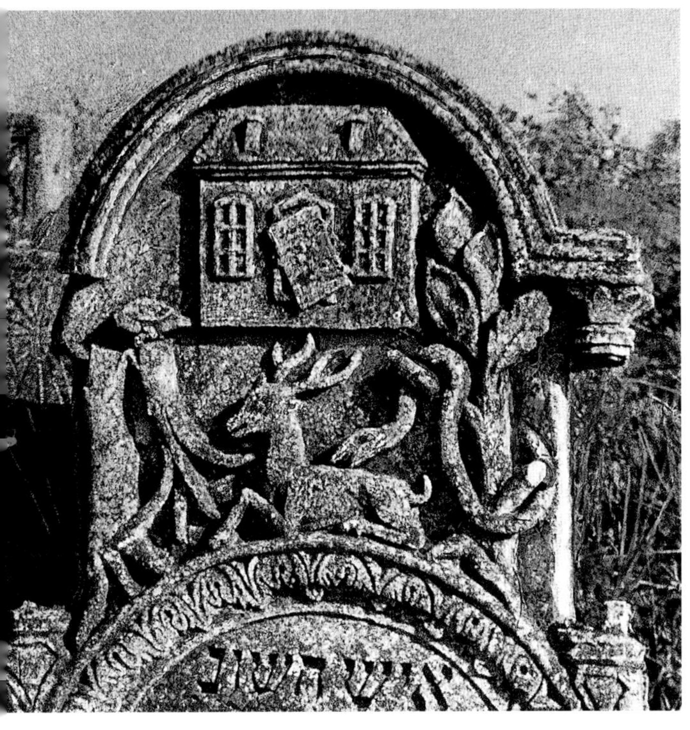

Kishinev. 1867.
An abandoned house (the door hanging by one hinge), a broken tree, and a deer being bitten by a snake.
Yakov, son of Naftali. An important person.

of the eighteenth century through the nineteenth, it is very interesting to see how the interpretation of motifs expands and becomes freer of symbolic content and more literal, how the artist's ideas are formed, and how ideas are executed. Thus, the symbolic meaning of a lion is reduced over time to simply representing the name Lev (in Hebrew, Aryeh or Judah). In the same way, the deer and the bear can signify the names Zvi (or Hirsch) and Dov, a fish the man's name Fishel, or birds the female name Feigl. The trend toward finding an artistic equivalent for a name led to perplexing situations in some of the later stones. A. Levi, researching Jewish gravestones in Poland, recalled a stone with the family name "Gut," which featured an image of a hat flanked by lions. There was a simple solution, however: "Gut" is pronounced like *Hut*, the Yiddish word for "hat." The image of a fish on the grave of a drowned person has an obvious meaning—but though it may seem superficial, one is disarmed by the simple spirituality of the image.

The stonecutter did not stop at simply illustrating something as external as a name. He might depict an animal pierced by an arrow, combining the symbol of the name with the thought of death. The stone of a girl named "Feigl" shows a bird flying away, allegorically portraying her life leaving her. The monument of a man named Hirsch shows a deer being bitten by a snake. Giving priority to his idea, the master does not simply render the animal tied to a name, but turns it into an independent symbol. Different subjects are used to convey the core idea; a broken tree, a smashed boat, a flower falling from a stem, an empty house, its door hanging from one hinge, turns into a symbol of death.

Seeking to intensify the impression, to evoke the inevitability of facing the final hour, the artist puts several images together. A rose on a broken stem is combined with an image of a snake about to bite. One stone in a Kishinev cemetery combines three symbols: a broken tree, a snake coiled around the tree biting a reclining deer, and, above them both, an abandoned house with the door hanging off its hinges, putting the finality of death in human terms. Sometimes the gravestones express a notion of death as a mercilessly severe force: a fierce lion crushing a blooming tree with its paw. Other times the image is dramatic: an evil bird extinguishes a candle with the sweep of its wing.

In some cases the artist did not hesitate to show the deceased. He or she could be portrayed as a lion in a tightly confined "eternal home" or as a dead bird fallen to the ground. One Kishinev stone depicts a tree with a split trunk. On the left side is a dead baby bird; on the right, mourning survivors under the shade of the tree. The drama of the sad event is captured in the image of the tree, which becomes the emotional center of the story. In this case the artist is using a well-known folk method, merging human subjects with nature. In some cases the graphic imagery also captures the specifics of a family situation. Thus, in one case, the poetic epitaph speaks of a young mother of six children and the stone depicts six baby birds under a tree with a broken trunk.

The stone reliefs often indicate the intellectual and human characteristics of the deceased. A squirrel, nibbling a bunch of nuts: a sign of wisdom. A crane killing a snake illustrates the idea that the virtues of the deceased overcame his sins. A pelican feeding its nestling with its own blood is an allegory for maternal love. One interesting stone shows a lion holding by the throat an eagle that has a lamb in its beak.

One set of images specifically relate to the profession or craft of the deceased. A bookcase with books is evidence that the deceased was a learned man. A gravestone of a musician might be decorated with a violin or a flute; a craftsman's stone with a saw and a plane; a tailor's stone with scissors and an iron; a water-carrier's stone with a cart carrying a barrel. The depiction of these mundane aspects of the deceased's life on holy stones reflects the democratic sentiments of the art, as well as the value the culture placed on labor. There is no lack of concrete meaning for plant life, although its primary role is decorative. Blooming plants and flowers, pomegranates, and bunches of grapes express the fruitfulness of human life.

The images on the stones do not always convey concrete symbols. Though strongly defined at the outset, they received many interpretations over time. The meaning of religious images were transformed the most, since the artists had varying levels of religious training and could not necessarily grasp the finer points of meaning. Incorporated into folk art, these religious symbols changed their significance as they passed from hand to hand and became purely decorativc. The artistic preference of the master carver took precedence over innate meanings.

In many cases, the artists freely improvised. Having lost any connection to the text and freed of the burden of ideas, they brought to life a whole world of folk art imagery on the stones. Animals, birds, and plants cease to express any specific message. There are lions baring their fangs with tails raised high, deer with gorgeous antlers, bears, rabbits, and squirrels with fuzzy tails, snakes coiling around trees, birds, fishes, mystical unicorns, mysterious creatures of the sea—a carved stone bestiary. Surrounding these creatures are plants, ornamentation, and elegantly lettered Hebrew script. The artist's sole purpose has become the creation of a work of art. And by accomplishing that goal, the artist breathes new content into the gravestone, and one that contradicts its essential meaning: in stones that are created to remind us of mortality and death, we can hear the voice of life and praise of nature's generosity and beauty.

Chernovtsy. 1876.
A lion.

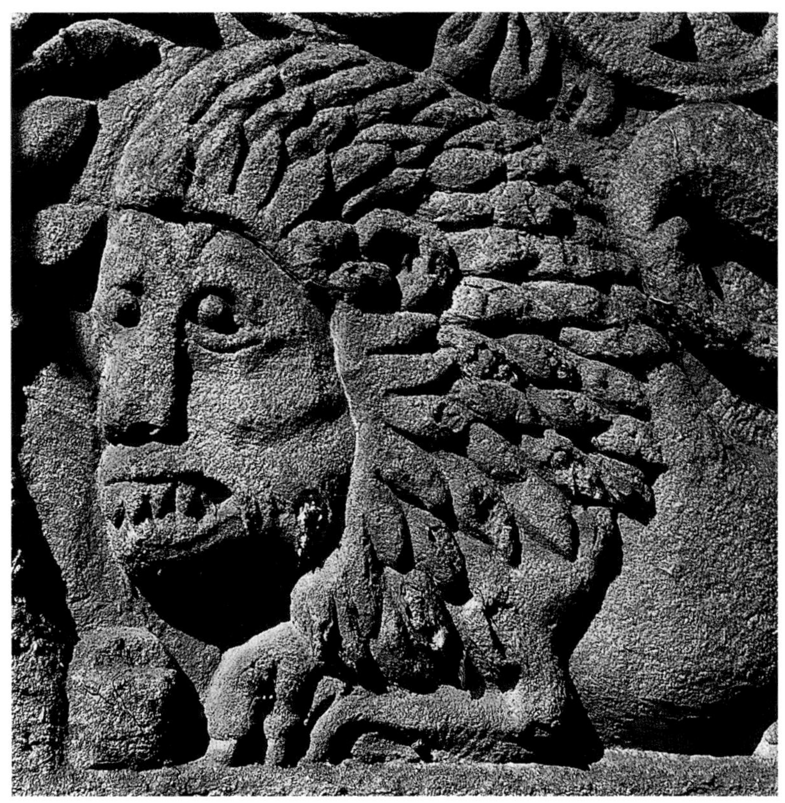

Aesthetically, Jewish gravestones are intriguing. The carving captures a stylistic duality, the merging of high professional requirements and folk art, with one or the other element predominating to varying degrees. Some reliefs are distinguished by the exquisite, intricate quality of design of the animals and birds, fancy acanthus scrolls, palmettes, volutes, rocaille forms, and other Renaissance and Baroque motifs, which are combined with Eastern woven images to create incredibly beautiful, if coldly professional, compositions. Alongside these,

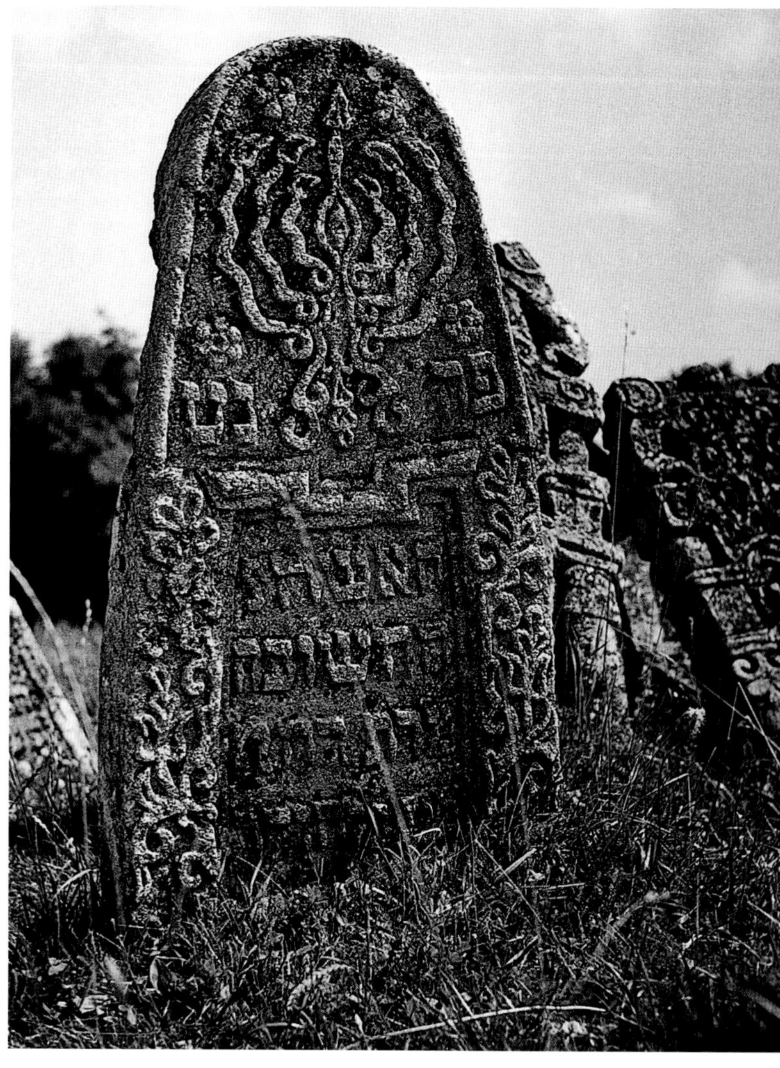

the folk-art stones, carved with forms chosen by an independent master, more than make up for the lack of "study" by a spontaneity that conveys simplicity and sincerity.

Stone carving draws on the diverse potential of the material. An image can be executed in contour lines, creating relief mainly through varying depths, or sometimes in high relief, or even through rounded shapes—a bowl, a pitcher—that project outward from the face of the slab. Sometimes the background is notched, varying the contours of the image. Script was either done in relief or inscribed.

The artist's life experience plays a major role in the realization of his work. He draws on his own world for the images of familiar items. The Levite jug is drawn from clay or metal vessels that he knows in everyday life. It could be a clay cup he uses himself, or an embossed pitcher with a wide mouth and the sharp fluted lines of embossed copper. And if the artist's vision inspires him to show the full cleansing ritual, he will show a piece of the interior with a barrel of water and a towel on a carved wooden shelf. A bookcase with carved columns and a characteristic front, chimneys, shutters, iron hinges, a lock on the skewed door of an abandoned house, a steam iron with the top ajar, a high-heeled boot—all are interesting because they capture the reality of a life long past.

Sniatyn. Late 1800s.
Seven branched menorah, lighted.
The married woman Rachel.
An important woman.

The artistic language of carving was simple and convincing. It had its own methods derived from specific understanding of form, space, and dimension. Every grave must have a gravestone and therefore the cost had to be low, which defined the parameters of the artistic expression itself. The master had to achieve the greatest possible expressiveness with the most modest means. Aside from that, the stone itself—its porosity and fragility—put limits on the level of detail the artist could employ. But limits imposed by cost and materials cannot explain the powerful laconic quality so common to the majority of the reliefs. Most often the artist stopped carving well before the stone sent a "warning." The specifics of the artist's methods — the simplicity and generality of forms, cleansed of secondary or accidental influences — reflects a defined system of artistic expression characteristic of folk art.

Conventional images in relief are invariably associated with clarity of depiction. There is no foreshortening or perspective. Images of animals and birds are always in profile, their silhouettes firm and clear. We never find an image of an animal coming "toward the viewer," or a hand outstretched "from the picture." Leaves and flowers are fanned out, as if displayed in a herbarium, and all components of the composition are placed so they will not overlap, their forms remaining clearly visible. Some design elements exhibit a characteristic of peasant art. The stonecutter will show a flower as if it were dissected, exposing some parts that would otherwise be hidden by the petals. A pitcher might be shown with both the top and bottom visible at the same time. The same freedom and conscious contradiction of reality allows the artist to change proportion according to his own needs. It is not surprising to see a house, a bird, and several leaves of a tree all the same size.

The artist's imagination gives rise to unlimited variation and improvisation. Variations on the design of menorahs, for example, would make an interesting study in itself. Some objects are rendered simply and seem less like a representation of an object than a schematic. Others are rendered realistically and capture authentic designs of the period. Often forms that create ornamental compositions of an Eastern style are entwined. Menorahs in a Baroque style are particularly popular; especially interesting are menorahs in the shape of a tree, following the Biblical prototype, with lamps shaped like flowers with pistil-like wicks.

Some stonecutters demonstrated a fine sense of composition. It is most evident in asymmetrical works where an artist has chosen not to balance one side of the work with the mirror image. It is easy to observe, however, that even in compositions with central and flanking elements, symmetry was not necessarily so strong. Each element of a dual image has its own interpretation—clearly the result of a free form of expression.

In the search for variety, the master carver combined different elements of the major components of the stone, images and text. In some cases, the epitaph is clearly separated from the images, providing a decorative balance; in others, the transition from text to image is softened with the help of ornamentation. Text could frame the image, or break into the image, most frequently with the phrase "here lies" (*poh nikbar* or *poh nitman*), which would flow organically into the design of the image.

The epitaph deserves special attention. Very brief, it usually consists of just the deceased's name and the name of the father (without a family name); one or two descriptive terms; date of death with day, month, and year in the Jewish calendar; and the inevitable five-letter abbreviation of the farewell blessing: **תנצבה** * ("May his/her soul be bound in the bond of [eternal] life").

Some epitaphs have more detailed text, describing the virtues of the deceased, sometimes with quotations related to a Biblical person of the same name. Even the rendering of the letters is interesting. The architectonics of the forty-nine letters, following the classic Hebrew tradition of thin vertical elements connecting heavy horizontal ones, provides a certain monumentality, and in the realization of blocks of text, a strength and finality. Sometimes the lines are justified by the elongated final character that is common in ancient Hebrew manuscripts. Thanks to the quiet rhythm of the lines of text, sometimes set apart by rules, and the lack of empty space or especially dense sections, the text can be viewed as pure design. The impression given by the ancient gravestones, for which the sole design element is the epitaph, is unforgettable (see illustration, page 26).

The stonecutters' creations speak to their highly developed and artistic feeling for the material, and a reasonable and respectful attitude toward its natural beauty. The master might leave untouched an uneven area of the slab, giving a lively and unforced quality to the whole composition. Sometimes the surface of the stone is uneven, and the artist carves on that face of the stone. Generally trusting in his feeling, the cutter rarely used a ruler or a compass, even when the design was symmetrical, but worked freely with his chisel from the main points of orientation. As a result, the same motif is realized in a variety of shapes.

* תהא נפשם צרורה בצרור החיים (tiheyeh nishmato [nishmatah] tserurah bitseror hahayyim)

Finally, we would note the artists' interest in color, which, though not often seen, is distinct and clear when present in traces. The application of paint might strengthen a design when the hardness of the material prevented the execution of a deep relief. A customer might also find the effect of color appealing, since it would sharply differentiate the stone amidst a sea of colorless gray ones. Painting was also used to restore monuments. The pigments employed were yellow and terracotta mud, lime, and a blue mixed from egg yolk and ashes. The painting did not last very long. The color was washed away by rain, and only in carved surfaces does some color remain to remind us of the past brightness of these decorated stones.

In conclusion, we would like to underscore the historic and artistic importance of this expression of the Jewish folk art, we call the art of carved stone. Humble anonymous craftsmen, true artists in their own right, breathed life into the stone, inspired by their thought, trembling with their own vitality. Their legacy has survived many dramatic crises, and it is extremely important that the surviving work be kept for future generations.

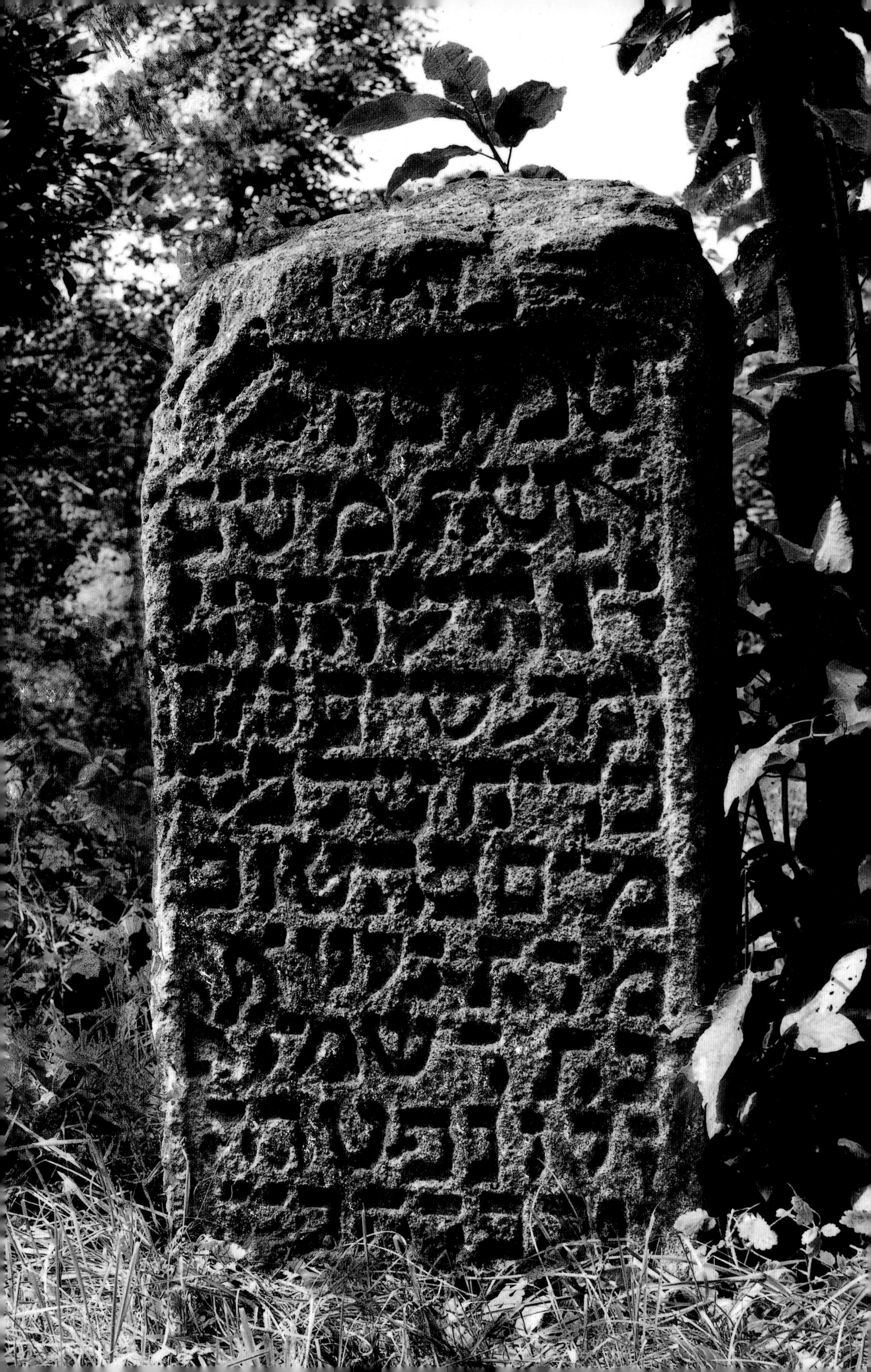

GERSHON DAVID HUNDERT

Jewish Life in Eastern Europe

There is an ancient rabbinic tale, adapted by a seventeenth-century Polish rabbi to apply to his fellow East European Jews. In the original version, Jews are depicted wandering in the sea searching for a place to settle. In Rabbi Samuel Edels's adaptation, they wander in the heart of a metaphorical 'sea of exile' [*be`imkei metsulot yam hagalut*]. In both stories, they find a great, flat, fertile plain and settle there. "For they thought they had found dry land and forgot they were in exile" [*sevurim hem deyabashta hava veleika galuta*]. And, indeed, the self-confidence of the actors in the tale, and the reduced level of their consciousness of living in exile, are characteristic of the Jewish experience in Eastern Europe. In the words of the eighteenth-century mystic, Pinhas of Korzec, "in Poland exile is less bitter than anywhere else."[1]

When I, as a historian, try to recover the experience of Jews in Eastern Europe, I confront a number of obstacles or existential problems. The first of these is the desire to see one's ancestors in a favorable light. It should be stressed that the vast majority of Jews in the United States and the former Soviet Union, and about half of the Jewish population of the State of Israel, are descended from the East European community. There is a reluctance to accept impiousness in the generations of the past and a natural tendency to romanticize, even to sanctify, the historical record. A second, more difficult obstacle is the Holocaust. Our knowledge of the end of the story forms a sort of distorting prism, impeding our vision of what came before. One must try to avoid the fallacy of seeing all of East European Jewish history as leading inexorably to the Nazi genocide and to see the earlier periods directly; many centuries elapsed before the Holocaust, centuries of life and vitality.

If one asks various members of a contemporary American Jewish family where their ancestors lived, they might each name a different country for the same town. And they would all be correct! Many of the towns represented in this book were within Polish borders in the mid-eighteenth century (a few were in the Ottoman Empire), in the Habsburg or Russian Empires in the nineteenth century, and in Romania, Hungary, Czechoslovakia, the Soviet Union (Ukraine), or Poland

Medzhibozh. 1556.
Archival photo.
Zelda, daughter of Shmuel.

again in the period between the two world wars. When David Goberman took these photographs, the towns were all within the borders of the U.S.S.R., in the republics of Moldova and Ukraine. Today, Moldova and Ukraine are independent.[2] Since the photographs were taken, many, if not most, of the gravestones seen in this book have disappeared, either destroyed by the Soviet authorities, or simply neglected by a community whose circumstances no longer allowed for attention to them. The locus of memory that they represent is preserved now only in the ephemeral images of Mr. Goberman's photographs.

Before the end of the eighteenth century, though, the primary home of East European Jewry was the confederated state of Poland-Lithuania. Virtually no Jews lived in Russia before the last decades of the eighteenth century. It was because of the annexation of almost the entire eastern half of the Polish Commonwealth that about 800,000 Jews came to live under Russian rule by the beginning of the nineteenth century.[3] Simultaneously, the Habsburg Empire annexed southern Polish territories that were named the Kingdom of Galicia and Lodomeria. Jews there numbered about 220,000—roughly nine percent of the population. Romania appeared on the map of Europe, after a long struggle, in 1878. Several of the towns included in this book were part of Romania in the period between the two world wars. Still, despite these bewildering movements of national borders, the traditional culture of Jews who lived in these lands was unitary. Within the culture, though, variation and difference abounded.

In the course of the centuries, millions of Jewish lives were lived in these territories. Virtually all of the heterogeneity and diversity of which so many human beings are capable were played out. No generalization, no single adjective would fit such a large and polychromatic group of people, the largest Jewish community in the world from the seventeenth century on. They followed spiritual regimens that were at times uniform, at times anarchic. Chastity and licentiousness, fasting and feasting, perfunctory prayer and mystical intensity, proprietary sadness and God-intoxicated joy, vast wealth and dire poverty, orderly patriarchal solemnity and rebellious and impudent youth—all were to be found among these Jews.

If one *had* to choose a single word to reflect the experience of Jews in Polish lands, that word would be *vitality*. Vitality and an indomitable, and indomitably positive, sense of self. The Jewish community was vibrant, creative, proud, and self-confident; "for they thought they had found dry land and forgot they were in exile." Their neighbors knew this about Jews as well. They referred to Poland as Paradisus Judaeorum—*rajem dla Żydów*. The full expression was: Poland is heaven for the nobility, hell for the peasants, and paradise for Jews.[4] This is hyperbole of course, but it serves as a corrective to the predominant popular image of the Jewish experience in Eastern Europe, one that is altogether too dismal and profoundly colored by events in the twentieth century.

Three main strands in the complex web of the historical experience of East European Jews are: the sheer size of this Jewry; the longevity and rootedness of the community; and the Ashkenazic character of its culture, language and politics. The demographic development of Jews in Eastern Europe is fundamental to understanding their history. In 1500, Jews were less than one half of one percent of the Polish-Lithuanian population, but by 1672 the proportion was roughly 2.5 percent and by 1765, almost 5.5 percent.[5] The Jewish population was growing at a substantially faster rate than that of the general population. Almost three-quarters of Jews lived in the eastern half of the Commonwealth in a broad north-south belt from Lithuania, through Belarus, to Ukraine and Ruthenia. These were among the territories annexed by Russia and the Habsburg Empire at the end of the eighteenth century. In 1765, two-thirds of Polish Jews lived in towns, one-third in the countryside. The proportion of Jews in villages declined progressively, beginning at that time and throughout the nineteenth century.

Even in the eighteenth century, however, many village Jews were only temporarily rural and maintained residences in towns, or returned to towns after the expiration of the economic contract that had brought them to the villages. That contract was usually a license from the lord of the estate entitling the Jew to distil and brew alcoholic beverages. Roughly equivalent numbers of Jewish workers were involved in commerce and in artisanry. Contrary to what we might expect, there was no occupational ghetto in Eastern Europe. We must emphasize here the overwhelmingly urban character of the Jewish community in a society that was even more overwhelmingly rural and agricultural because the striking and remarkable consequence of this concentration in the towns was that *half* of the urban population of Poland was Jewish.

In the areas annexed by Russia (and the Habsburg Empire), the rapid growth of the Jewish population became a veritable explosion. The roughly 800,000 Jews in 1800 (2 percent of the Russian population as a whole) became 5.2 million (3.7 percent of the Russian population) by 1897 despite the beginnings of a substantial emigration movement. Tsarist Russia confined its Jews to a geographical ghetto made up of the provinces along its Western border. In this so-called Pale of Settlement, Jews made up 11.6 percent of the population. Here too, the concentration of Jews in urban areas must be stressed. About one and a half million Jews lived in some 700 towns and cities with Jewish majorities. These conditions also prevailed in the Galician province of the Habsburg Empire. The roughly 220,000 Jews in 1800 had become 811,000 by 1900 (11.1 percent of the population).[6]

Thus, the use of the term "minority group" to describe Jews in Eastern Europe is singularly inappropriate. Throughout the eighteenth century and for much of the nineteenth century, at least, *a significant proportion of Jews lived in towns where there was a Jewish majority*. An even larger proportion can be said to have *experienced* living in towns where there appeared to be a Jewish majority because much of the Christian population of the towns was urban only in the geographic sense, while they actually pursued agrarian occupations, farming plots outside the town. Most of the shops and stalls on the marketplace, the inns, and the taverns belonged to Jews. In other words, most Jews resided in communities that were large enough to support the living of the dailiness of life in a Jewish universe. Their experience was not the experience of a minority. Through the eighteenth century and into the nineteenth, these Jews were all Yiddish-speaking, living in accordance with the rhythms of the Jewish calendar and, for the most part, the demands of the traditional way of life. (Even in 1897, 96.5 percent of Jews in Russia said their mother tongue was Yiddish.) This Jewry created a vast and heterogeneous cultural universe using elements primarily drawn from its own traditions.

Polish Jews and their neighbors shared the sense that Jews were an ancient, rooted, and permanent community.[7] Jews had come to live in Polish lands as early as the eleventh and twelfth centuries. Their legends of origin betray a positive attitude and a conviction of antiquity of residence. Best known is the tale associated with a pun on the Hebrew word for Poland, *Polin*. A group of exiled Jews is supposed to have crossed the Polish border and to have heard a divine

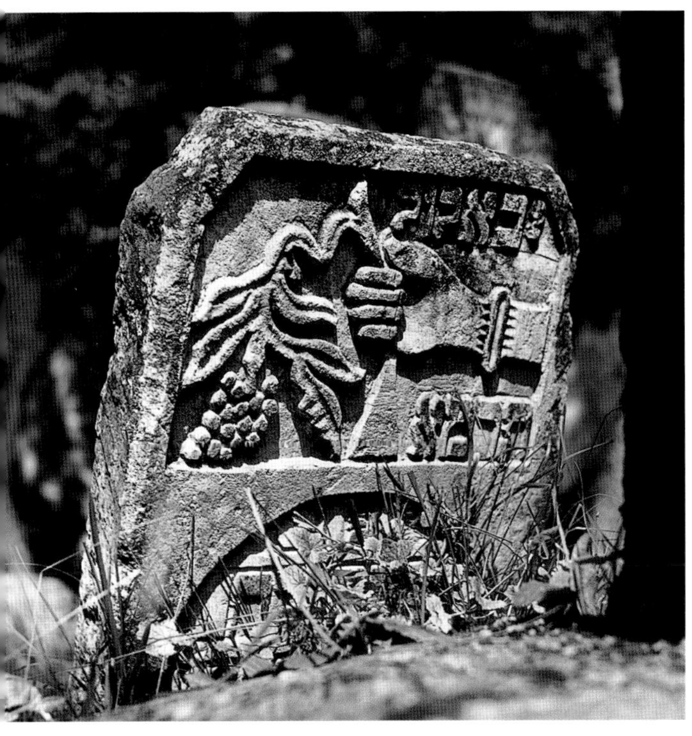

voice saying to them, "*poh lin*," that is, "dwell here." Other traditions played on a different version of the name of the country, parsing it "*poh lan Yah*," that is, "here dwells the Lord."

The legendary etymologies of *Polin* and *Polanyah* betoken a Jewish understanding of their residence as divinely ordained. It is very striking indeed that this huge Jewry, resident in East European lands for so many centuries, produced no messiahs. There were messiahs from Spain, from Italy, from Yemen and elsewhere, but there were none from Poland.[8] The great movement of religious revival that arose in Poland at the end of the eighteenth century did not have a messianic character. The emphasis was on personal, not national, redemption. The Baal Shem Tov (Israel the son of Eliezer of Medzhybizh, 1700–1760), putative founder of Hasidism, is supposed to have interpreted the prayer *karva el nafshi ge'alah* ("draw near to my soul to redeem it") as a prayer for the individual's soul, *nafshi davka* ("my soul," in the singular), and not *nafsheinu*—our souls. Each person has to seek the redemption of his own soul.[9]

Kosov. 1881.
The hand of God with a broken grape vine bough, referring to the Song of Songs, "God's hand went down and plucked a flower."
Ten days into Elul, 5641.

Some of the towns represented in this book were in the very heartland of Hasidism. Among these were Kosov and Kuty, towns associated with companions of the Baal Shem Tov. Vizhnitsa was the home of an important Hasidic dynasty. Sadgora was the headquarters of Ruzhin Hasidism, which, together with Belz, was a dominant movement in Ukraine during the nineteenth century.[10]

When did Jews first come to Eastern Europe? The first Jewish visitor may have been a diplomat from Spain during the tenth century called Ibrahim ibn Jakub. He provided the first report of Poland to his monarch and to the civilized world. By the early eleventh century, there were some Jewish communities in Poland, but we do not know whether these turned out to be permanent settlements. We also have archaeological evidence indicating the presence of Jews in the western parts of the country in the twelfth and thirteenth centuries. There was a Jewish community in Kiev, perhaps as early as the tenth century, but eventually they were expelled from the city. Boleslaw the Pious issued the first charter or privilege to Jews in Poland in 1264. It included no restrictions on Jewish rights of residence or economic activity. In fact, the legal status of Jews improved continuously during the ensuing centuries.

Migration of Jews to Poland continued during the fourteenth, fifteenth, and sixteenth centuries, chiefly from contiguous lands in the West: Czech, German, and Bohemian territories. Royal charters and privileges guaranteed Jews not only residential and occupational rights, but also, after some negotiation in the fifteenth and sixteenth centuries, a kind of autonomy that in some ways approached self-government. As Shimon Dubnow wrote: "From the days of the Medieval centers in Babylon and Spain, no other land had such a large concentration of Jews and such wide latitude for autonomous development."[11] Indeed, Polish Jewry developed the most elaborate and ramified institutional structures in European Jewish history: from artisan guilds and voluntary societies, communal governments and regional assemblies, to a national council or parliament usually called the Council of Four Lands. In these institutions the Jews saw, as an eighteenth-century memoirist put it, "a fragmentary redemption and a bit of honor."[12] Although the Council of Four Lands was disestablished in 1764 and the Russian government in 1844 abolished the *kahal* or communal self-government, strong traditions of communal autonomy persisted throughout the nineteenth century.

These traditions were a manifestation of the third strand, namely the Ashkenazic character of this community. Although in the early centuries of the Middle Ages a few Jews may have come to Polish lands from Byzantium and from Kievan Rus, the overwhelming majority came from the west, from Ashkenaz. The expulsion of Jews from the Iberian Peninsula had no significant impact in Poland. Only a tiny number of Spanish exiles came to Poland, mainly via the Ottoman Empire or Italy.[13]

East European Jewry was Ashkenazic in every respect. The migrants from Central Europe brought their culture with them: their language—which became Yiddish; their political strategies and behavior; their autonomous institutions; their liturgical and halakhic traditions; and their spiritual values. The leaders and the rabbis were generally all drawn from the same thin stratum at the top of Jewish society. And this, I hasten to add, was in line with traditions established in earlier centuries in Ashkenaz and was seen by contemporaries as right and just.

The middle years of the seventeenth century saw the worst disaster in European Jewish history to that date. In the years following 1648—*gezeres takh vetat*—Jews were attacked and murdered in succession by Ukrainian Cossacks and peasants, by the Russian army, and by Polish forces during what Polish historiography refers to as the *potop*, the period of the deluge. Thousands of Jews lost their lives; others fled westward, anticipating a movement that would become a veritable flood in subsequent centuries. The Jewish population, however, recovered rather quickly from these blows. Major centers of Jewish settlement were re-established precisely in the regions of the Cossack attacks, except for the east bank of Ukraine, which was annexed by Russia and where Jews were forbidden to reside.[14]

During the seventeenth century and thereafter, because of a long list of developments and changes including the enormous and growing popularization of Kabbalah (the mystical tradition), there was a substantial complication of the configuration of the Jewish elite as well as the emergence of striking manifestations of popular religious consciousness. In the leadership of the community in spiritual matters, learned rabbis were now joined by masters of esoteric lore known as *ba`alei shem*. These became a professional group distinguished by knowledge of the secret divine names and expertise in the realm of practical Kabbalah. *Ba`alei shem* enjoyed relatively high status and were very much part of normative communal existence. Their appearance was an expression of the growing popularity of kabbalistic ideas and their diffusion among the masses of Jews.[15]

Just as there was a complication of the religious elite in this period, the lay communal leadership changed as well. At the side of wealthy merchants, who traditionally led the community, men with particular ties to powerful aristocrats appeared. These Jews managed various dimensions of the monopolies enjoyed by the feudal lords on the mills, the tolls, the forests, and especially on the distilling and brewing of alcoholic beverages. Since about two-thirds of Polish-Lithuanian Jewry lived in towns and villages considered "private," that is, belonging to these magnate-aristocrats, those Jews who had special ties to the town-owners wielded particular influence. This political and economic alliance between Jews and magnates was powerful and beneficial for both sides, although it was the noblemen who reaped most of the material profits. It was the progressive collapse of the old order in the course of the nineteenth century that eventually contributed to the appearance of messianic thinking among the Jewry.

Beginning some time before the middle of the nineteenth century, there was an enormous and enormously diverse activization of this community. Polyvalent, leaderless "messianisms" arose, leading people to take radical decisions, all of which were characterized by a desire to gain control of their own fate, to cease floating like so much flotsam and jetsam on the currents of history. This new urgency manifested itself among the Hasidim and in the yeshivas as much as among the revolutionaries, the Zionists, and the emigrants.

Russia, especially in the second half of the nineteenth century, was fraught with contradictions: rapid industrialization and a waning feudal system. Ninety million serfs had been "emancipated" in 1861—two years before Lincoln freed the slaves—but their poverty and backwardness were not alleviated. An autocratic government co-existed with the spread of democratic and progressive ideas about government. Liberal and reactionary regimes alternated. Among Jews who had been economically tied to the "feudal" system that was now dying, some adjusted with enormous success, while others were cast adrift to join the growing ranks of vocationless, homeless poor.

Given the population pressures and the encouragement of the Russian government, many Jews migrated within the Empire to the sparsely settled regions of the south and southwest of the Pale of Jewish Settlement. Jews in Russia were confined to a geographical ghetto—a band of provinces from the border of East Prussia in the North to the Black Sea and Odessa in the south. Many moved south to relatively unsettled areas within the Pale of Settlement. Most dramatically, Odessa, which had been an insignificant village in 1800, became a booming port city and a major center of Jewish modernization by the last decades of the century. Kishinev, the capital of Moldova, had a Jewish population in excess of 50,000 by 1897. This trend of internal migration preceded and accompanied the massive emigration movement that began in the 1870s and eventually brought two million Jews to America.

In seeking to give our imagination access to the traditional Jewish society of Eastern Europe, we might try to join Western travelers of the eighteenth and early nineteenth century. Their descriptions, from a viewpoint as close to our own as any contemporary document could be, were almost all reflections of what they saw, unqualified by any intimacy with their subjects. The distance between them was great. Still, one could maintain that the impressions of these travelers would be like our own, at least at first. They provide a tenuous port-of-entry to this distant and foreign society.

Indeed, the sight of East European Jews, at once exotic and familiar as the Bible, sometimes set off striking associations in the observers. Adam Neale, for example, who visited Poland in the early years of the nineteenth century, asserted of Jewish men that,

> The enjoyment of liberty and civil rights seems to have produced a strong effect on the physical constitution and physiognomy of this singular race; bestowing a dignity and energy of character upon them which we may in vain look for in those of other countries. The men, clothed in long black robes reaching to their ankles, and sometimes adorned in front with silver agraffes, their heads covered with fur caps, their chestnut or auburn locks parted in front, and falling gracefully on the shoulders in spiral curls, display much manly beauty. Nay, I have frequently contemplated with astonishment many amongst them, whose placid, yet melancholy countenances recalled strongly to my recollection the heads depicted by Raphael, Leonardo da Vinci, Carlo Dolce, and the earlier Italian painters; and which, until I visited Poland, I had conceived to exist only amongst the fine ideal forms of art. More than once an involuntary awe has seized me on contemplating on the shoulders of a Hebrew villager, a head presenting those traits of physiognomy, which, by a long association, I had always conjoined with the abstract ideal countenance of the Saviour of the World.[16]

John Thomas James (1786-1828), an English academician who took holy orders when he returned from the continent and eventually became Bishop of Calcutta, "could not help being struck with the beauty of this race of people, for they seem by no means to have degenerated by limiting themselves to intermarriage with their own breed."[17] To be sure, many others found male Jews "lank and squalid,"[18] asserting that "few of the Jews enjoy a robust and healthy constitution."[19]

The descriptions of the Jewish women vary just as widely. Robert Johnston, who seems to have had an animus toward Jews in general, nevertheless provided considerable detail:

> They are clad in a most ridiculous and gaudy dress of silken rags; on their head is a large white napkin rolled around, with three tails hanging over their shoulders; and, under this

head dress, a kind of flapping cover of pearls, with dangling steel ornaments, hangs over the ears and forehead. The body is covered with a loose silk vest, and a large petticoat of same; the arms are hidden in long loose shirt sleeves, terminated with a deep worked frill. The shoes are made without leather at the heels, and every one appears slipshod. Over their dress they wear a large silk gown (and in some instances even two), the sleeves of which hang down the back; a fur cloak is suspended from the neck. All this superfluity of dress seems constantly employed in detaining it on the body. They take peculiar pride in their head dress of pearls; the more valuable denotes the distinction of wealth. In other respects, their dress seems a bundle of dirt and rags. [20]

John Ledyard (1751-1789), a young American adventurer and Columbia College graduate, had a different view of the women's costumes:

The Jewish Women have beautiful Complexions. A fine Skin & as happy a Mixture of Colour as ever I saw; long black Hair which among the Demoiselles hangs down behind in one & sometimes two plaits, the rest is hid, as the Married Women do all theirs under one or more Handkerchiefs. They have large full Jet black Eyes, which like all others of that Sort, rather surprise than convince me into the Idea of Beauty. They have good Teeth & some very pretty Features. ... but they are disguised under a vile Eastern Dress. The Child of damned Jealousy or damned Superstition called into existence expressly to turn the Eyes of Man from viewing a Work of Nature as expressly formed to attract Attention, Admiration, Esteem & Love. [21]

The most recurrent observation about Jews in Poland-Lithuania found in this literature of travel recounts the numerousness of the Jewish population:

We now crossed the frontier of Poland, and passed from the land of the credulous to the habitations of the unbelievers, for every house we saw was in the hands of Jews. They seemed, indeed, the only people who were in a state of activity, exercising almost all professions, and engaged in every branch of trade; millers, whitesmiths, saddlers, drivers, ostlers, innkeepers, and sometimes even as farmers. Their constant bustle makes them appear more abundant in number than they really are; and although the streets of Zytomir seemed full of them, we were informed that out of a population of 6,000, not more than one third were of this sect, ...we could easily have imagined the contrary to have been the fact. [22]

James's explanation needs to be supplemented only with the fact that Jews were generally identifiable by their costumes and appearance, which also made them stand out against a general and undifferentiated background.

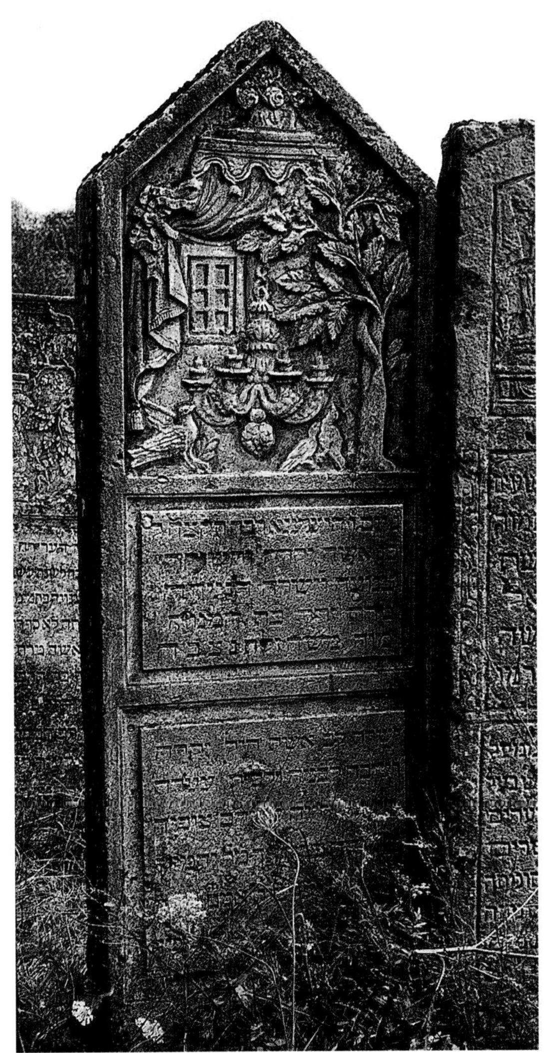

Brody. 1834.
Archival photo. Interior of a prosperous house, with drapes, valences, an ornate chandelier, and the tree of life.
A dear and modest woman with a steadfast heart. A woman of valor.

Traditional Jewish society was eroded progressively in the nineteenth and early twentieth centuries by the modernizing trends in the countries of Eastern Europe and by the more brutal imposition of change by the Bolshevik regime in the Soviet Union. During the Second World War, the Nazis destroyed most of what remained.

Beginning late in the seventeenth century a novel architectural type of wooden synagogue appeared in the southeastern regions. These synagogues were characterized by elaborate, high, multi-tiered roofs, a wide, domed interior with hidden sources of light, and richly colored, figurative decoration that drew on the iconography of Jewish folk and midrashic traditions. They were constructed in prospering small and middle-sized towns. The interior decoration, at least, was the work of a school of itinerant Jewish artists like Yehuda Leib, Dawid Friedlander, Eli`ezer Zussman of Brody, and Hayyim ben Yitshak Segal of Sluck.[23] The architects of the buildings are unknown. While these buildings obviously reflect the vernacular architecture of the region, the particular combination of elements that characterizes them, and especially the domed interior, makes them unique.[24]

In the context of this exhibit, it should be noted that at almost precisely the same time the form of the gravestones in Jewish cemeteries changed as well. Around the beginning of the eighteenth century, the gravestones, which had previously been virtually unornamented, began to display a growing variety of symbols and other forms of decoration. Historians have not yet addressed the interesting question of the reason for the sudden appearance of concern with the visual among East European Jews at this moment. We can say that it was contiguous with the spread of kabbalah and with indications of a more individualized quest for spiritual meaning. In the last decades of the eighteenth century, this quest exploded in the form of Hasidism, which engulfed much of East European Jewry.

There is a legend recounted by the kabbalists, often cited by Hasidic masters as well, that begins as follows:

> Thus we learn from one incident, recorded by Rabbi Isaac of Acre, of blessed memory, who said that one day the princess came out of the bathhouse, and one of the idle

> people saw her and sighed a deep sigh and said: 'Who would grant me my wish, that I could do with her as I like!' And the princess answered and said: 'That shall come to pass in the graveyard but not here.' When he heard these words he rejoiced, for he thought that she meant for him to go to the graveyard to wait for her there, and that she would come and he would do with her as he wished.
>
> She did not mean this, but wished to say that only there [in the cemetery] are great and small, young and old, despised and honored, all equal, but not here, so that it is not possible that one of the masses should approach a princess.[25]

The fate of the man in the story and his subsequent mystical insights need not concern us here. Except for distinguished rabbis and Hasidic leaders over whose gravestones simple structures called *ohalim* were sometimes built in the nineteenth century, Jewish gravestones were equal in size for men and for women. Smaller grave markers indicated the resting-place of children. The inscriptions for most were similar but not identical; differences in wealth and scholarship were revealed. Still, most women were called important and modest; most men, simple and upright, like the Patriarch Jacob. The location of the graves could also reflect status; suicides and renegades were buried in distant corners, while distinguished scholars might have a special row, usually at the highest point of the cemetery. People of priestly descent were often buried near the entrance for the sake of their (male) relatives, who, as priests, were forbidden contact with the dead. And the decorative motifs, as mentioned earlier, appeared on the gravestones around the beginning of the eighteenth century, after a century in which they were almost universally absent.[26]

The cemetery was designated in speech as "the house of the living" or "the house of eternity" (after Eccl. 12:5). The dead inhabited the Jewish town. At the High Holiday season or in difficult times, women in particular would go to the graves of their ancestors to pray for their intercession and/or for that of the Matriarchs and Patriarchs of Israel. Chava Weissler, the authority on Yiddish women's prayers, has noted that "the motif of graveside appeals to powerful intercessors clearly lived in the imagination of East European Jewish women." There is a prayer (*tkhine*) that women recited after following the custom of measuring the cemetery, or individual gravestones, with wicks. These would be dipped in wax and made into long-burning candles for the Day of Atonement when the "sentence" of every Jew was pronounced in the Heavenly Court.

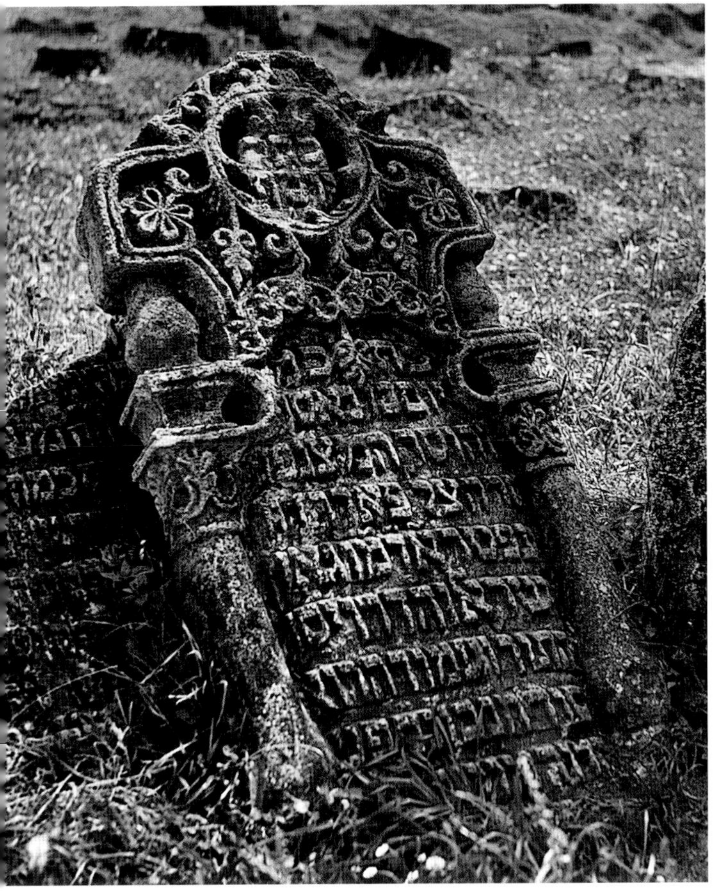

Sniatyn Late 1700s.
This is the gravestone of a Hasidic rabbi, probably a Cohain. It refers to the crown of Jacob.
The mantle has fallen. Our teacher, our master, the rabbi of all Israel and everyone who lives in [illegible].

The following is a passage from the prayer in Weissler's translation:

> May it be Your will, God, my God, the God of my forebears, Abraham, Isaac and Jacob, and of Sarah, Rebecca, Rachel and Leah, the God of righteous men and women, of male and female martyrs [that] for the souls who have already been forgotten, and for the souls who died before their time, in their youth, and for the souls who have no one to make lights for them in the synagogue; may it be Your will, God, my God, that they may have a portion in these lights, so that our lights will not be extinguished, Heaven forbid, before the [proper] time. As we have not forgotten the souls who sleep in their graves—we go to entreat them and to measure them—thus may we be measured for good in the Heavenly court. . . . Therefore, we entreat the dear God, blessed be He, that our sentence may be pronounced with great mercy, not Heaven forbid, with anger, so that we may not, Heaven forbid, leave any little orphans. May these souls inform the souls that sleep in the Cave of Machpelah that they should pray for us, that we may have a good year...that we may be delivered, and that we may have a year of mercy for good. [27]

Everything related to the burial of the dead of the community was entrusted to the Burial Society. Everyone was provided with a proper burial; the costs of the burial of the poor were provided by the Society. Each of the voluntary associations (*hevrot*) in the Jewish community was called "holy society" because they were identified with religious values. Of these societies, the most prestigious was the burial society, called the Holy Society of the Performers of True Good Deeds (*gomlei hesed shel emet*). The rabbis considered the performance of commandments in the service of the dead the only example of true benefaction, as the recipient would never be able to reciprocate. Because of its prestige and importance, the burial society was known as the *hevra kadisha*, the holy society. It also had charge of the cemetery and its maintenance.

Virtually none of the gravestones reproduced below includes a surname for the deceased. The inscriptions record only the name of the person together with a patronymic and sometimes the name of a woman's husband. Jews acquired formal and permanent surnames at the behest of the modernizing states of Europe beginning late in the eighteenth century. Within the community, a person was known officially and for the purpose of religious rituals by his/her personal name and the name of the father.[28] The imposition of surnames in the Russian Empire was not always enforced, and many families came to adopt them only when they arrived in America.

Alas, the vast, rooted, and traditional community of Eastern Europe has virtually vanished. The legacy of that millennium of Jewish culture and society can be found among American, Ukrainian, Russian, and a large proportion of Israeli Jewry. For all of the enormous diversity in the forms that Jewish identity has taken in this "postmodern" era, the core elements of East European Jewish self-understanding have survived. In many important ways, and in a myriad of different forms, the vitality, and the indomitably positive sense of self that distinguished East European Jewry continue to persist among their descendants even today.

I began my remarks with Edels's version of a rabbinic tale, but I did not reveal the end of the story. That broad plain of fertile land turned out not to be dry land at all, but the back of a great beast. After a while, the hearth fires in the Jews' homes disturbed the slumbering monster and it awoke, reared up, and threw them off. After so many centuries of relatively secure and confident life on what they thought was dry land, East European Jewry discovered that they had not been on land at all, but in the heart of the sea of exile—*be`imkei metsulot yam hagalut.*

Notes

1. As quoted from Cincinnati, Hebrew Union College, MS 62, by Abraham Joshua Heschel, *The Circle of the Baal Shem Tov: Studies in Hasidism*, ed. S. H. Dresner (Chicago: 1985), 40. In addition, see: M. J. Rosman, "A Minority Views the Majority: Jewish Attitudes towards the Polish-Lithuanian Commonwealth and Interaction with Poles," *From Shtetl to Socialism: Studies from POLIN*, ed. Antony Polonsky (London, Washington: 1993), 39–49.

2. The oblast of Transcarpathia has autonomous status within Ukraine. See Paul Robert Magocsi, *Historical Atlas of East Central Europe* (University of Toronto Press: 1993) and the literature cited there.

3. See Eli Lederhendler, "Did Russian Jewry Exist prior to 1917?" *Jews and Jewish Life in Russia and the Soviet Union*, ed. Yaacov Ro'i (Portland, Oregon: 1995), 15–27.

4. See Janusz Tazbir, "Images of the Jew in the Polish Commonwealth," *POLIN* 4 (1989), 18–30, and the references there.

5. Estimates of the total population of Poland before the first partition in 1772 range between 12.3 million and 14 million. W. Czaplinski and T. Ladogorski, eds., *Atlas historyczny Polski* (Warsaw: 1989); Irena Gieysztorowa, "Ludność," *Encyklopedia historii gospodarczej Polski do 1945r.* (Warsaw: 1981), 430. Most historians agree on only one number and that is the figure for 1764–65 established by Raphael Mahler: 750,000. Raphael Mahler, *Yidn in amolikn Poyln in likht fun tsifern* (Warsaw, 1958); Shaul Stampfer, "The 1764 Census of Polish Jewry," *Bar Ilan* 24–25 (1989), 41–147.

6. The Galician figures are not particularly reliable and almost certainly represent an underestimation. See Adam Wandruszka and Peter Urbanitsch, eds., *Die Habsburgermonarchie* (Vienna: 1980), v. 3, pt. 2, 881–903.

7. For surveys of the literature see: Gershon Hundert and Gershon Bacon, *The Jews of Poland and Russia: Bibliographical Essays* (Indiana University Press: 1984); Gershon Hundert, "Polish Jewish History," *Modern Judaism* 10 (1990); Joseph M. Davis, "The Cultural and Intellectual History of Ashkenazic Jews," *Leo Baeck Institute Yearbook* 38 (1993), 343–90; and annual surveys of the literature published in recent volumes of *POLIN* and *Gal-Ed*.

8. Gerson D. Cohen, "Messianic Postures of Ashkenazim and Sephardim," *Studies of the Leo Baeck Institute*, ed. M. Kreutzberger (New York: 1967), 114–56. In addition, see Gershon Hundert, "No Messiahs in Paradise," *Viewpoints: The Canadian Jewish Quarterly* 2, no. 2 (Fall 1980), 28–33, for a more extensive, though unannotated, discussion of this point.

9. On Hasidism, the most recent "state of the field" summary is in *Hasidism Reappraised*, ed. Ada Rapoport-Albert (London: 1996). See the extensive bibliography there, pp. 465–91. See also Gershon Hundert, ed., *Essential Papers on Hasidism* (New York: 1991).

10. See David Assaf, *Derekh hamalkhut: R. Yisrael miRuzhin umekomo betoledot hahasidut* (Jerusalem: 1997). This work is scheduled to appear in English soon.

11. Gershon Hundert, "On the Jewish Community," *Revue des études juives* 142 (1983), 349–72.

12. See Mark Vishnitzer [Wischnitzer], ed. and trans., *The Memoirs of Ber of Bolechow (1723–1805)* (London: 1922), 40.

13. One Polish nobleman building a new town attempted to restrict Jewish residence to Sephardim. A dozen or so Sephardi families were settled there. Soon enough, though, the community became indistinguishable from the rest of Polish Jewish society. Jacob Shatzky, "Sefardim in Zamoshch," *Yivo bleter* 35 (1951), 93–120; Janina Morgensztern, "Notes on the Sephardim in Zamość, 1588–1650," *Biuletyn Żydowskiego Instytutu Historycznego* 38 (1961), 69–82.

14. Bernard Dov Weinryb, *A Social and Economic History of the Jewish Community in Poland from 1100 to 1800* (Philadelphia: 1973), 195–99. And for the few Jews who remained in Russian territory even after the mid-seventeenth century see John Klier, *Russia Gathers Her Jews: The Origins of the "Jewish Question" in Russia, 1772–1825* (Dekalb, Illinois: 1986), ch. 2.

15. Emanuel Etkes, "Mekomam shel hamagiyah uva`alei haShem bahevrah ha'ashkenazit bemifneh hame'ot ha-17 ha-18," *Zion* 60 (1995), 69–104; M. J. Rosman, *Founder of Hasidism* (California: 1996), 11–26.

16. Adam Neale, *Travels through Some Parts of Germany, Poland, Moldavia and Turkey* (London: 1818), 147–148. Neale (d. 1832) was a physician, attached for some time to the British embassy in Constantinople.

17. John Thomas James, *Journal of a Tour in Germany, Switzerland, Russia, Poland, during the Years 1813 and 1814* (London: 1819), v. 2, 370.

18. Robert Johnston, *Travels through Part of the Russian Empire and the Country of Poland along the Southern Shores of the Baltic* (New York: 1816), 330. Johnston (c. 1789–c. 1853) was a British scholar.

19. Ebenezer Henderson, *Biblical Researches and Travels in Russia Including a Tour in the Crimea and the Passage of the Caucasus with Observations on the State of the Rabbinical and Karaite Jews, and the Mohammedan and Pagan Tribes Inhabiting the Southern Provinces of the Russian Empire* (London: 1826), 222.

20. Johnston, 331–32.

21. Stephen D. Watrous, ed., *John Ledyard's Journey through Russia and Siberia: The Journal and Selected Letters* (Madison, Wisconsin: 1966), 209.

22. James, v. 2, 367.

23. Ignacy Schiper, "Malarstwo Żydowskie (1650–1795)," *Żydzi w Polsce odrodzonej*, ed. I. Schiper et al. (Warsaw: n.d.), 324–28; Jozef Sandel, *Yidishe motivn in der poylisher kunst* (Warsaw: 1954).

24. Rachel Wischnitzer, *The Architecture of the European Synagogue* (Philadelphia: 1964); Maria and Kazimierz Piechotka, *Wooden Synagogues* (Warsaw: 1959); Thomas Hubka, "Beit hakenesset beGwozdziec—sha`ar hashomayim: hashpa`at sefer haZohar al ha'omanut veha'adrikhalut," *Eshel Be'er Sheva* 4 (1996), 263–316; *idem*, "Jewish Art and Architecture in the East European Context: The Gwoździec-Chodorów Group of Wooden Synagogues," *POLIN*, 10 (1997), 141–82.

25. Elijah de Vidas, *Reshit hokhmah* as cited by Moshe Idel, *Hasidism: Between Ecstasy and Magic* (SUNY Press: 1995), 61 (with minor changes).

26. See Sylvie-Anne Goldberg, *Crossing the Jabbok: Illness and Death in Sixteenth- through Nineteenth-Century Prague* (California: 1996) and the references there; useful bibliographies on East European cemeteries and tombstones can be found in the following works: David Goberman, *Jewish Tombstones in Ukraine and Moldova* (Moscow: 1993); Monika Krajewska, *A Tribe of Stones: Jewish Cemeteries in Poland* (Warsaw: 1993); Marcin Wodziński, *Hebrajskie Inskrypcje na Śląsku XIII–XVIII wieku* (Wrocław: 1996); *idem*, *Groby Cadyków w Polsce* (Wrocław: 1998).

27. Chava Weissler, "'For the Human Soul is the Lamp of the Lord': The *Tkhine* for 'Laying Wicks' by Sarah bas Tovim," *POLIN* 10 (1997), 40–65. And see her book: *Voices of the Matriarchs: Listening to the Prayers of Early Modern Jewish Women* (Boston: 1998).

28. More informally, some men were known by the name of their mother or mother-in-law. This includes some famous Rabbis such as Joel Sirkes [Sarah's] and Samuel Edels. There was also a kind of East European Jewish aristocracy, known by ascribed surnames long before the name-laws, including Landau, Heilperin, Rapoport, Horowitz, Katzenellenbogen, Ginzburg, and others. In the middle of the eighteenth century, for example, ten leaders of the Council of Four Lands, fifteen rabbis of different communities, and several other judges and heads of yeshivas were all drawn from the Heilperin family.

For Further Reading

Czaplinski, W., and Ladogorski, T., eds. *Atlas historyczny Polski*. Warsaw, 1989.

Gitelman, Zvi. *A Century of Ambivalence. The Jews of Russia and the Soviet Union, 1881 to the Present.* New York: YIVO, 1988.

Gitelman, Zvi. *Jewish Nationality and Soviet Politics: The Jewish Sections of the CPSU, 1917–1930*. Princeton University Press, 1972.

Goldberg, Sylvie-Anne. *Crossing the Jabbok: Illness and Death in Sixteenth- through Nineteenth-Century Prague.* University of California Press, 1996.

Hoshen, Sarah Harel. *Treasures of Jewish Galicia: Judaica from the Museum of Ethnography and Crafts in Lvov, Ukraine*. Tel Aviv, Beth Hatefutsoth, 1996.

Hundert, Gershon, ed. *Essential Papers on Hasidism.* New York University Press, 1991.

Hundert, Gershon, and Bacon, Gershon. *The Jews of Poland and Russia: Bibliographical Essays*. Indiana University Press, 1984.

Katz, Jacob. *Tradition and Crisis*. B. D. Cooperman, ed. and trans. New York, 1994.

Klier, John. *Russia Gathers Her Jews: The Origins of the "Jewish Question" in Russia, 1772–1825*. Northern Illinois University Press, 1986.

Krajewska, Monika. *A Tribe of Stones: Jewish Cemeteries in Poland*. Warsaw, Polish Scientific Publishers, 1993.

Magocsi, Paul Robert. *Historical Atlas of East Central Europe*. University of Toronto Press, 1993.

Rapoport-Albert, Ada, ed. *Hasidism Reappraised*, London, 1996.

Ro'i, Yaacov, ed. *Jews and Jewish Life in Russia and the Soviet Union*. Portland, Oregon, Frank Cass, 1995.

Seipel, Wilfried, ed. *Thorah und Krone: Kulturgeräte der Jüdischen Diaspora in der Ukraine*. Vienna, Kunsthistorisches Museum, 1994.

Stanislawski, Michael. *Tsar Nicholas I and the Jews*. Philadelphia, Jewish Publication Society, 1983.

Weinryb, Bernard Dov. *A Social and Economic History of the Jewish Community in Poland from 1100 to 1800*. Philadelphia, Jewish Publication Society, 1973.

Weissler, Chava. *Voices of the Matriarchs: Listening to the Prayers of Early Modern Jewish Women*. Boston, Beacon Press, 1998.

Wodziński, Marcin. *Hebrajskie Inskrypcje na śląsku XIII–XVIII wieku*. Wrocław, 1996.

Wodziński, Marcin. *Groby Cadyków w Polsce*. Wrocław, 1998.

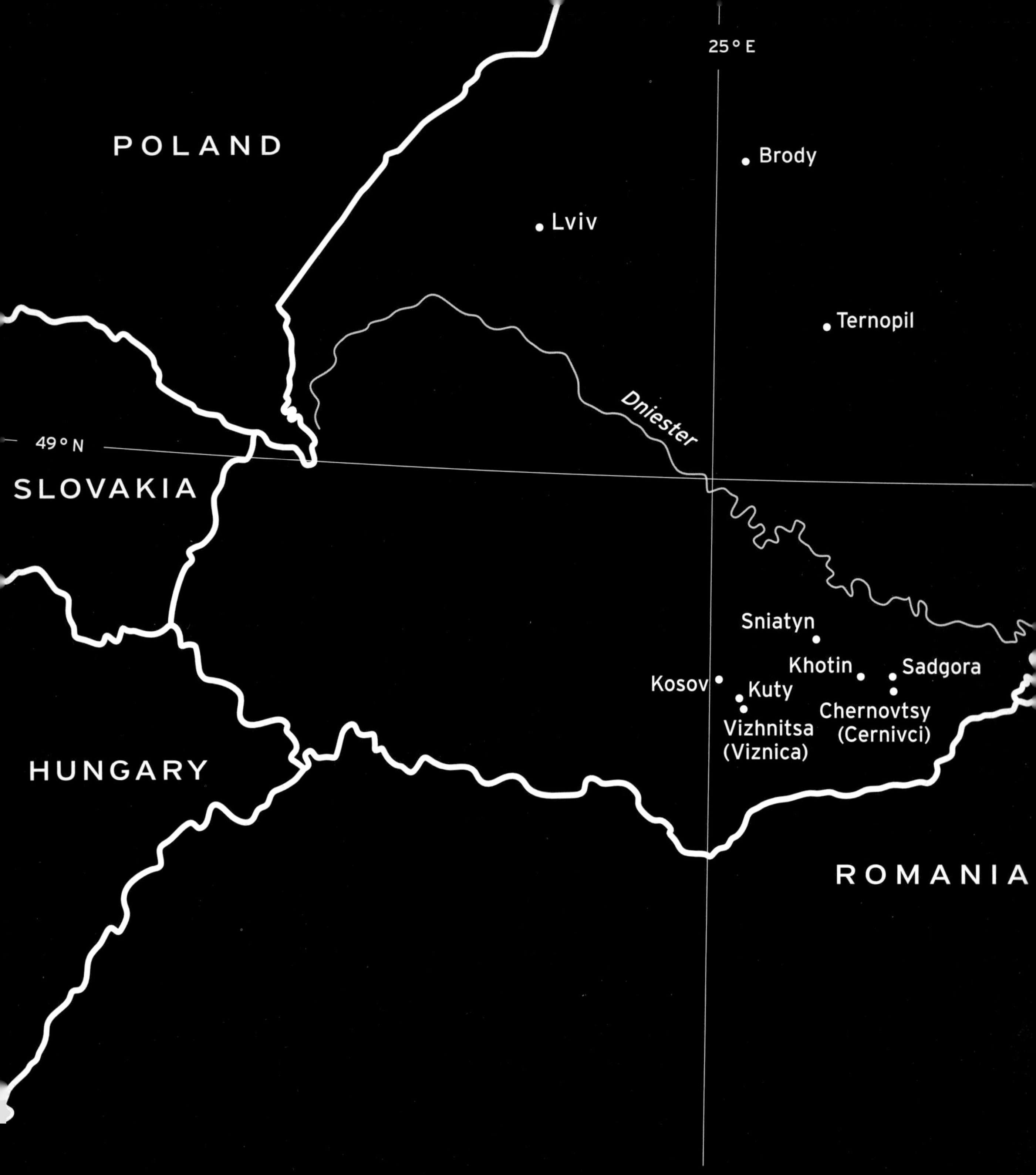

25° E

POLAND

Brody

Lviv

Ternopil

Dniester

49° N

SLOVAKIA

Sniatyn

Khotin

Sadgora

Kosov

Kuty

Chernovtsy (Cernivci)

Vizhnitsa (Viznica)

HUNGARY

ROMANIA

46° N

West Central Ukraine

In the 1730s the Ba'al Shem Tov, founder of Hasidism, stayed in the vicinity of **Kosov**, then part of Poland, and the town later became a center of Hasidic activity. **Kuty** also had a strong Hasidic element. Jews owned eleven houses in the town of **Sniatyn** in 1592. **Khotin's** Jewish population grew after Bessarabia became part of Russia in 1812 and by mid-century it had become a center for Haskalah (the movement promoting Jewish involvement in the secular world), and had a private school for girls. **Sadgora**, established in the 18th century, had a famous old synagogue, known as the "Great Schul," and became the seat of the rabbis known as the "Ruzhiner." **Chernovtsy** was a major regional Jewish center whose cemetery is the resting place of notable poets and actors as well as scholars and religious figures.

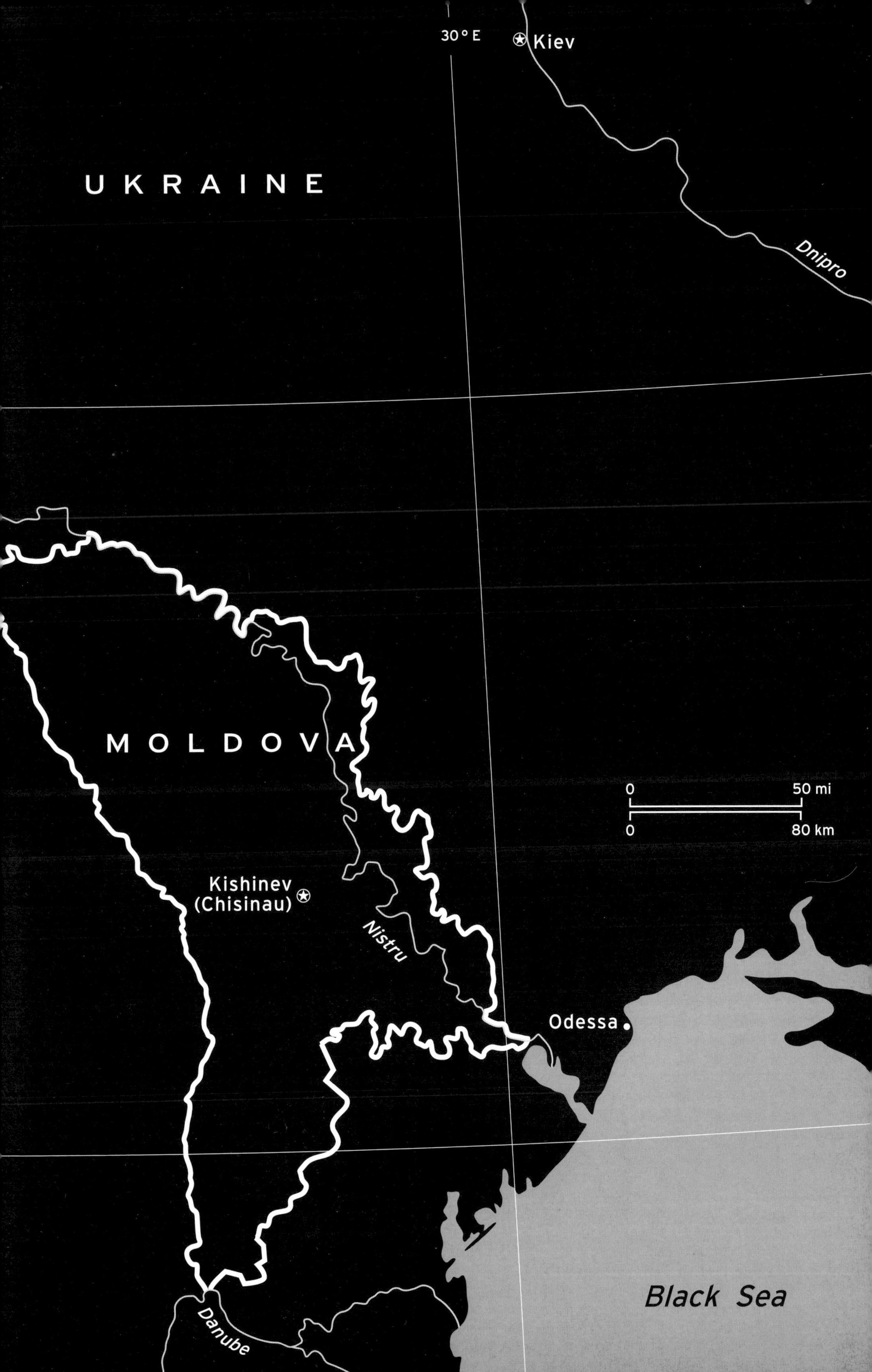
30° E
Kiev
UKRAINE
Dnipro
MOLDOVA
0
50 mi
0
80 km
Kishinev
(Chisinau)
Nistru
Odessa
Black Sea
Danube

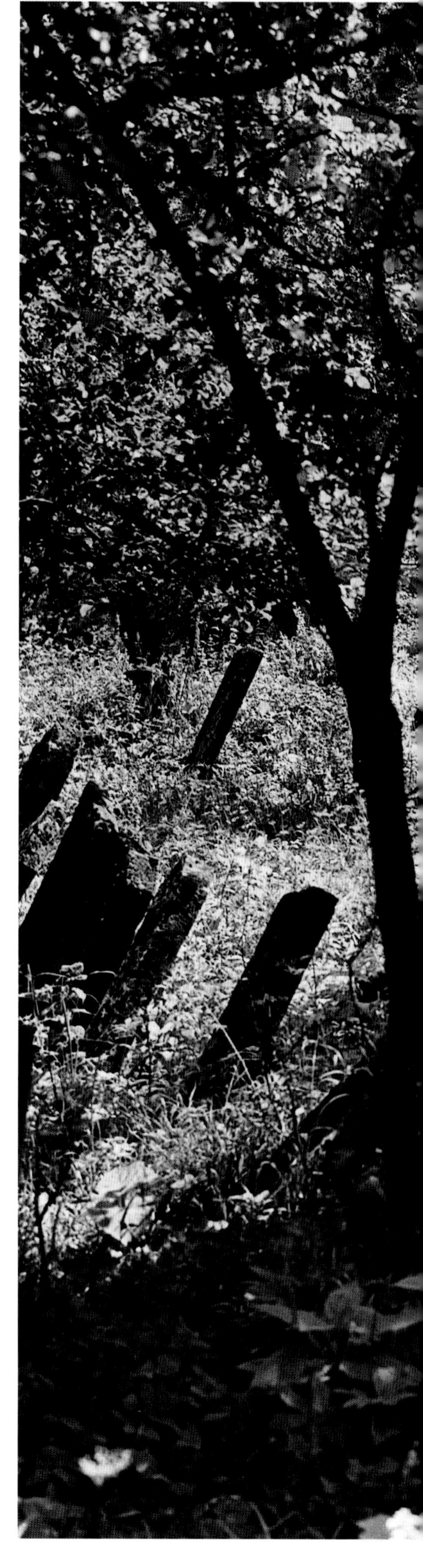

Kosov cemetery.

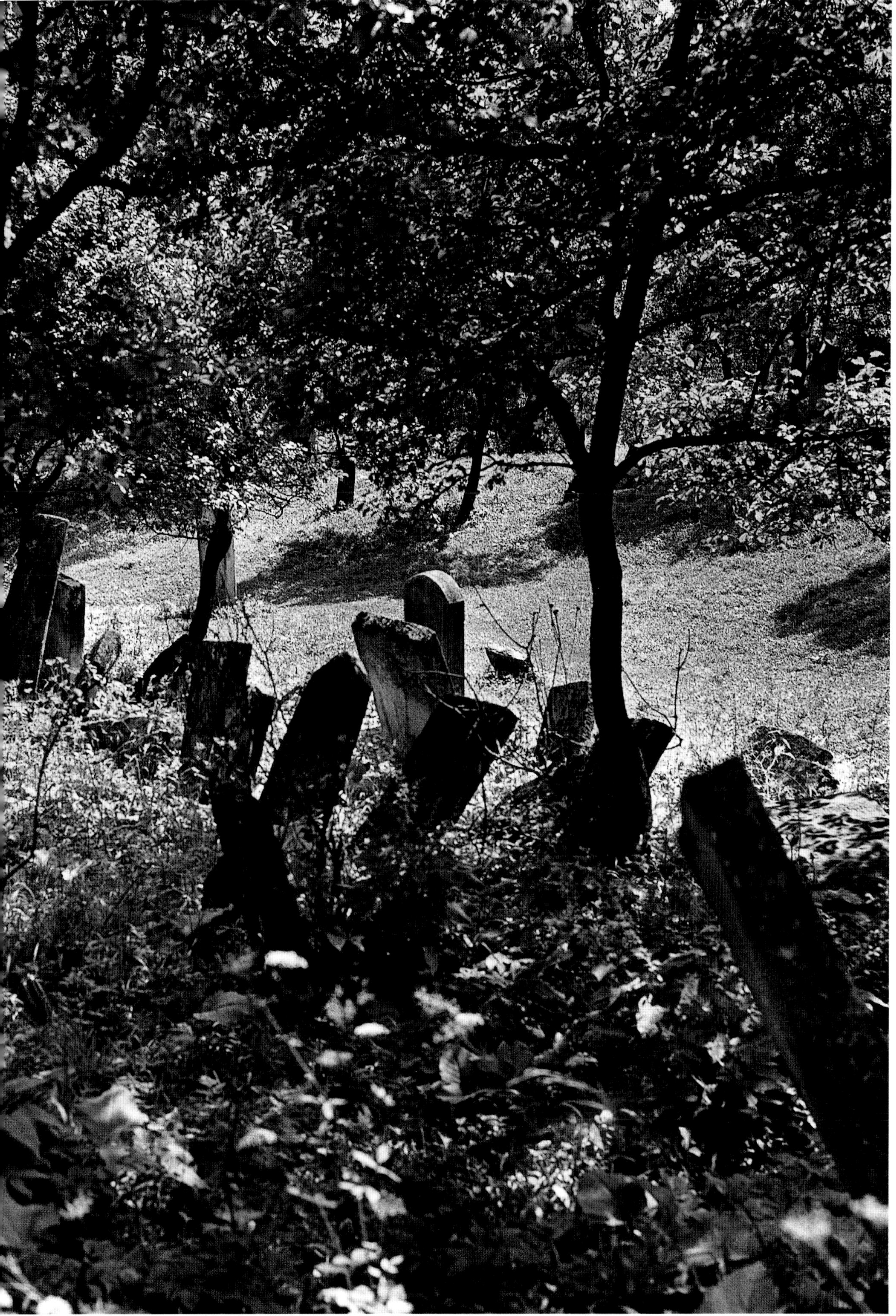

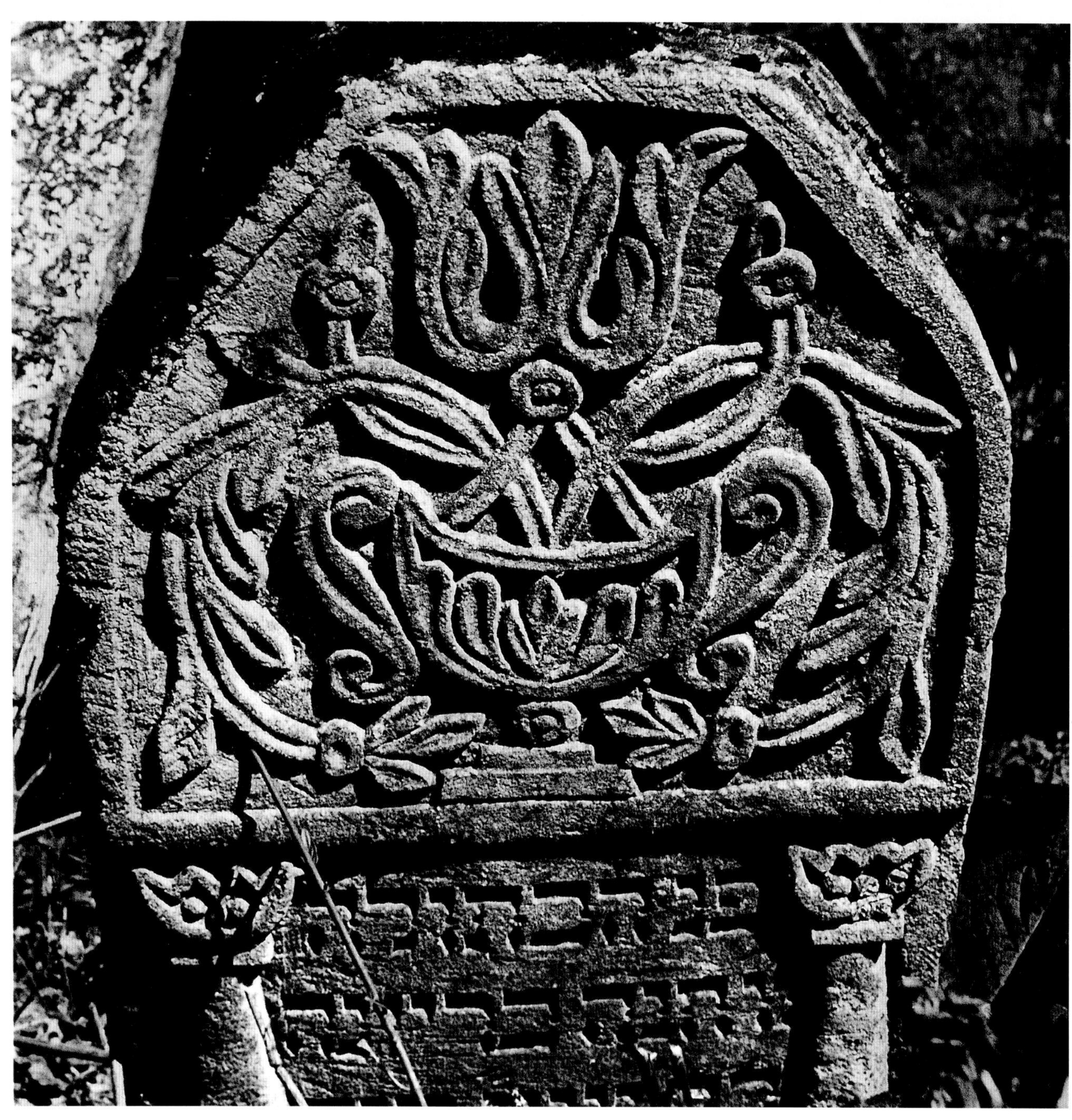

Kosov. Mid-1850s.
Drooping flowers in a pot.
A young woman (maiden), Chaya Brayna, daughter of David.

Opposite:
Kosov. Between 1700 and 1750.
Pitcher flanked by starfish.
Here is interred the Levite Shlomo, son of Jacob Siegel.

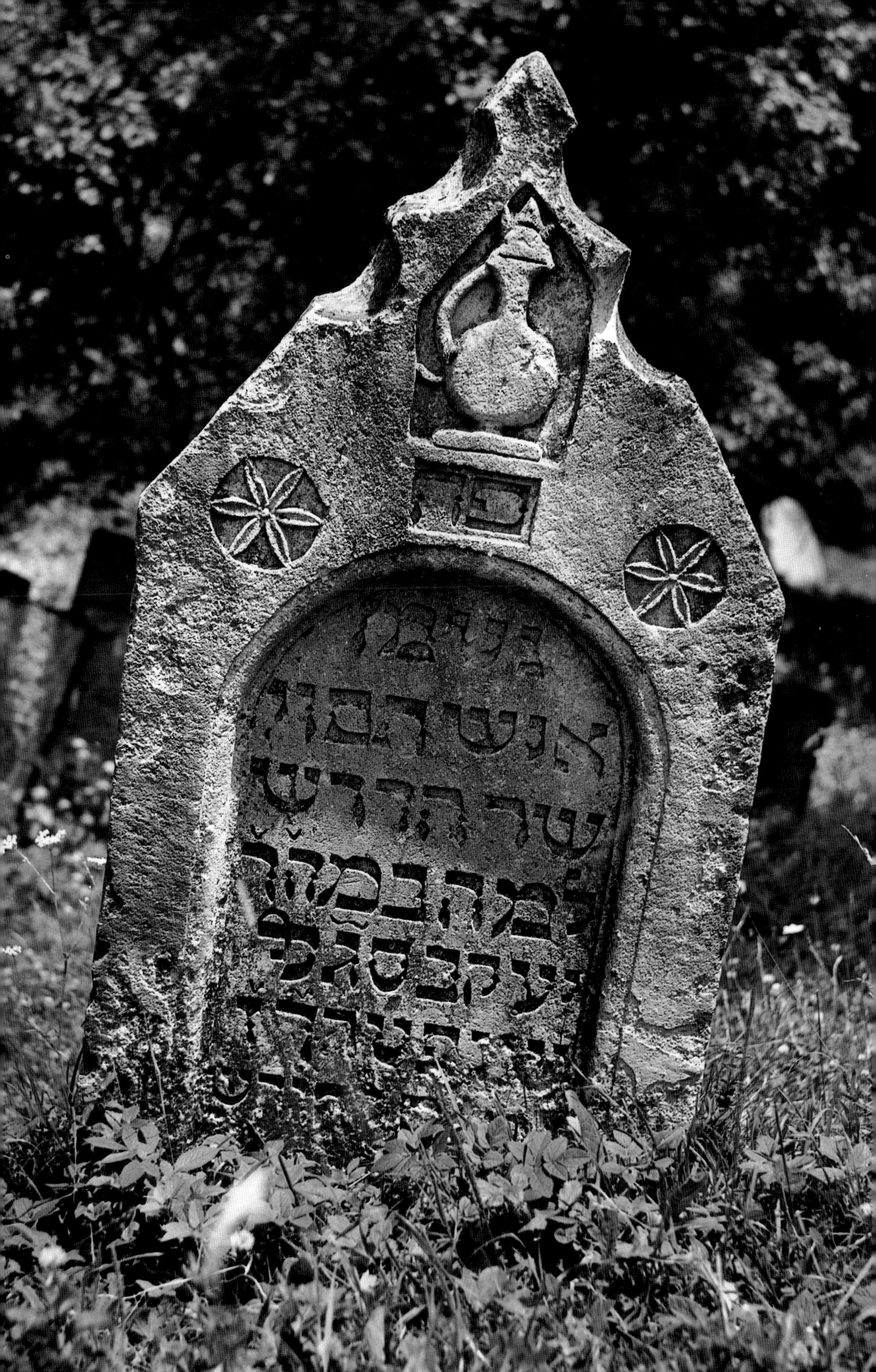

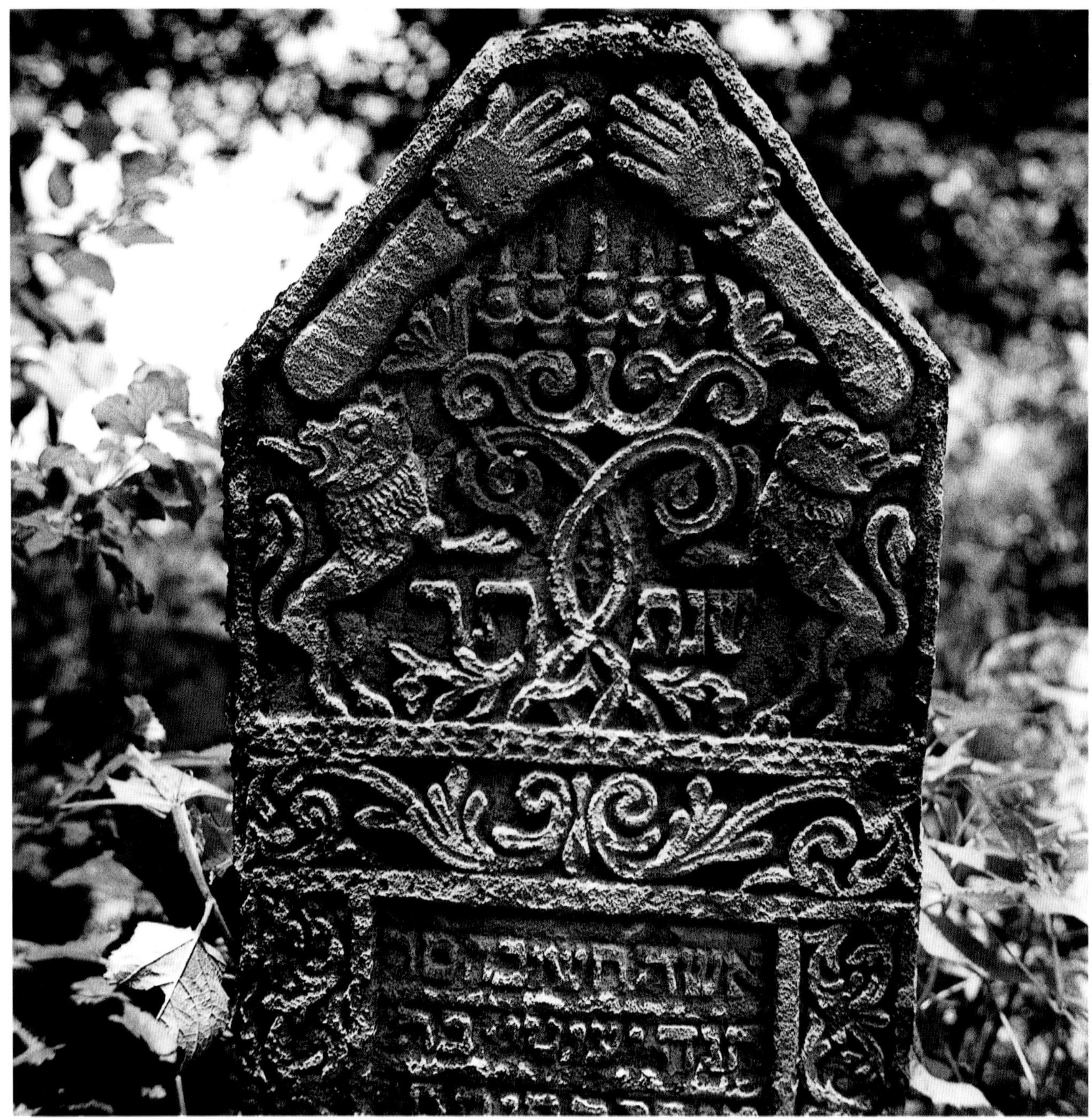

Kosov. 1840.

A lighted candelabra flanked by lions and with hands above the flame. The woman's hands, covering her eyes as she prays, are in a traditional pose, associated with the lighting of the Sabbath candles and symbolizing faith and devotion. The ruffles at her wrist show that she is dressed in Sabbath finery.

Opposite:

Kosov. 1865.

Lighted candlesticks, flanked by a woman's hands about to be raised for the Sabbath blessing. The name Fruma means "pious" in Yiddish.

A modest woman, Fruma.

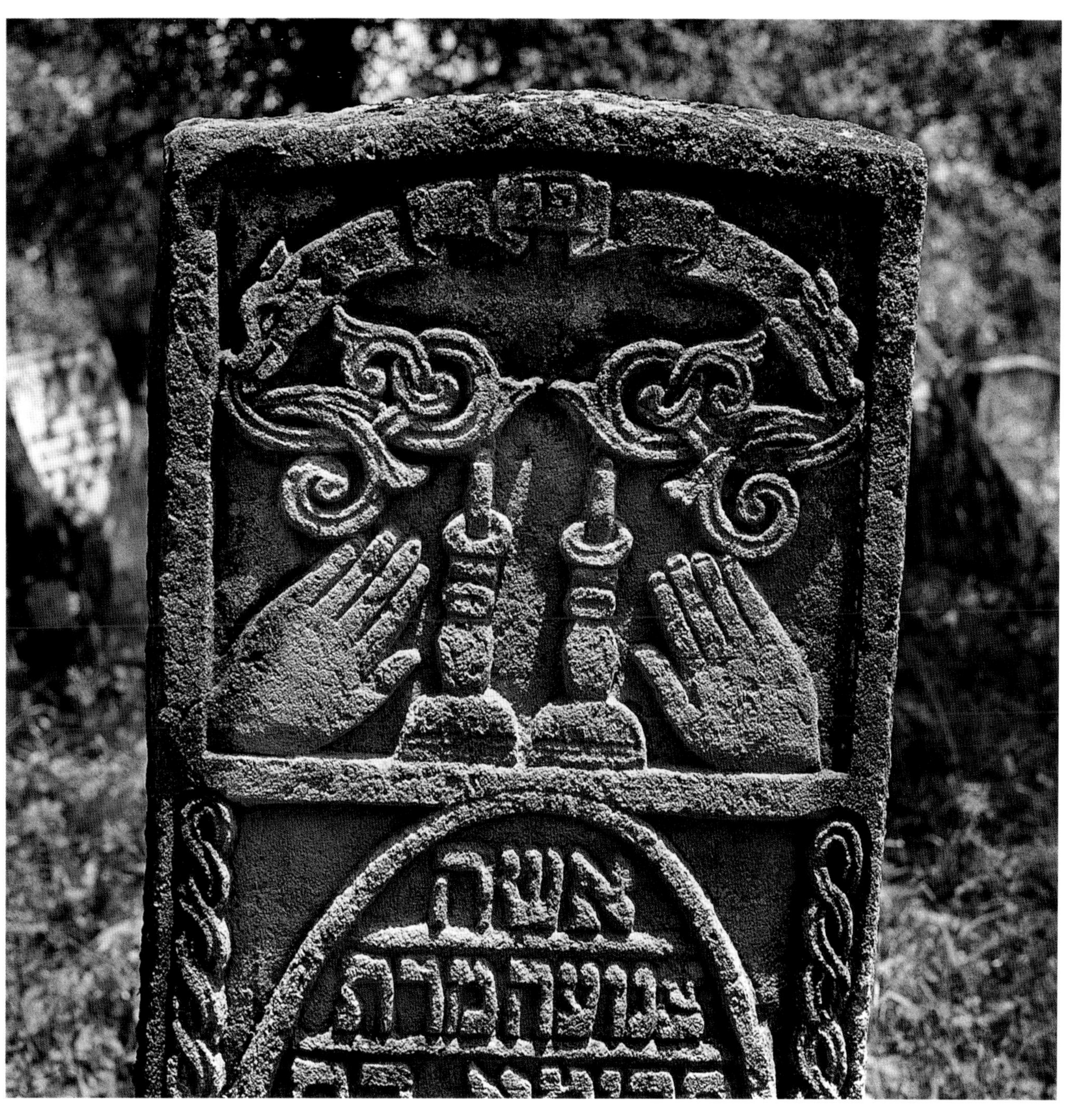
אשה
צנועה מרת

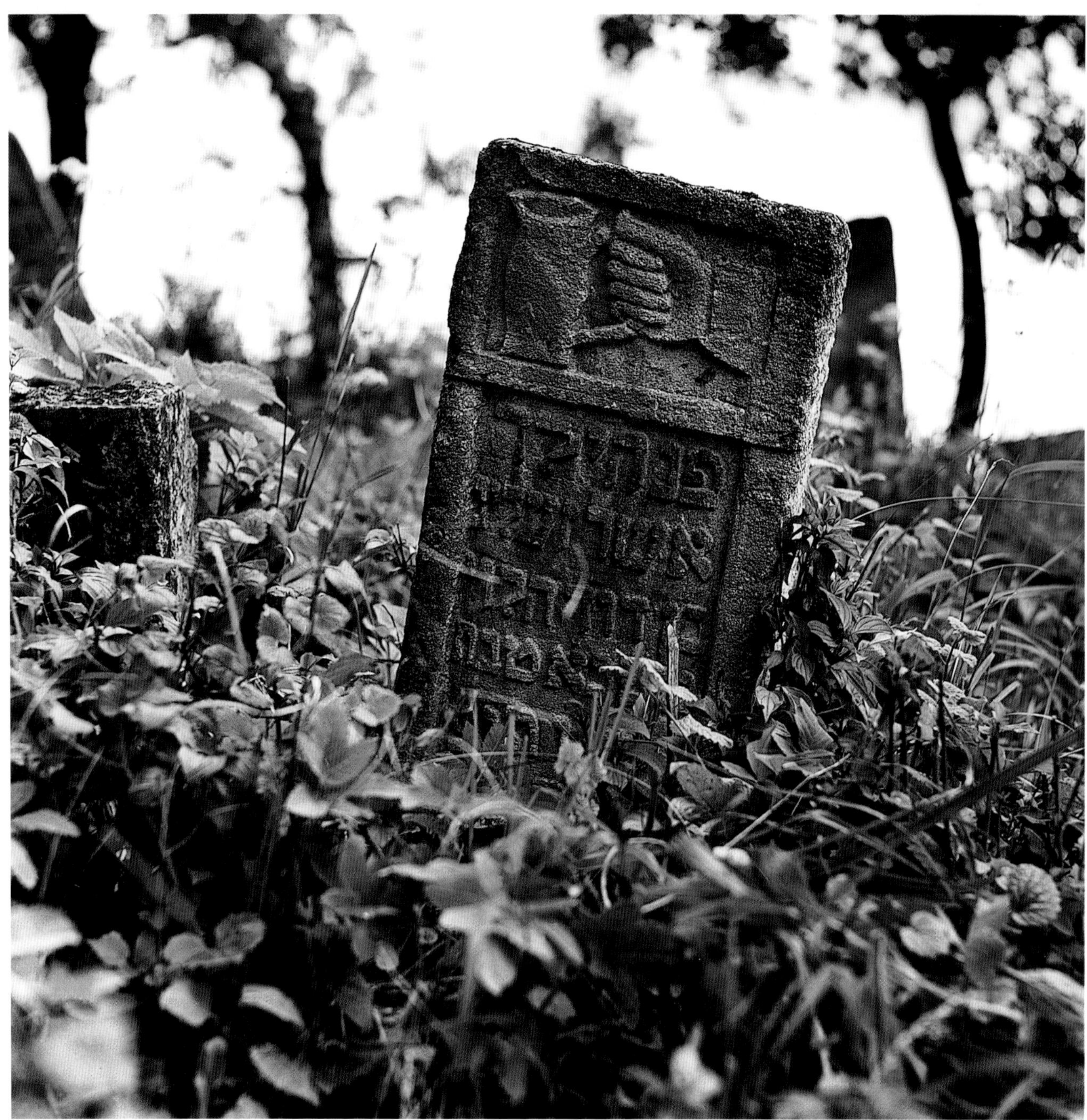

Kosov. 1870s.

A hand holding a pitcher: the tombstone of a Levite.
Here lies the child Zelig, son of David.

Opposite:
Kosov. 1880.

A hand descending from a pot of flowers, flanked by candlesticks. The ribbon above the flowers terminates in griffin-like heads.

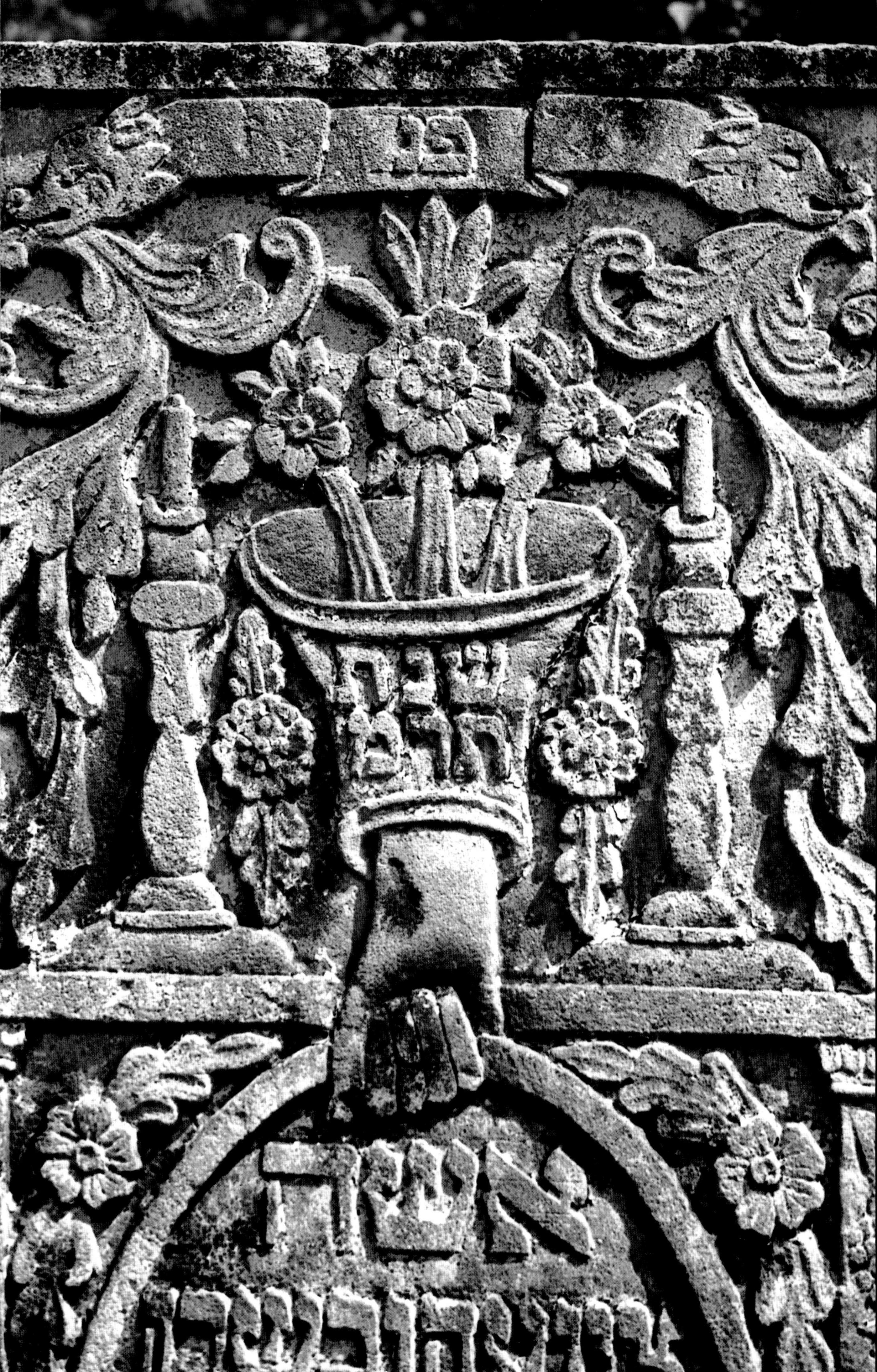

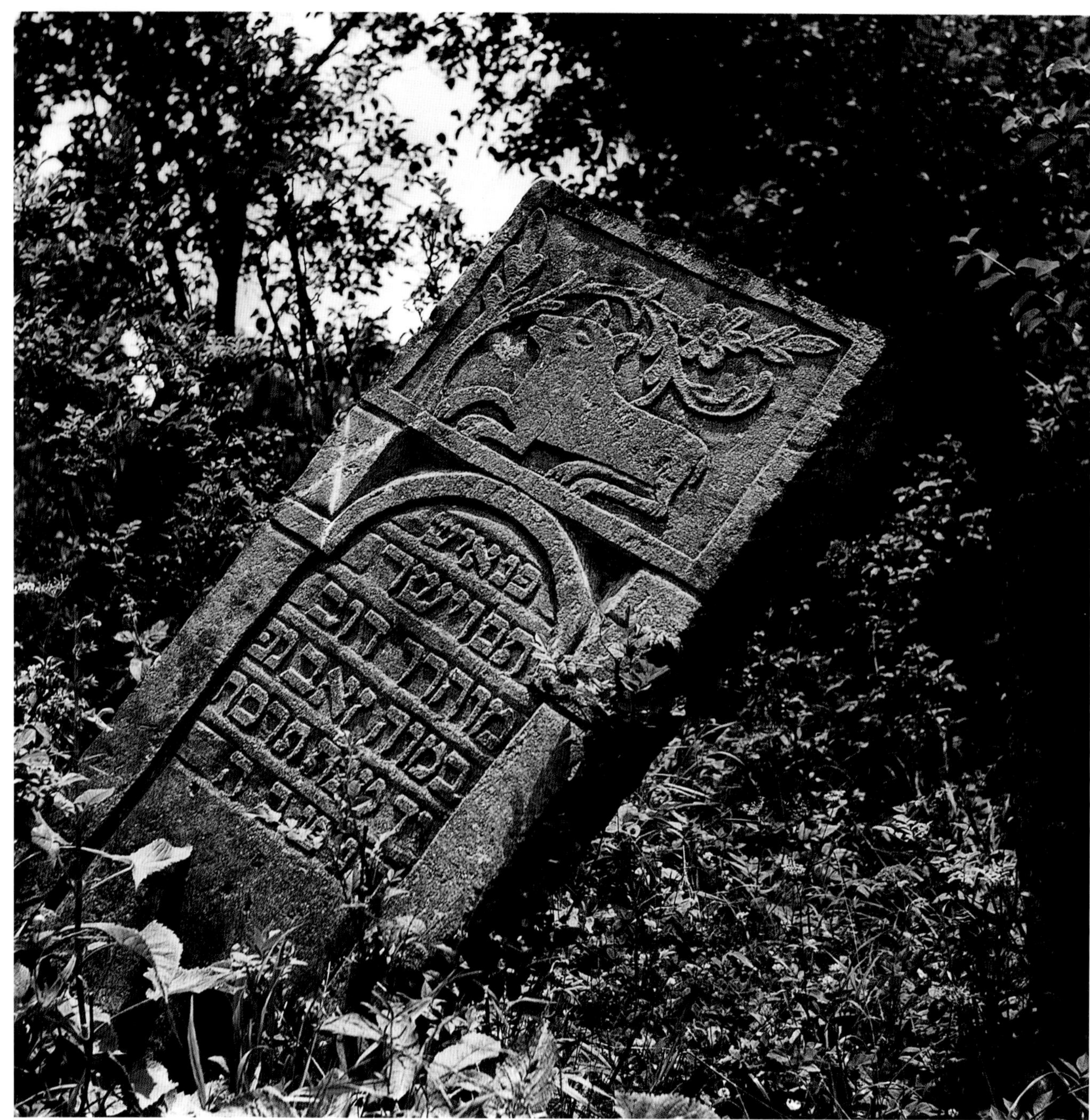

Kosov. 1908.

A bear reclining under a tree.

A pure and upright man. Dov [the name means "bear" in Hebrew], son of Zev. Died in 5667.

May his soul be embraced in the bond of life.

Opposite:

Kosov. 1866.

A lion with the throat of an eagle in its jaws.

The eagle has killed a lamb, which is in its beak.

Pure and honest. Joel Yitchak, son of Shmuel.

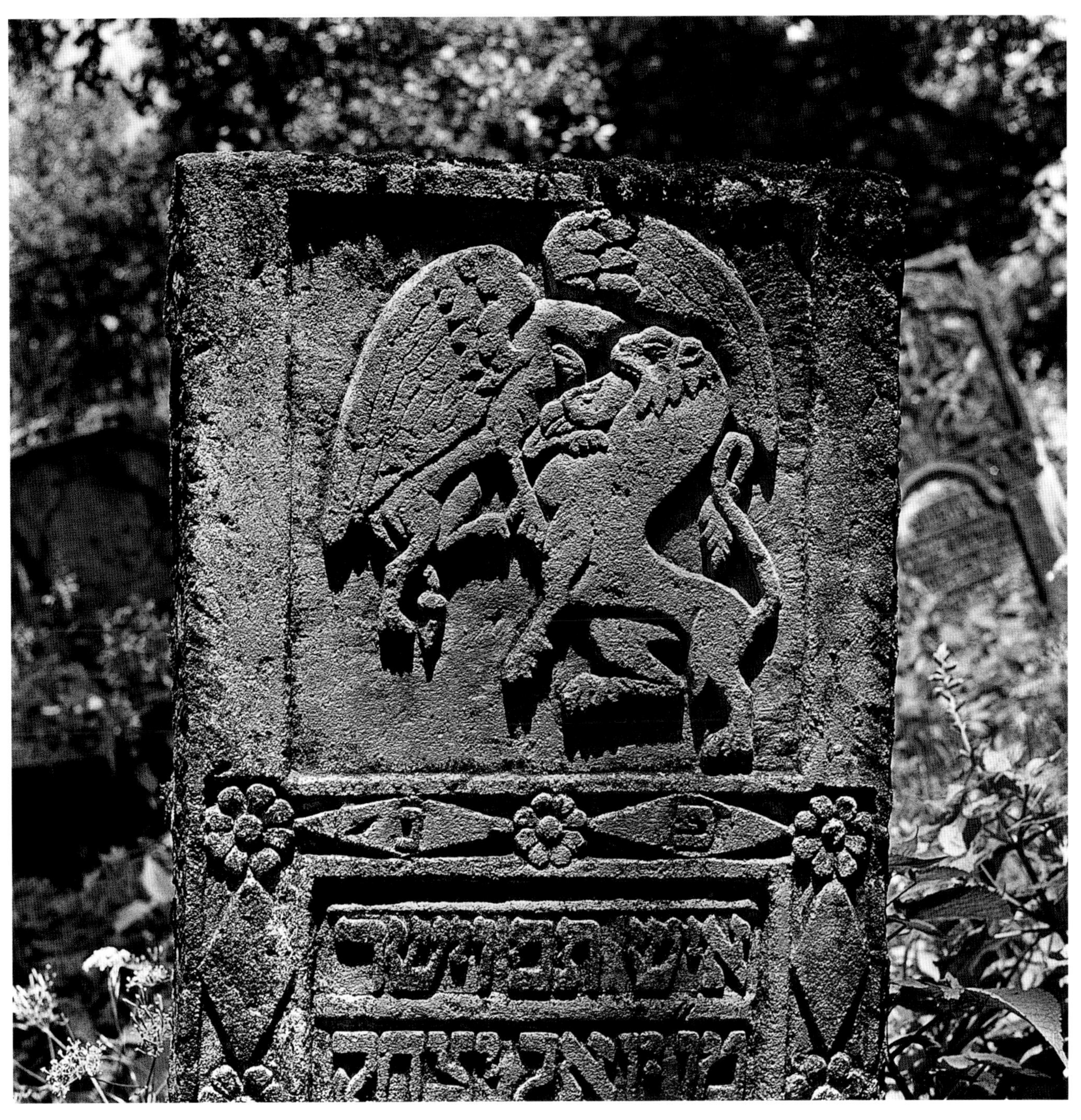
פ נ

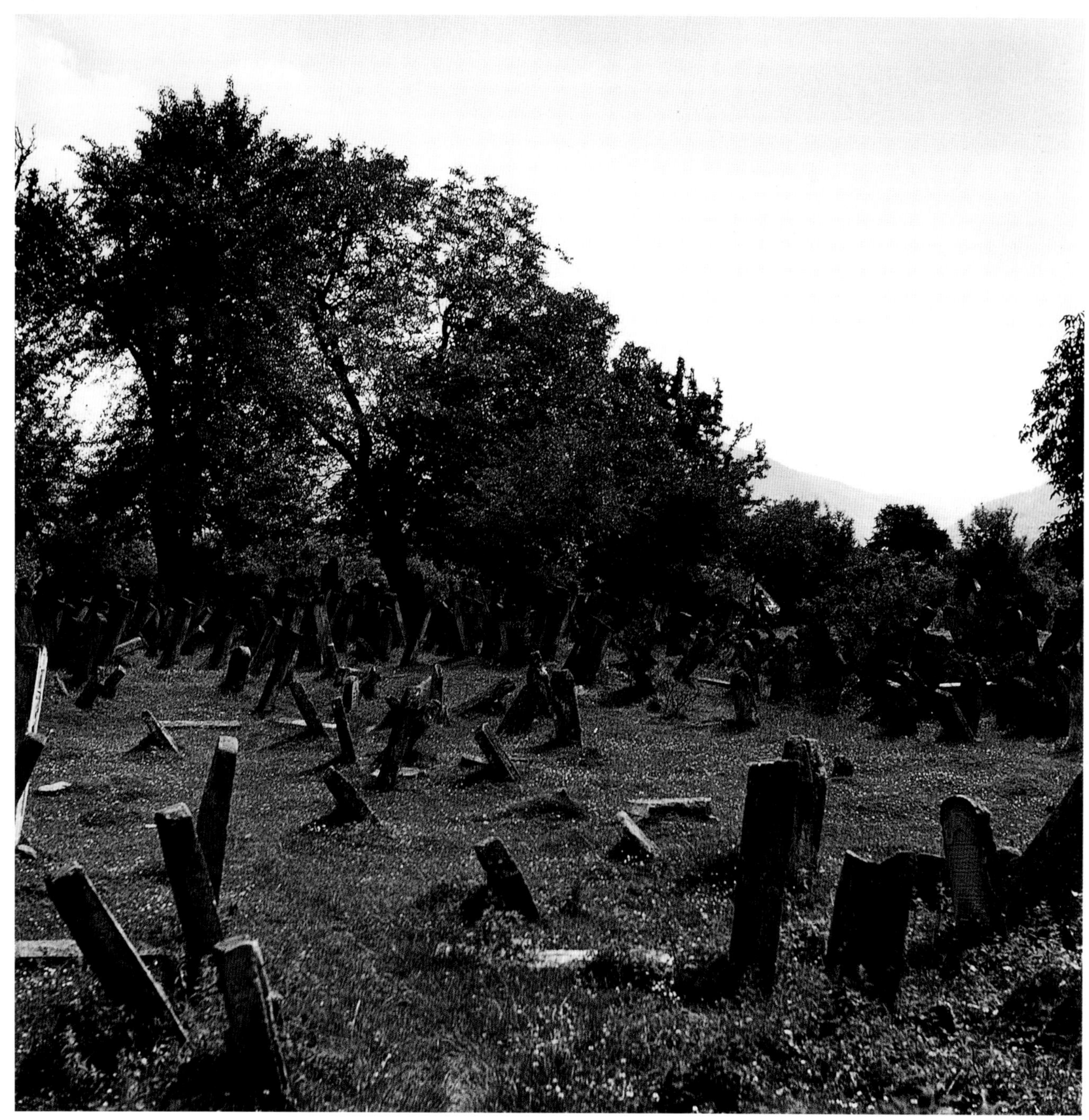

Kuty cemetery.

Opposite:
Kuty. 1788.
Probably the stone of a husband and wife. The upper part is decorated with fallen flowers. The double-sided design is meant to recall the Ten Commandments. Inscribed on the left is the wife, Yetta, and on the right, Simcha Bunem Yisroel, son of Eleazar Pinchas.

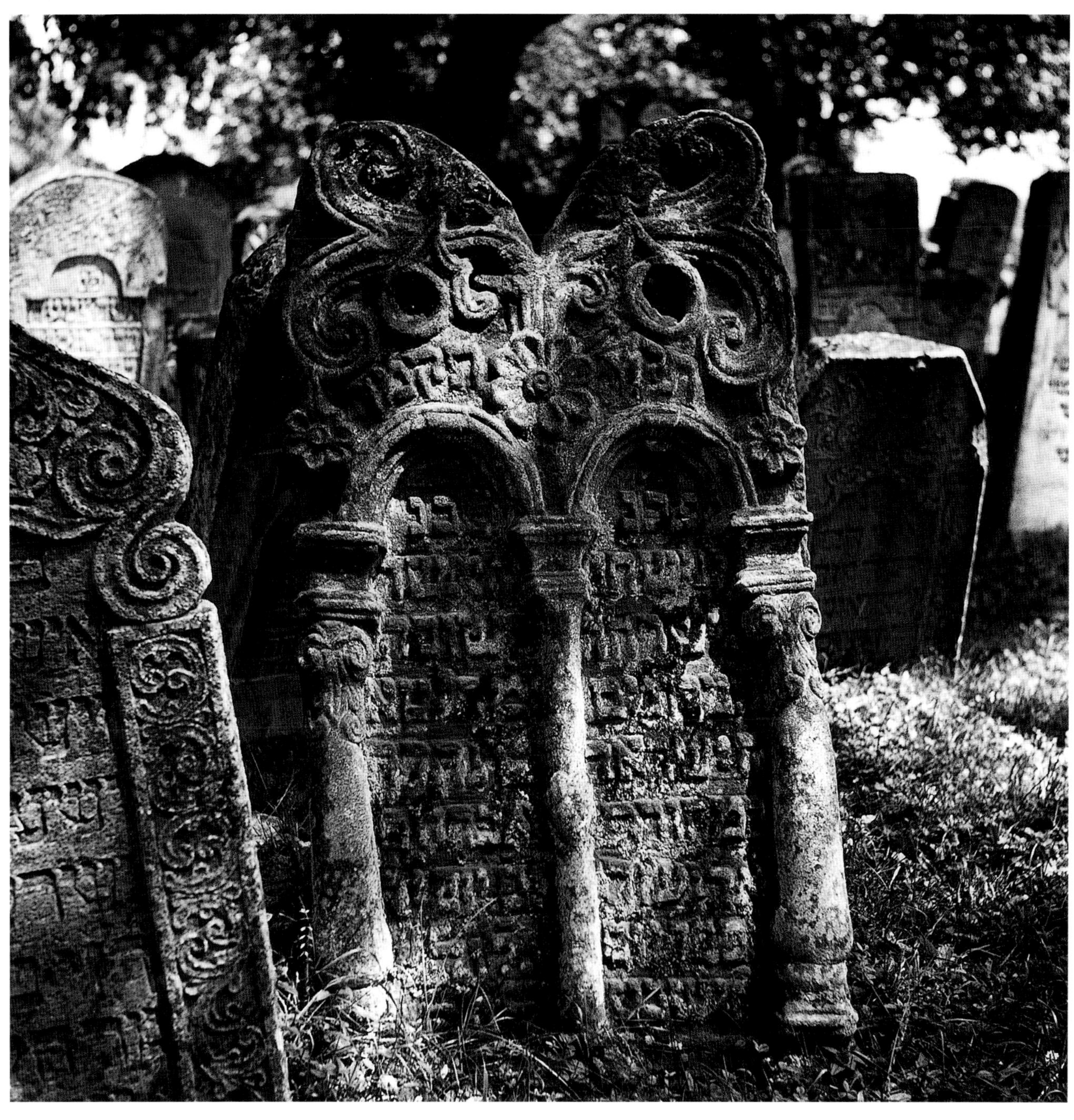

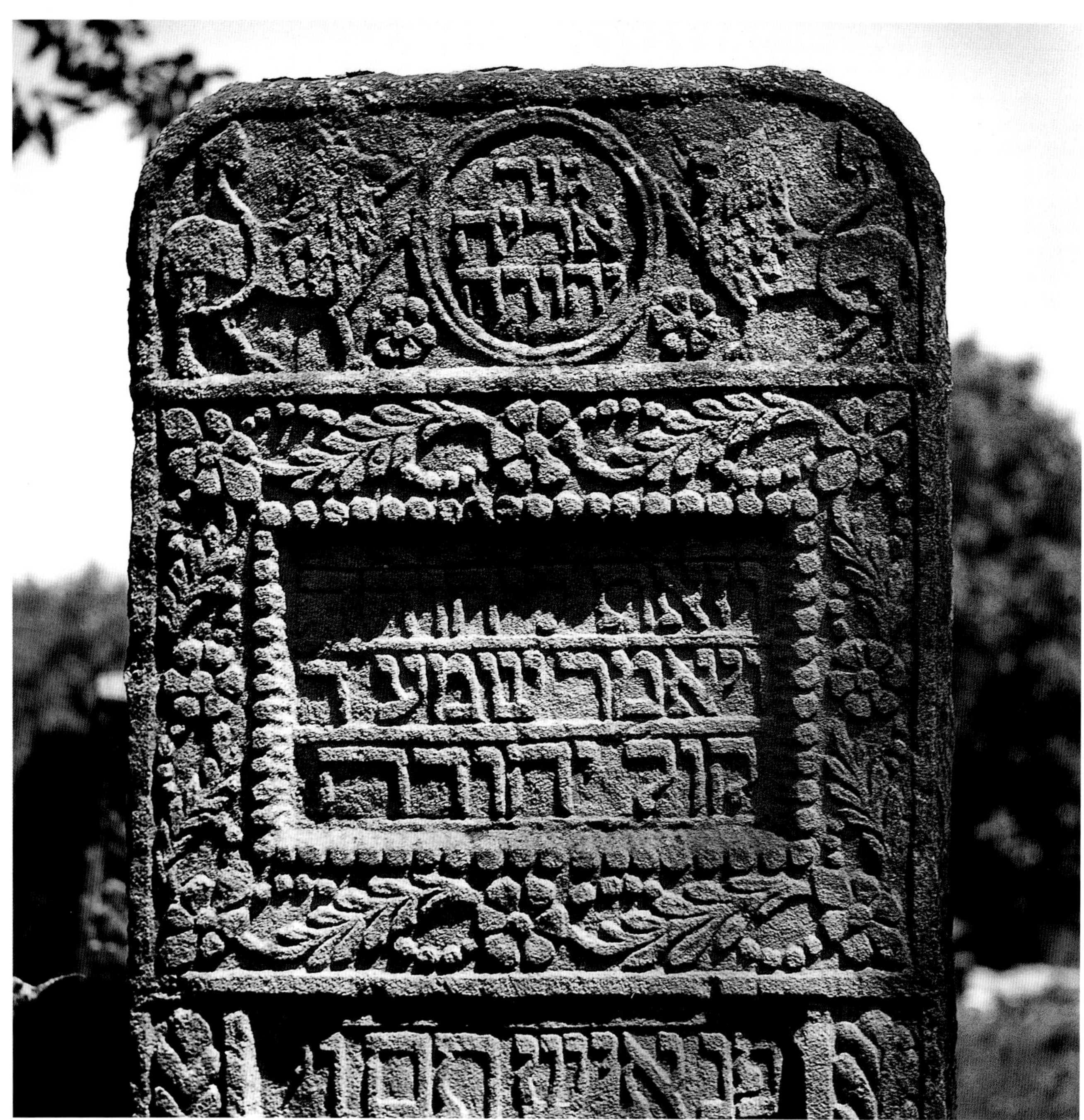

Kuty. Late 1700s.

Decorated with leaves, flowers, and lions. Commemorating a man, Arie Yehuda, the inscription quotes Deuteronomy, 3:37, a blessing that Jacob bestowed upon his son Jehuda (or Judah, a lion cub):

May God hear Yehuda's voice and bring him to his people.

The text below the recessed box reads: *He has the face of a righteous man.*

Opposite:

Kuty. 1840.

Detail. Unicorn with the tail of a sea serpent.

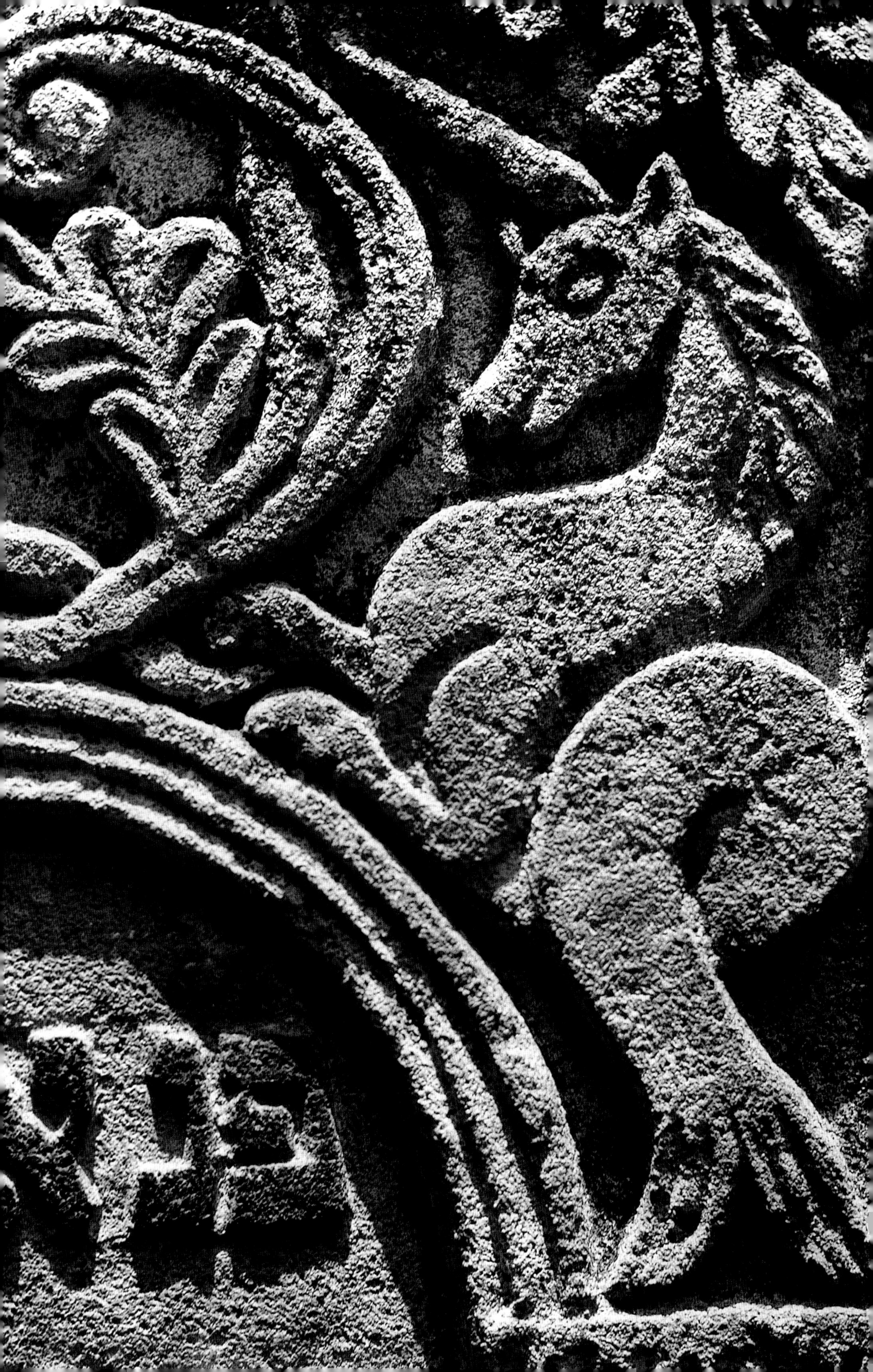

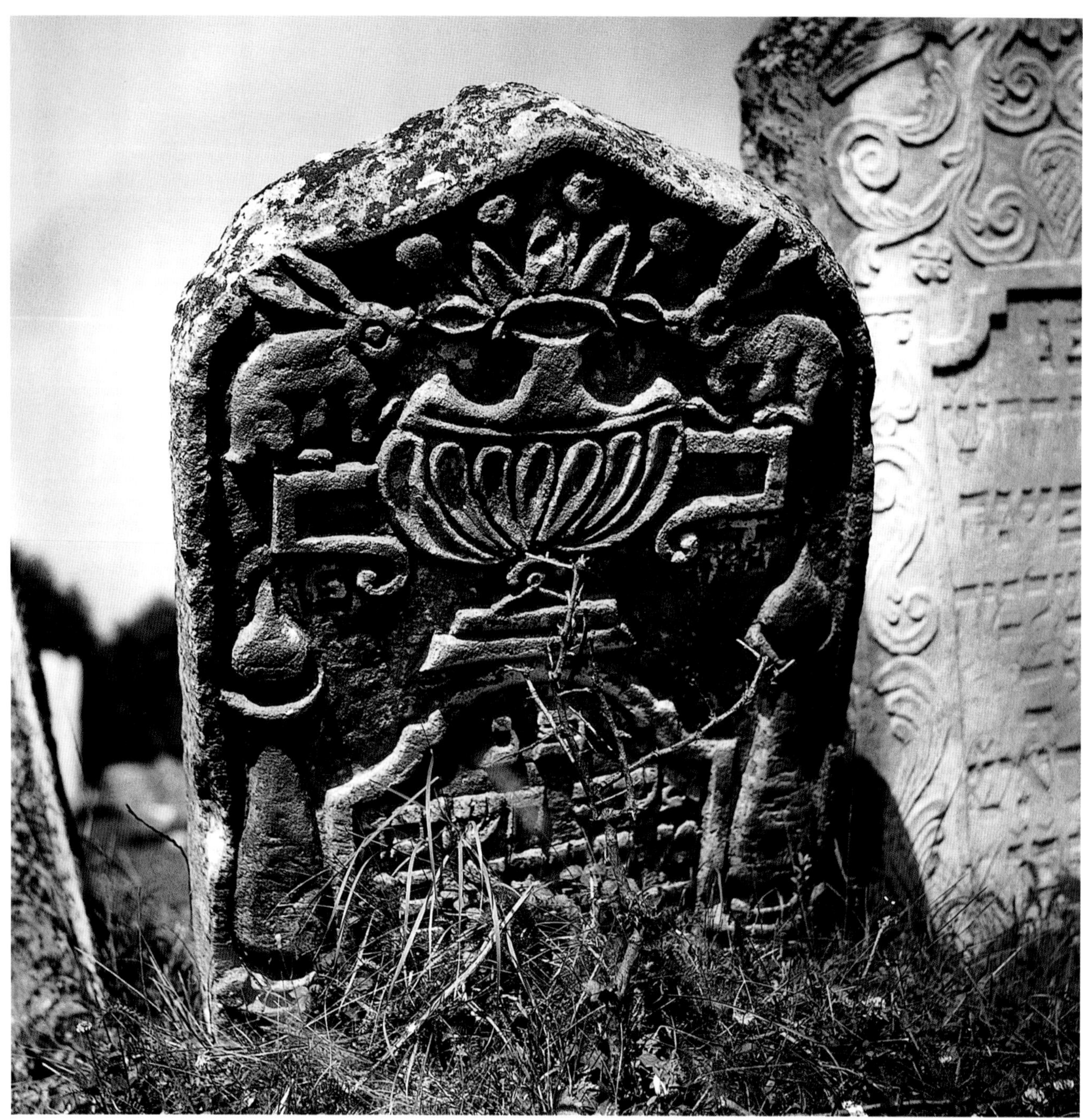

Kuty. 1826.
Two rabbits nibbling on a flower in a pot, a female reference. The rabbit represents fecundity

Opposite:
Kuty. Between 1850 and 1900.
A lion and a unicorn in battle. The inscription on this tombstone is unusual in being written in Yiddish rather than in Hebrew.
Here lies David Peltzil.

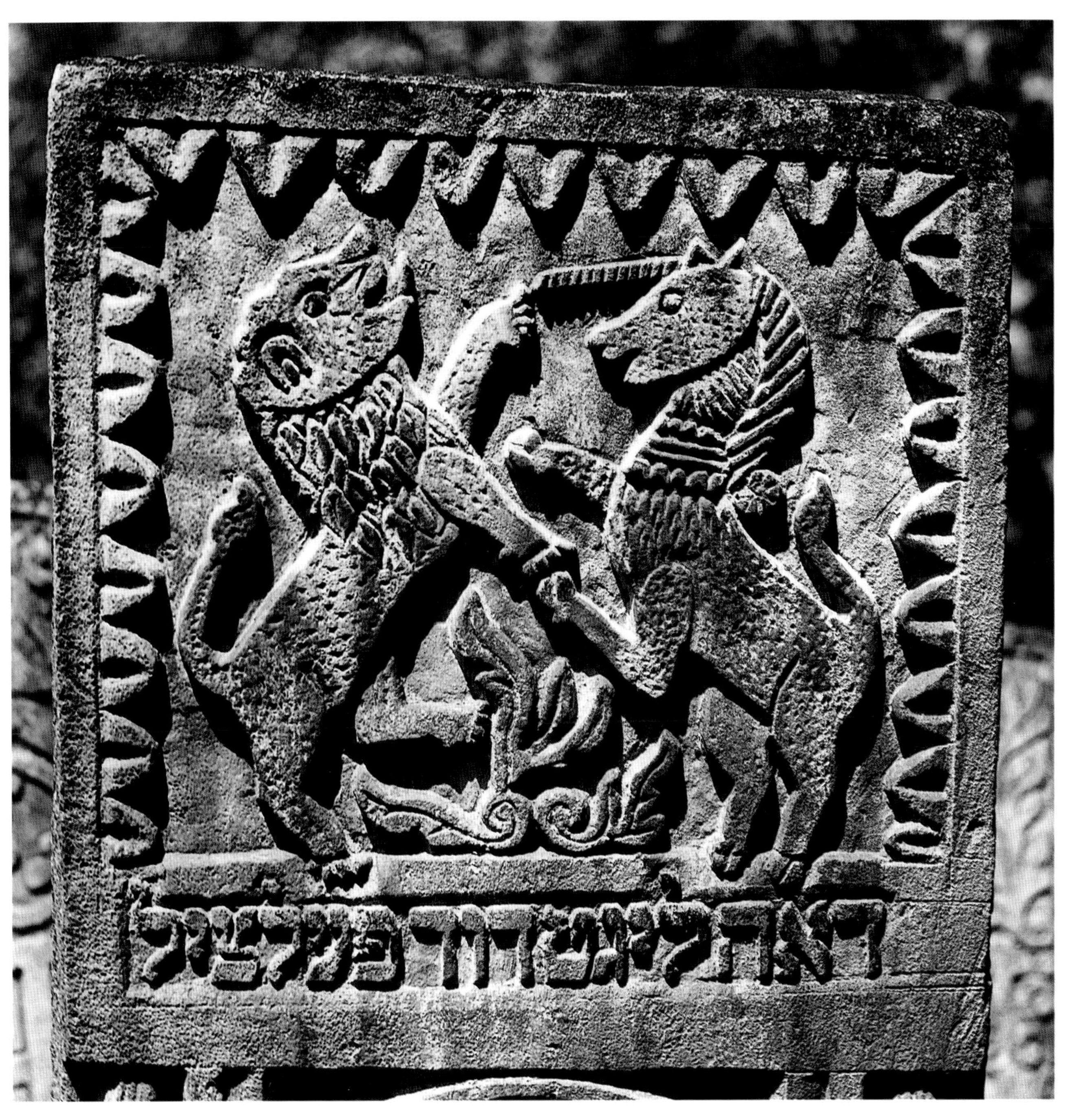

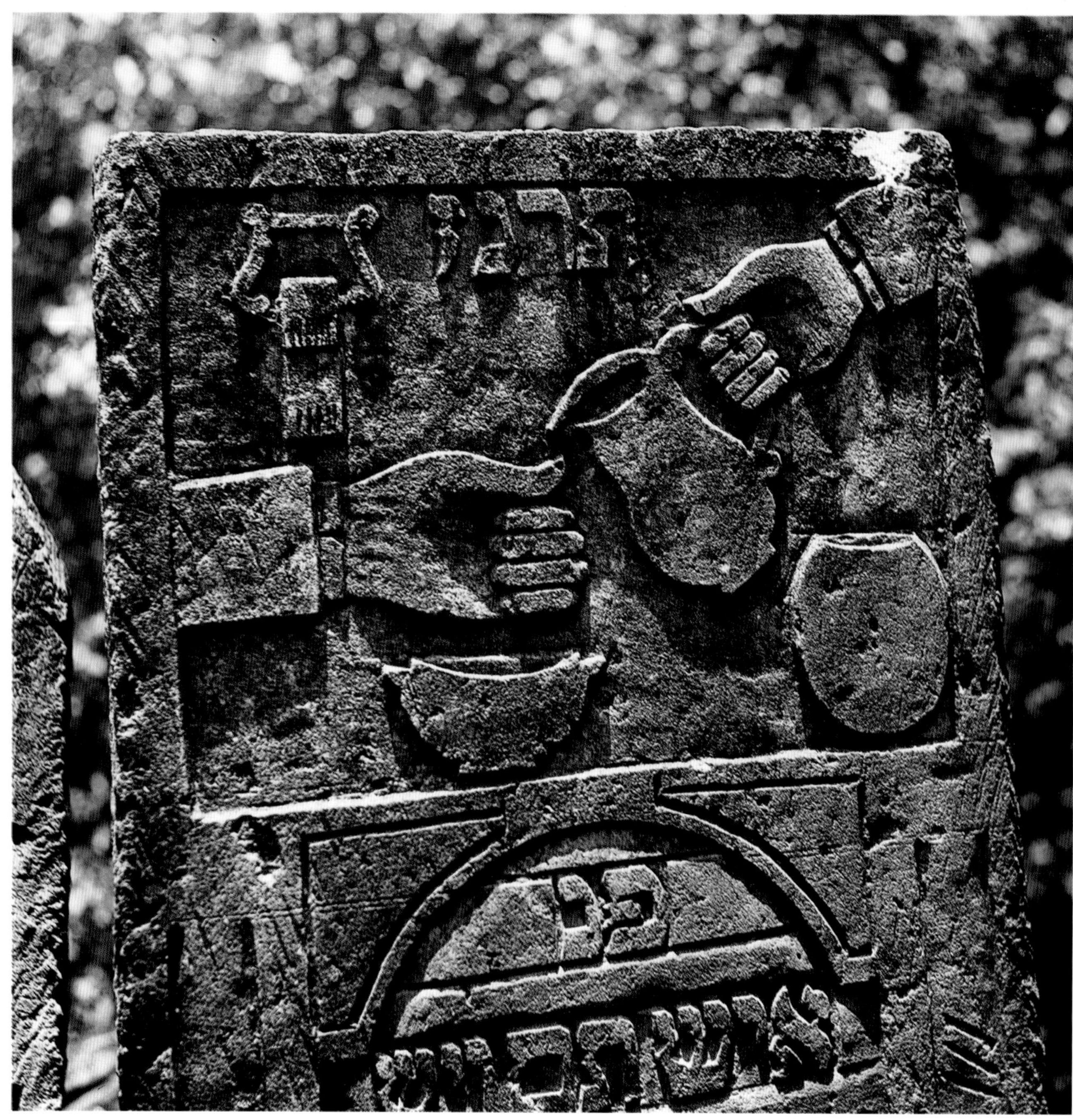

Kuty. 1897.

The ritual washing of the Cohain's (priest's) hands by a Levite, with a pitcher, basin, and towel, indicating that the deceased was a Levite.

A righteous and honest man.

Opposite:

Kuty. Between 1850 and 1900.

A lion beneath a tree.

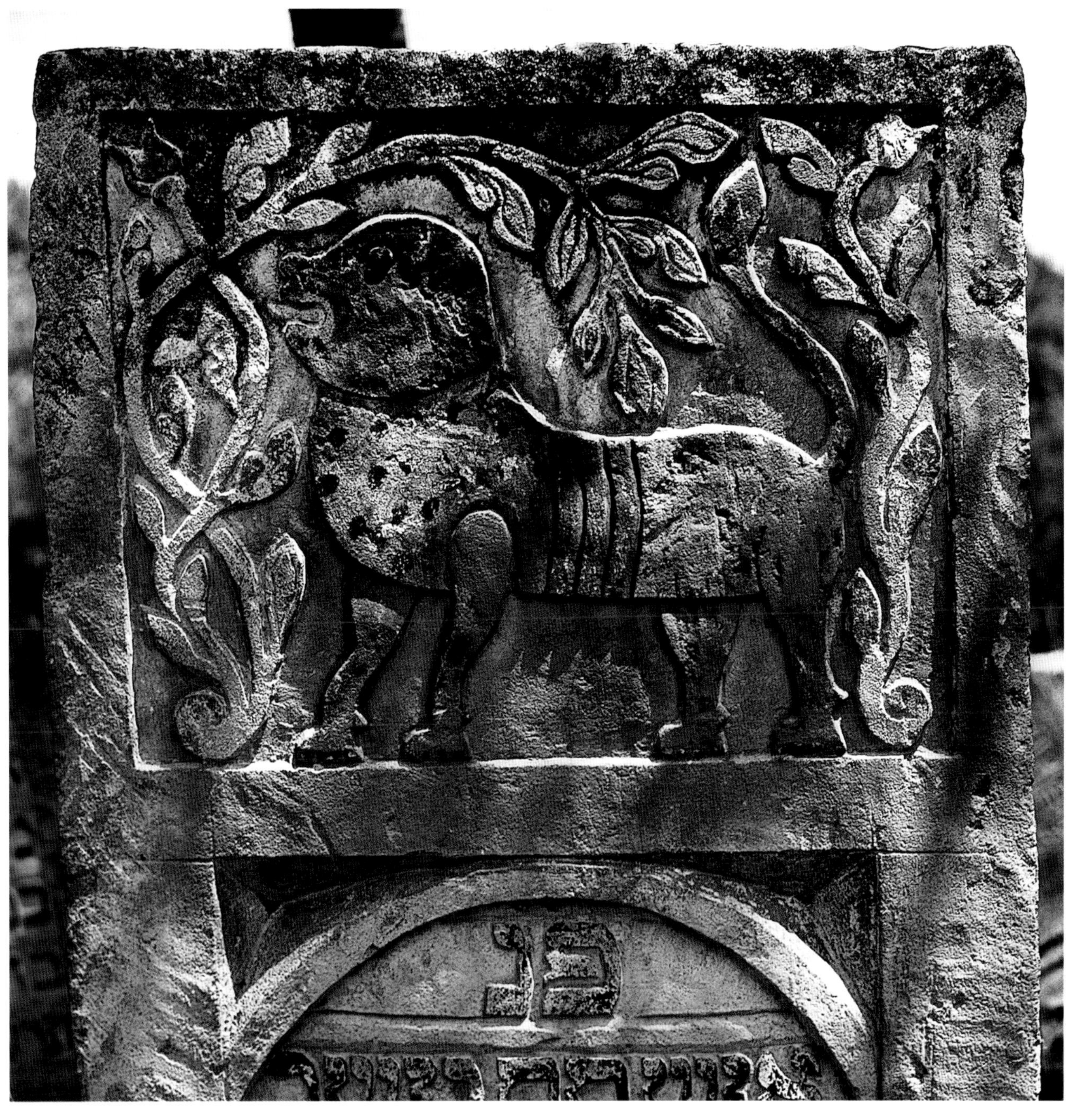
פנ

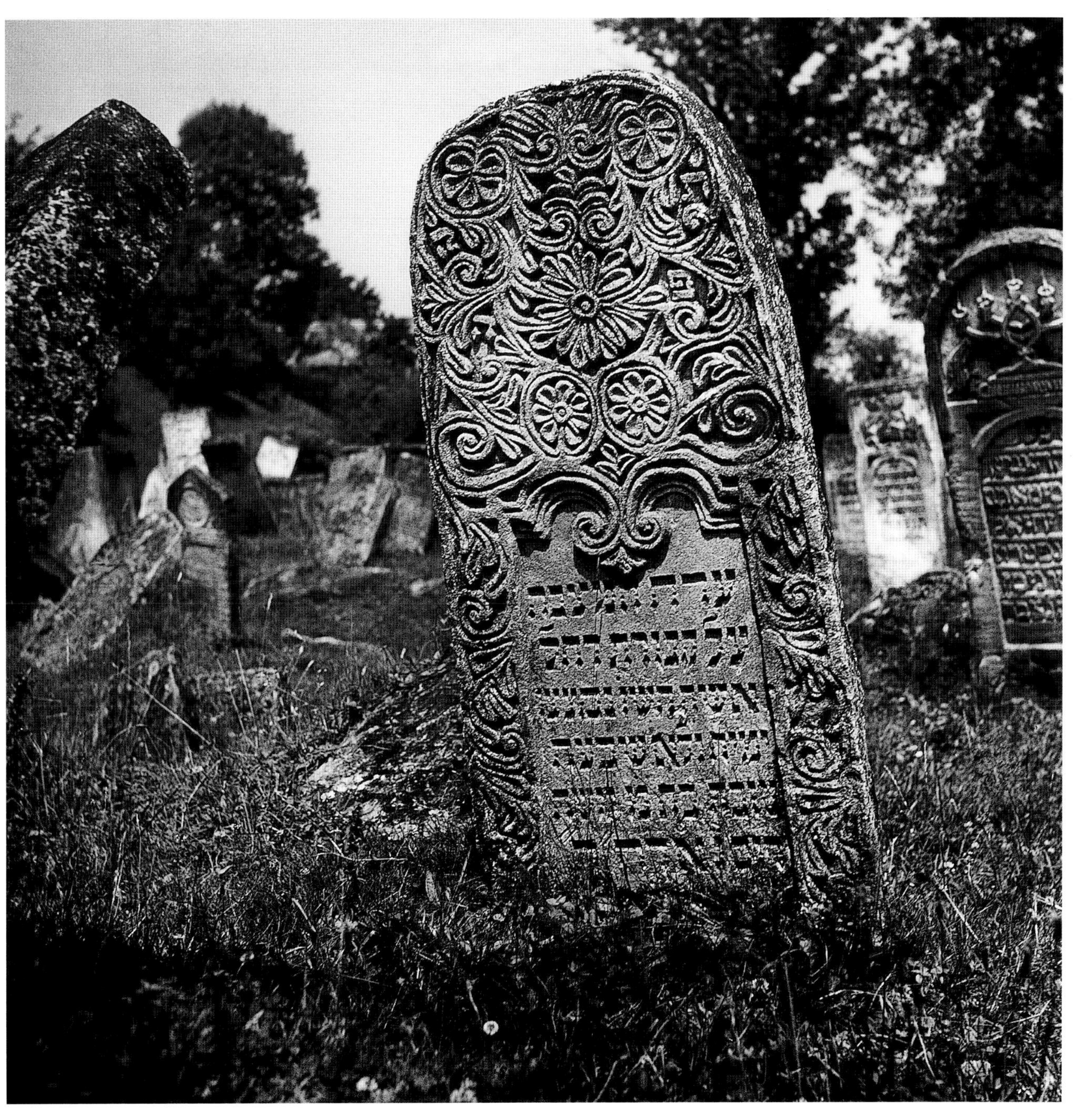

Kuty. 1825.

Ornate floral design bordered by leaves, with a fallen flower in the center. The stone is a monument to Rachel, an important woman, daughter of Moshe David. The year 5585 is inscribed in the floral design. Rachel died at the age of forty. The Hebrew inscription refers to the burial by Jacob of his thirty-seven year old wife, also named Rachel, in which he placed a stone to her memory.

She had trouble all her days and did not have years.

Opposite:

Detail.

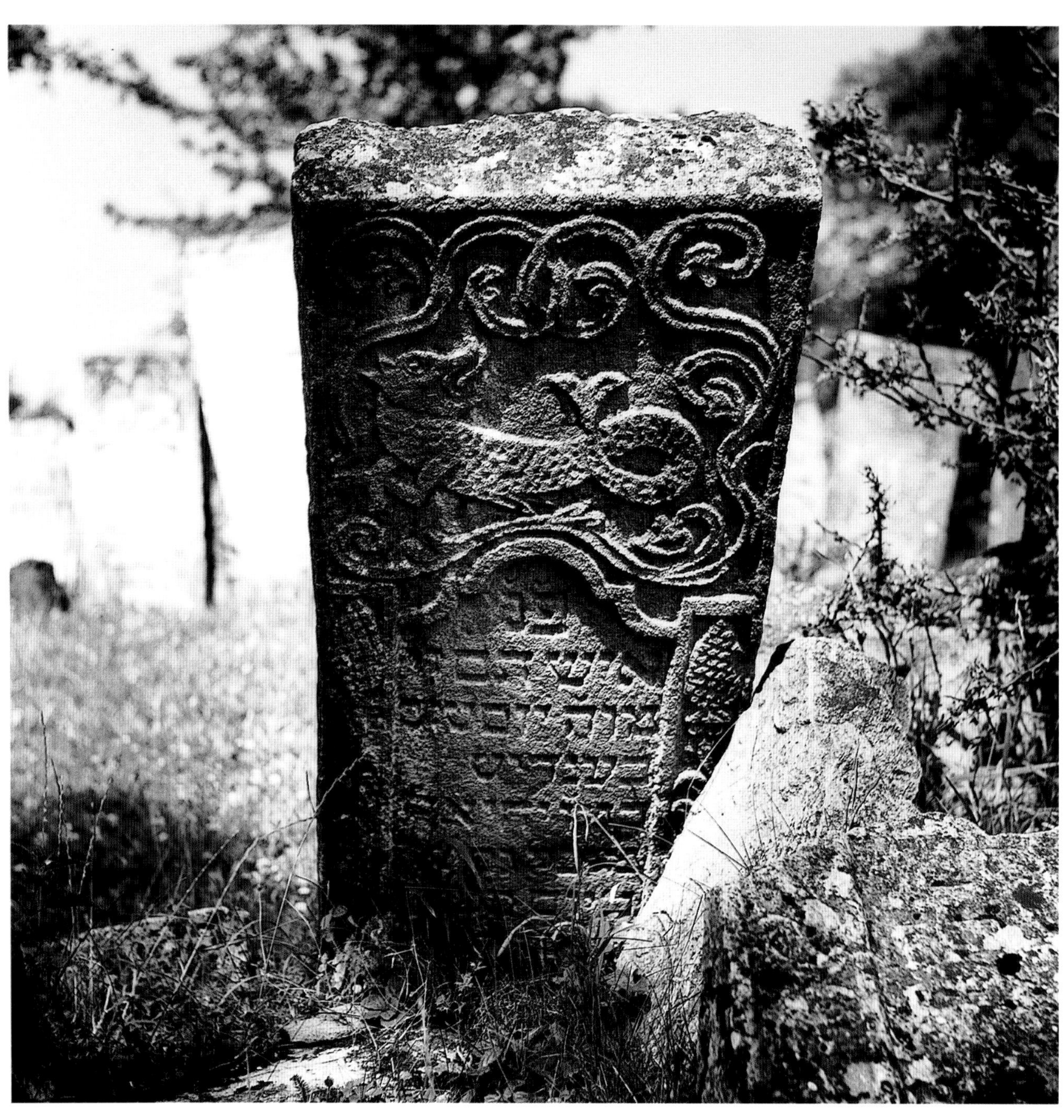

Kuty. Between 1800 and 1850.
A leviathan looking backward.
Here lies an honest and upright person, Haim Bendit.

Opposite:
Kuty. Between 1850 and 1900.
A sunflower with drooping leaves in a pot.
A young woman (maiden).

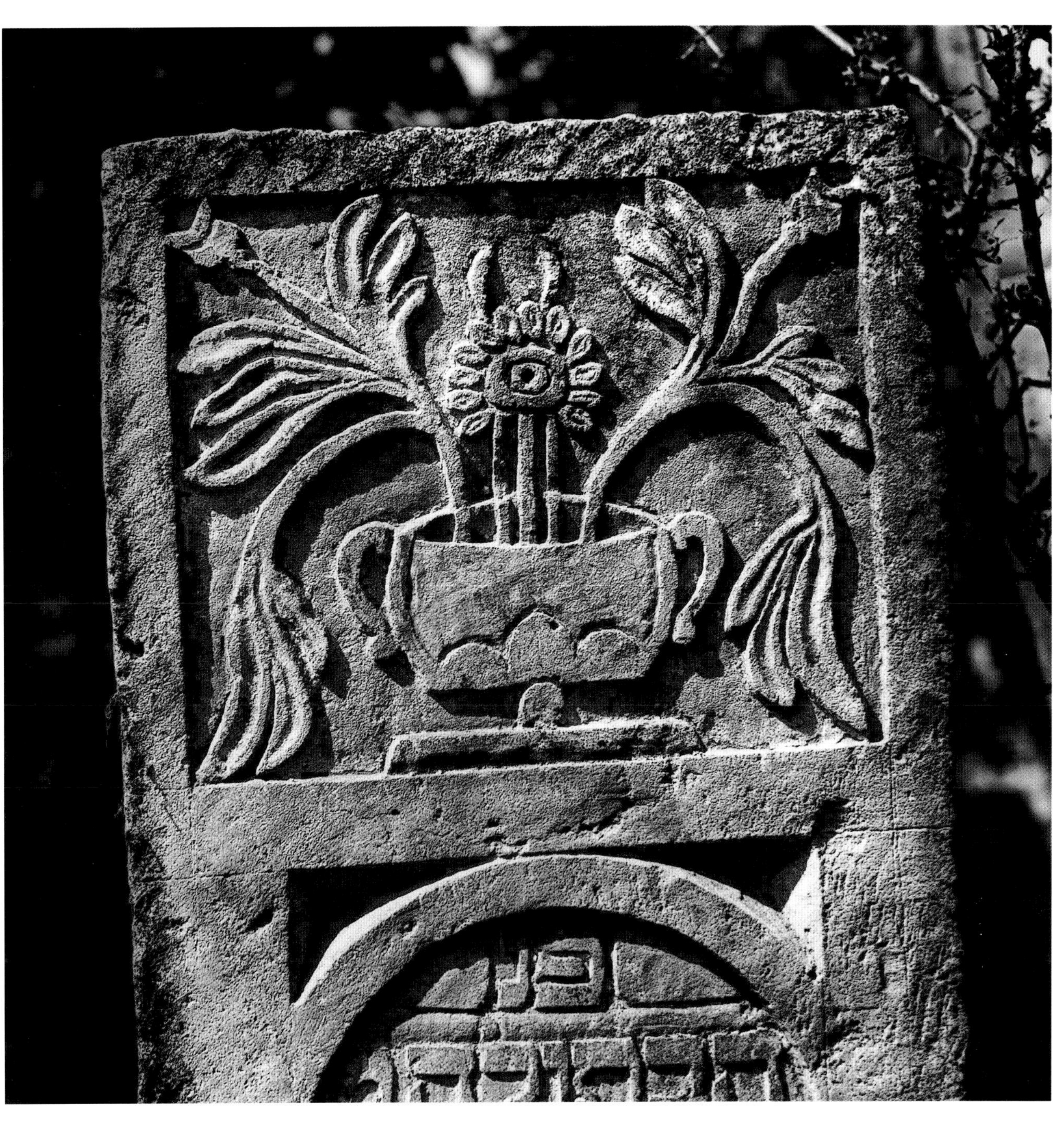

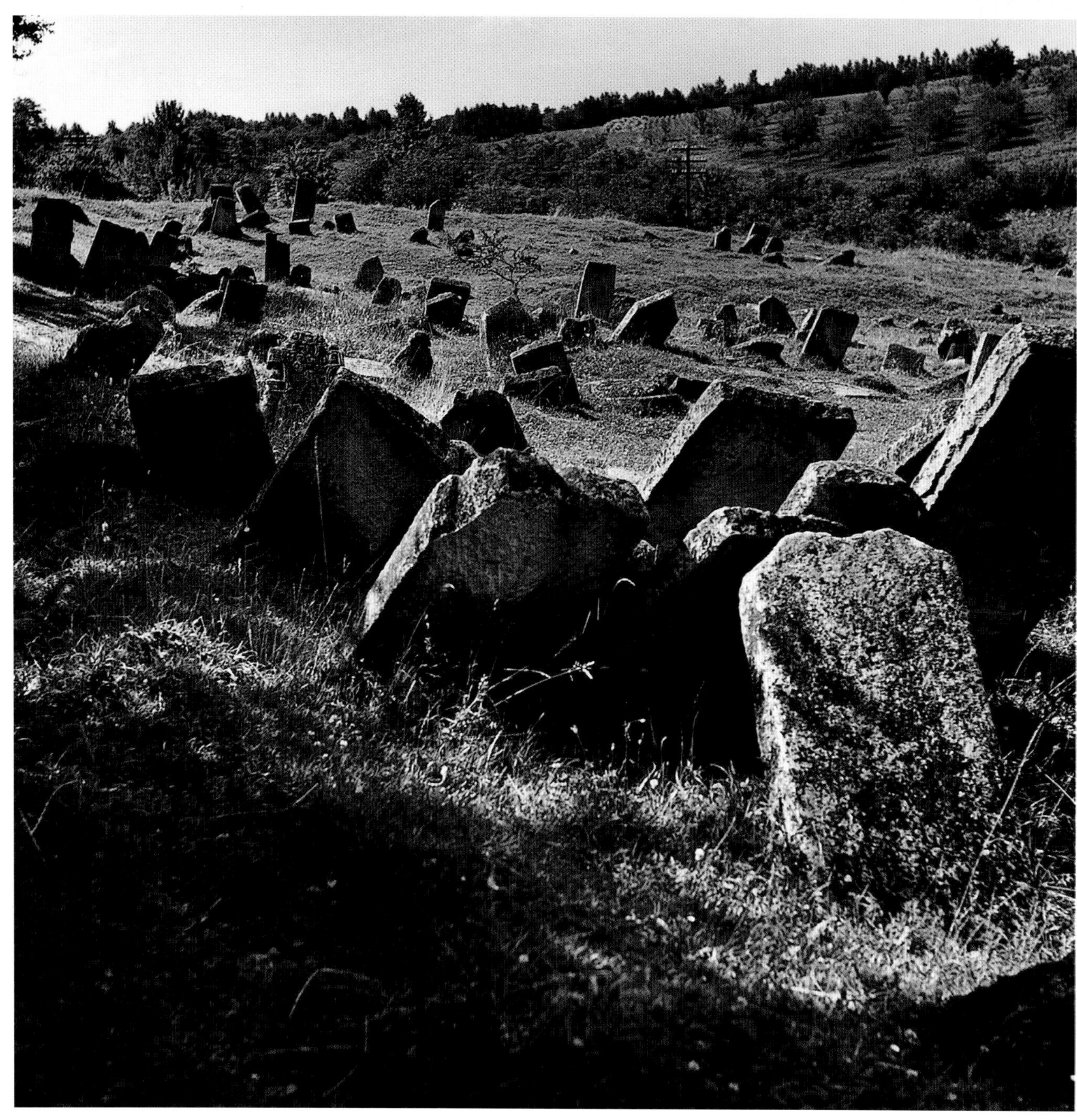

Sniatyn Cemetery.

Opposite:
Sniatyn. 1694.
The father of the deceased may have been a victim of the Cossack rebellion of 1648.
Israel, son of Abraham the Martyred.

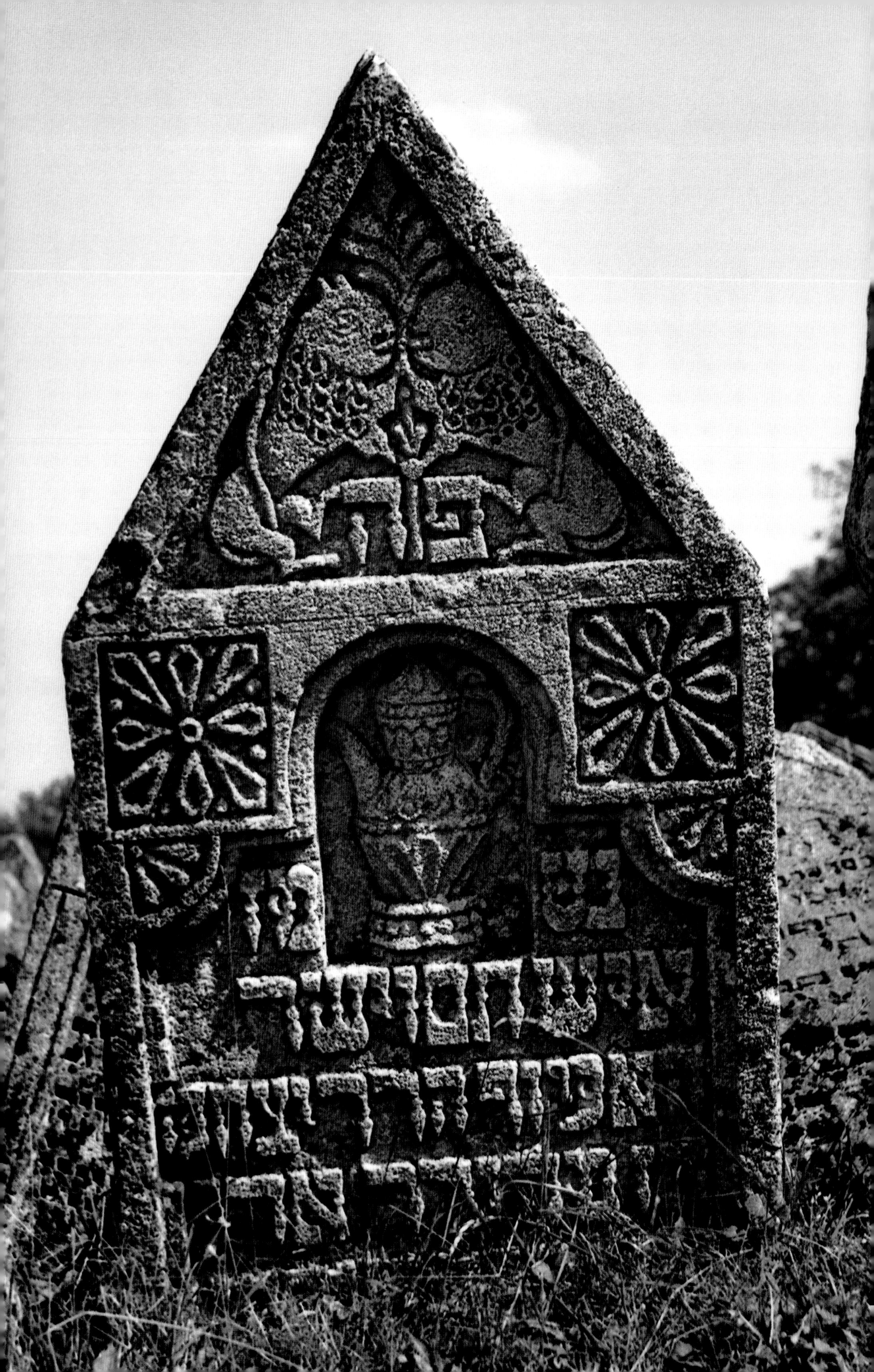
פנ

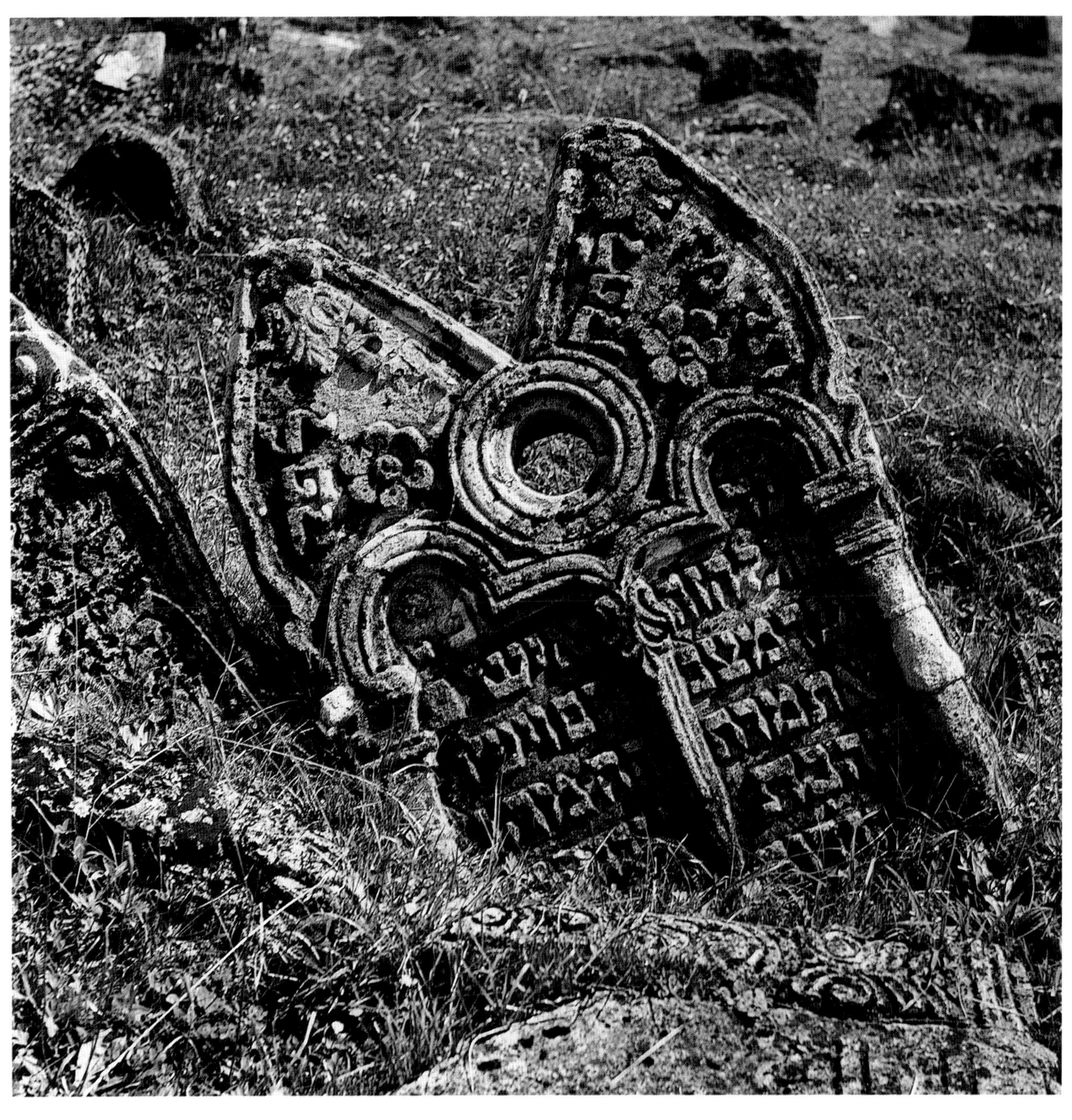

Snyatin. Between 1850 and 1900.

This tombstone is designed on the motif of the Ten Commandments. The panel on the left is for a man, and on the right for a woman—probably husband and wife. The inscription, from Genesis 31:52, is a reference to Jacob's creation of a monument to commemorate his peace treaty with Laban.

This heap of stones is a monument. This monument is a witness.

Opposite:

Snyatin. Early 1800s.

A water pitcher, signifying a Levite, and lions embracing a tree of life. The highly decorated pitcher is well preserved thanks to the recessed arch under which it was carved.

Yitzak son of Jacob. A very upright man.

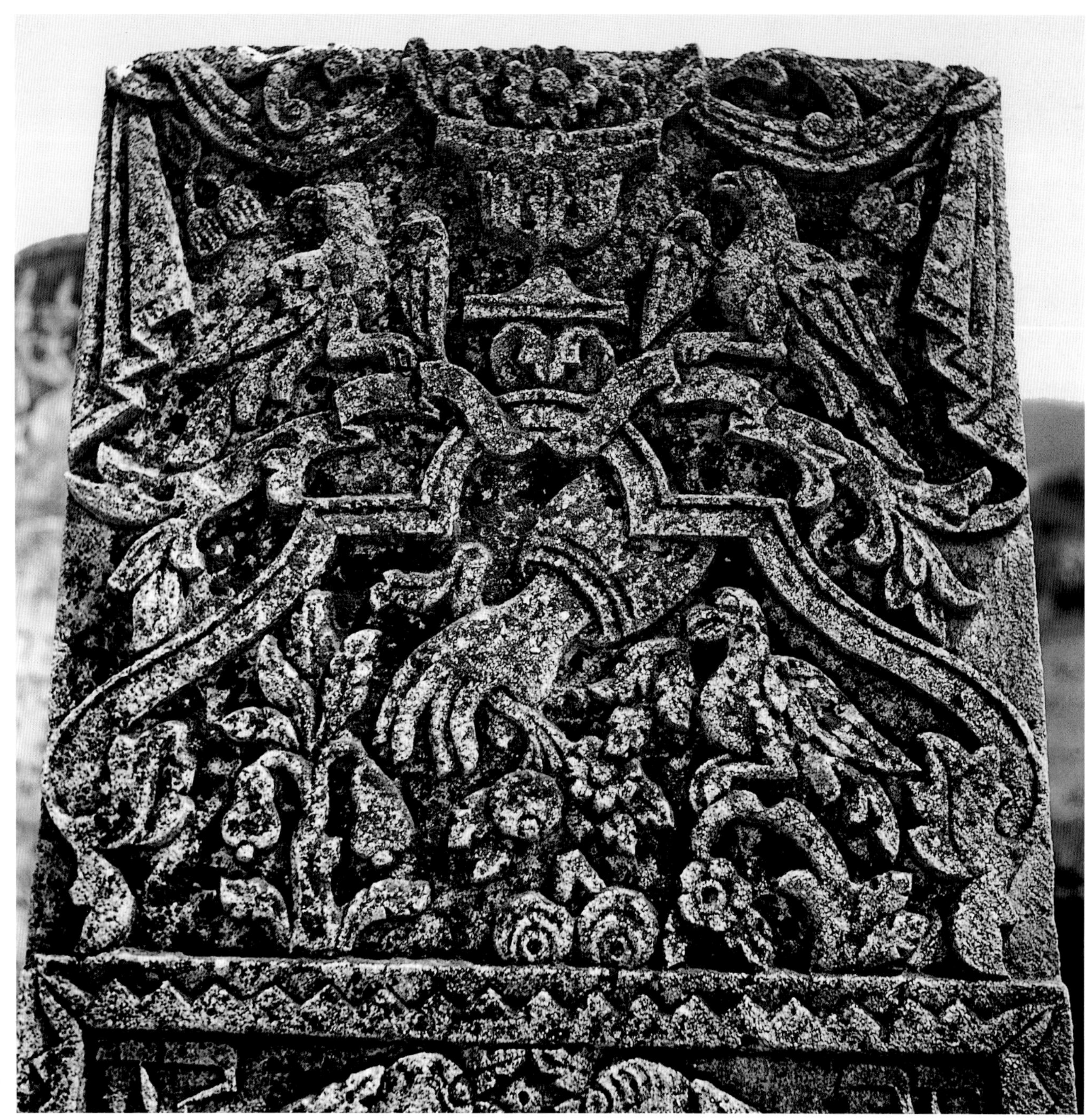

Snyatin. Between 1850 and 1900.
God's hand breaking a flowering branch with birds, curtains, and dove of peace.

Opposite:
Snyatin. Late 1700s.
Three-dimensional decoration with lions, rabbits, a wolf, deer, and a stag. The double-sided design refers to the Ten Commandments, and the inscription recalls Jacob's peace treaty with Laban.
This heap of stones is a monument. This monument is a witness.

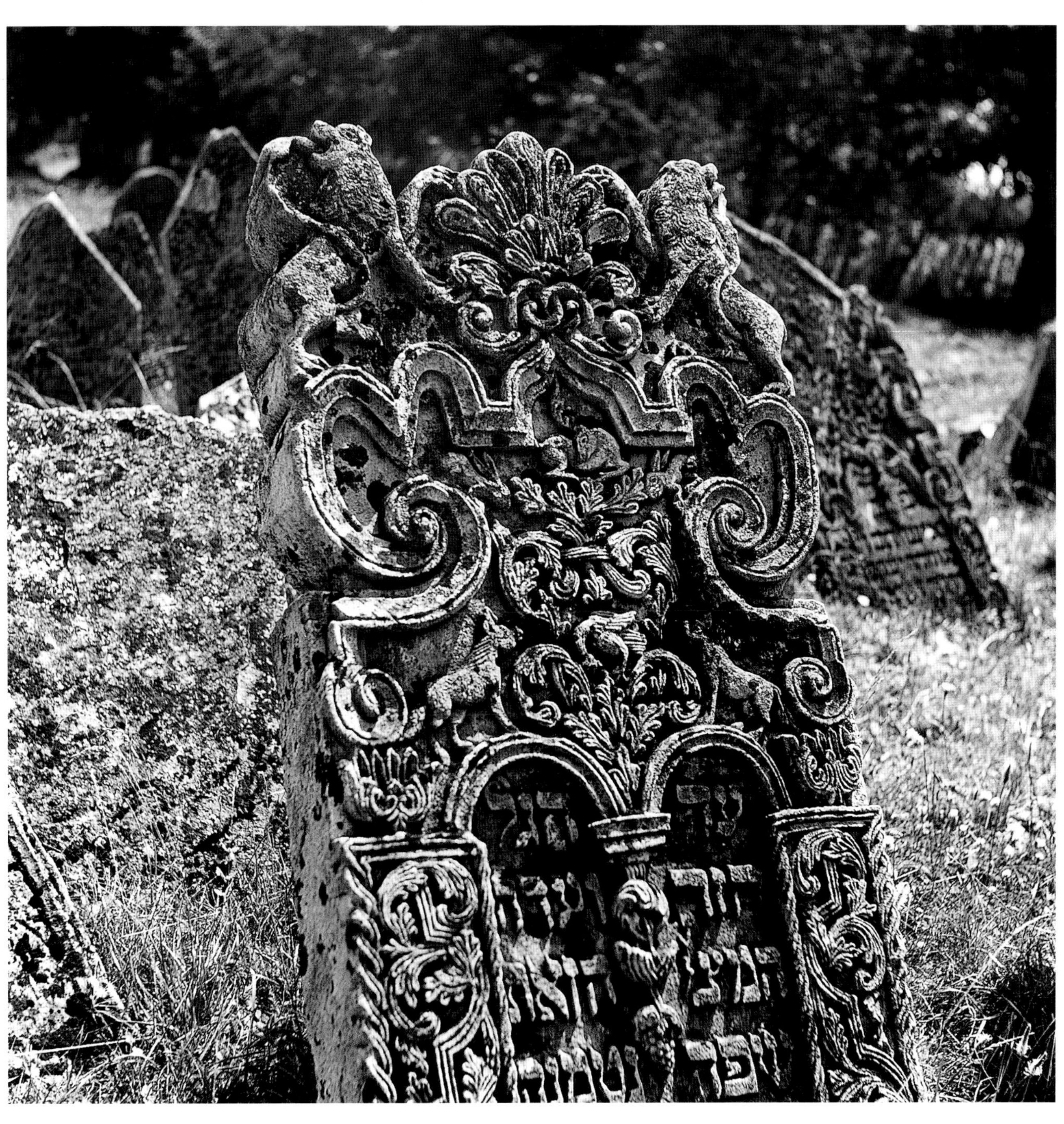

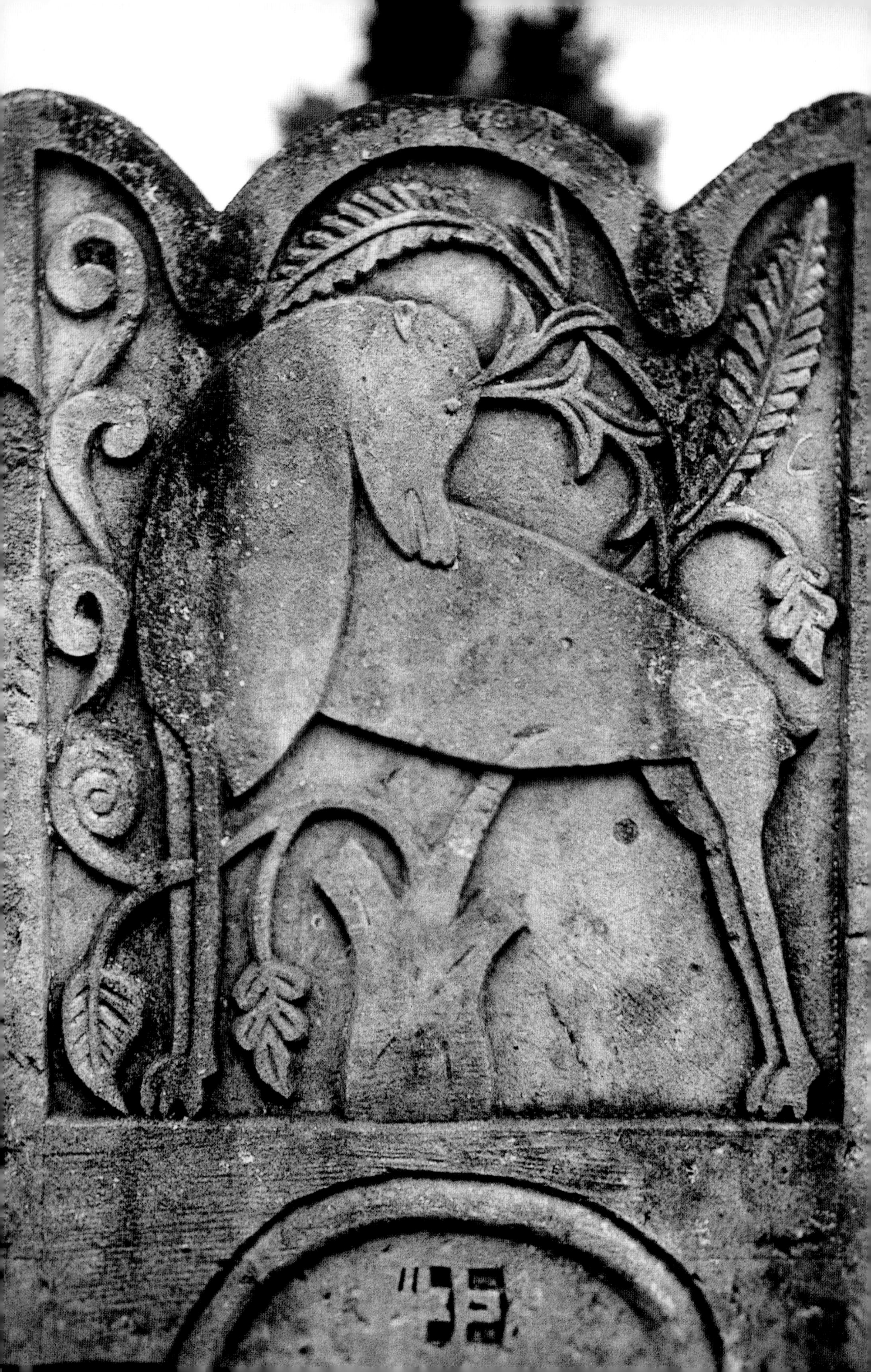
פ״נ

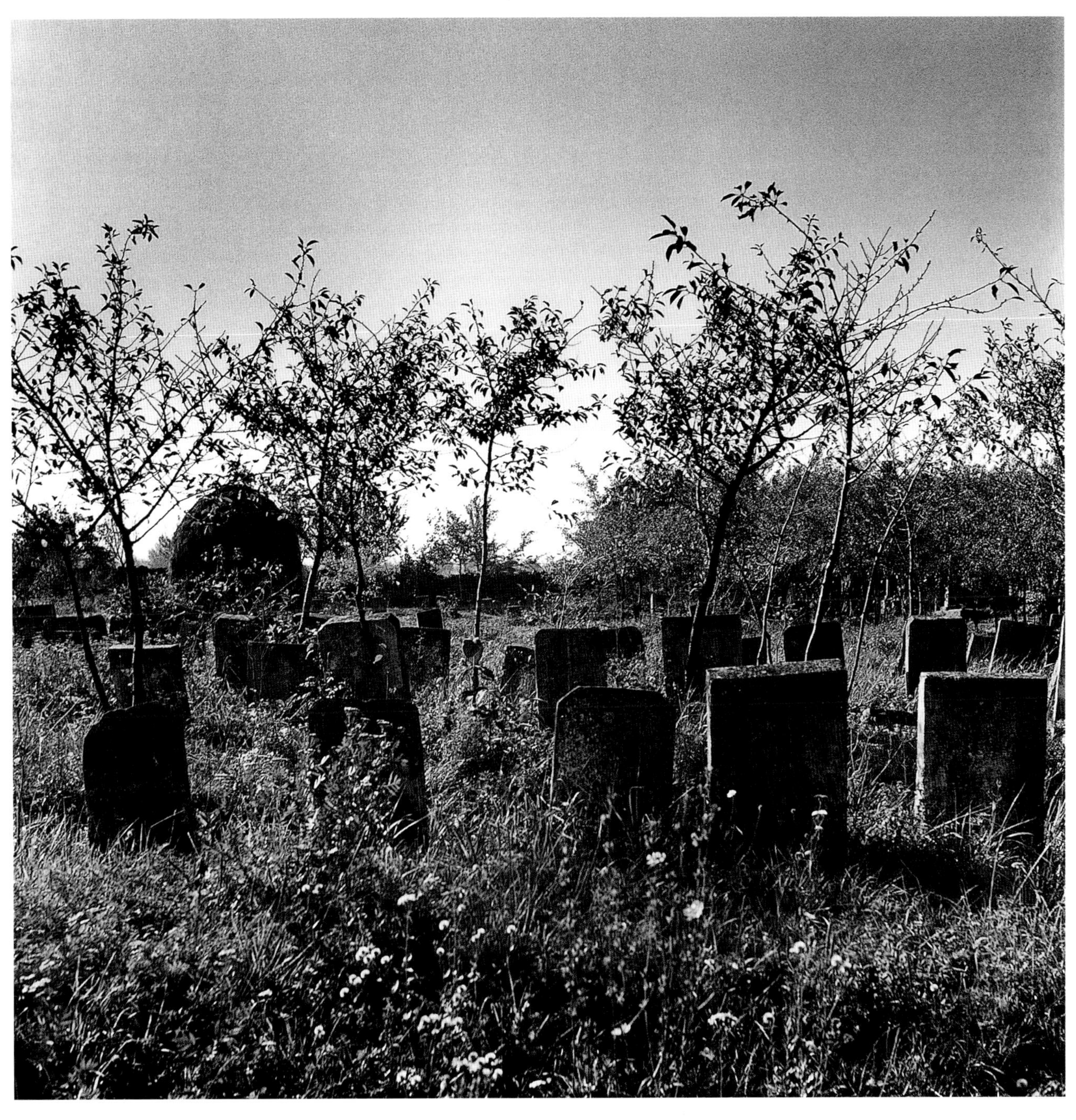

Khotin cemetery

Opposite:
Zastavna. Between 1650 and 1700.
A deer in Hebrew is "Zvi," a common name in the Pale of Settlement, and in Yiddish is "Hirsch," also a common name. The deceased's name may have been Hirsch. The stylized deer in front of a tree is looking back as if to remind the living to contemplate the life of the deceased.

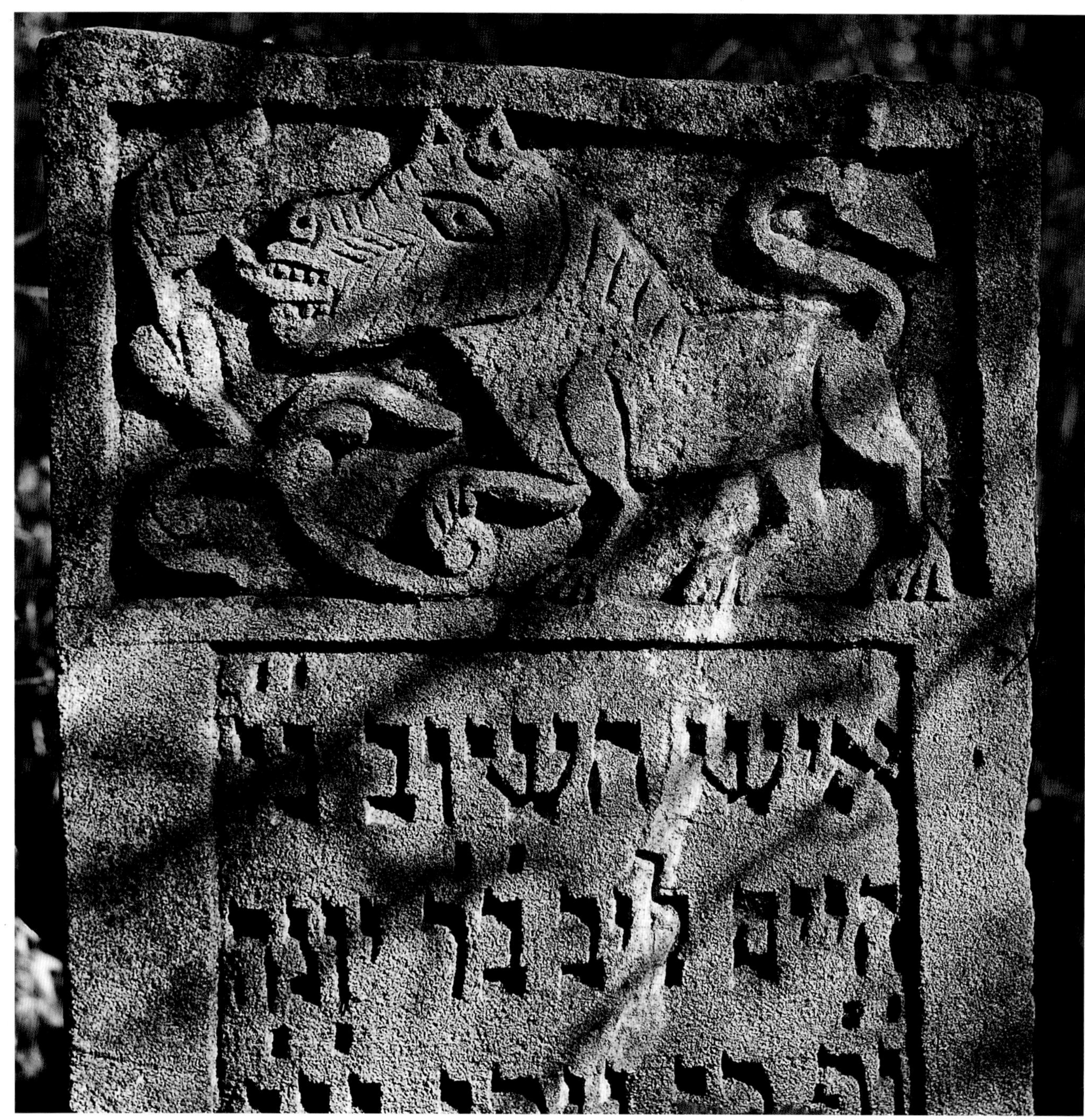

Khotin. Between 1850 and 1900.

A ferocious lion trampling a blooming tree.

A prominent man. Chaim Leib [or Lev, meaning lion] son of Jonah. An important man. May his candle burn brightly.

Opposite:

Khotin. Late 1800s.

A fish (for the name Fishel) beneath a simple flower.

Levi, son of Yekhiel Fishel. He was sated with years [an old man] when he died. Died on the twenty-sixth of Tivet. Let his spirit rest.

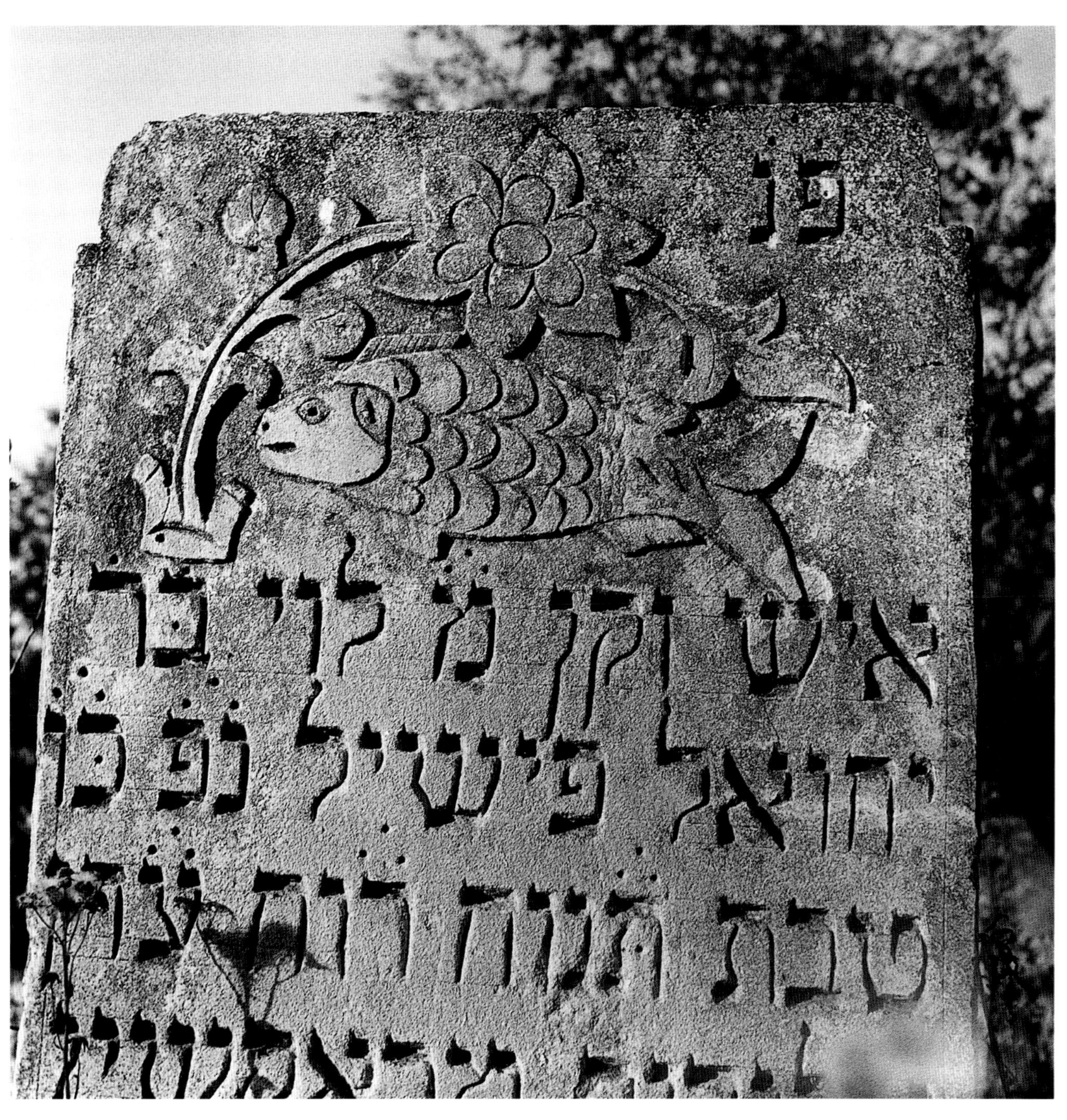
פנ
איש זקן מ לוי בר

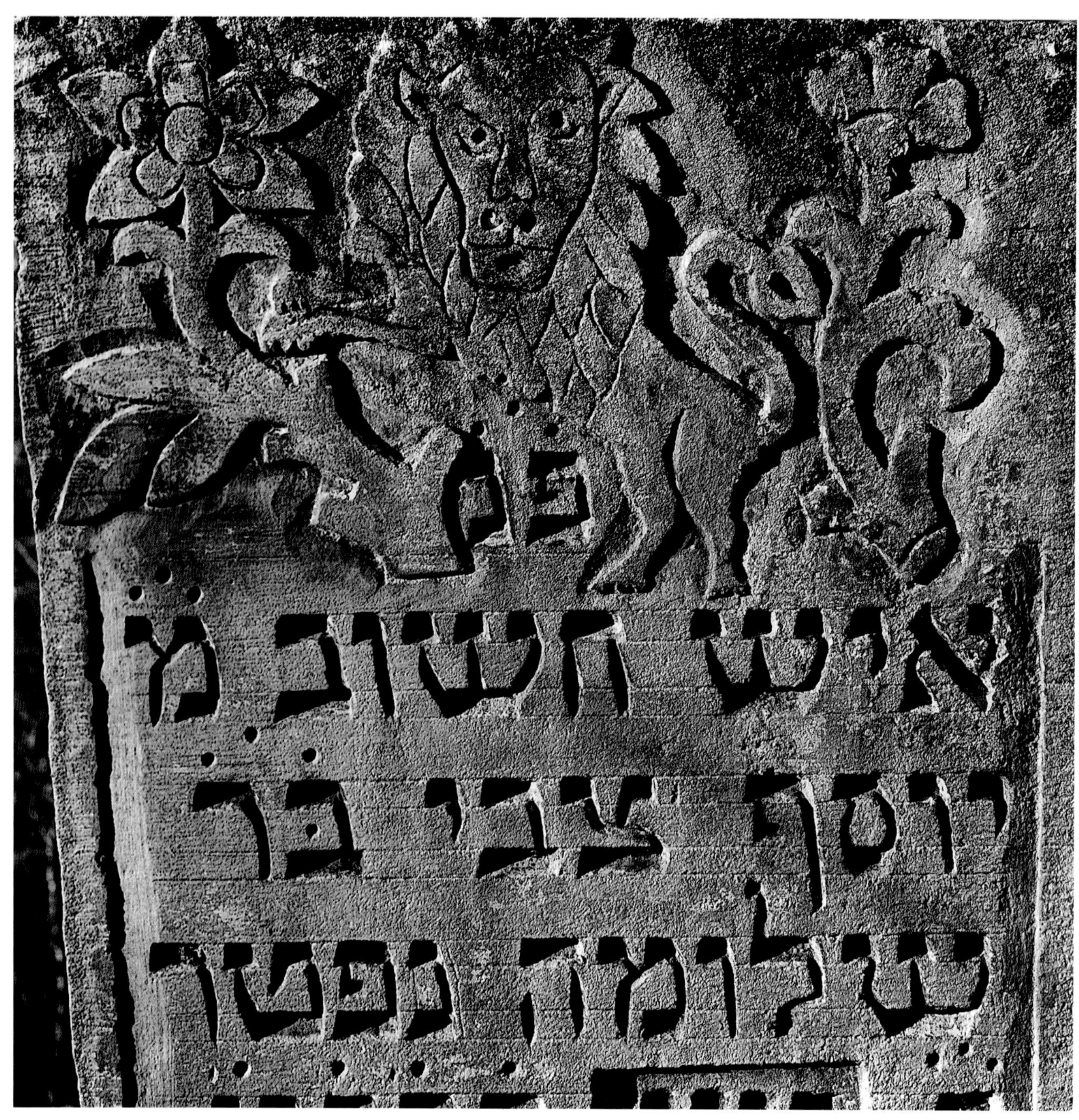

Khotin. 1909.

A lion pushing down a flowering tree rampant, while the tree to the right remains standing.

A prominent man. Mr. Joseph Zvi son of Shlomo.

Opposite:

Khotin. Between 1850 and 1900.

A lion with a ridged mane.

An important woman. Feiga, daughter of Jacob.

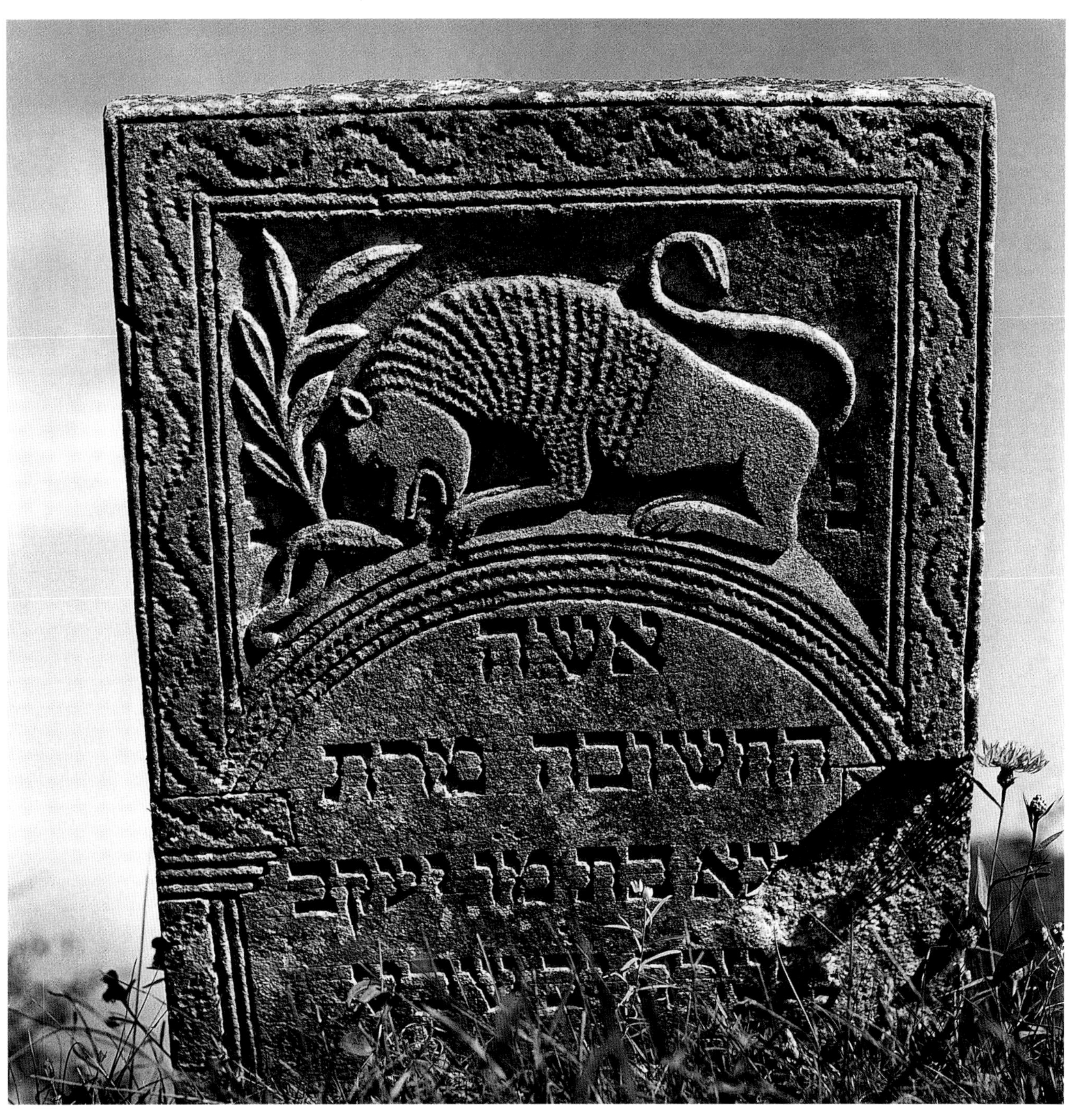
אשה
החשובה מרת

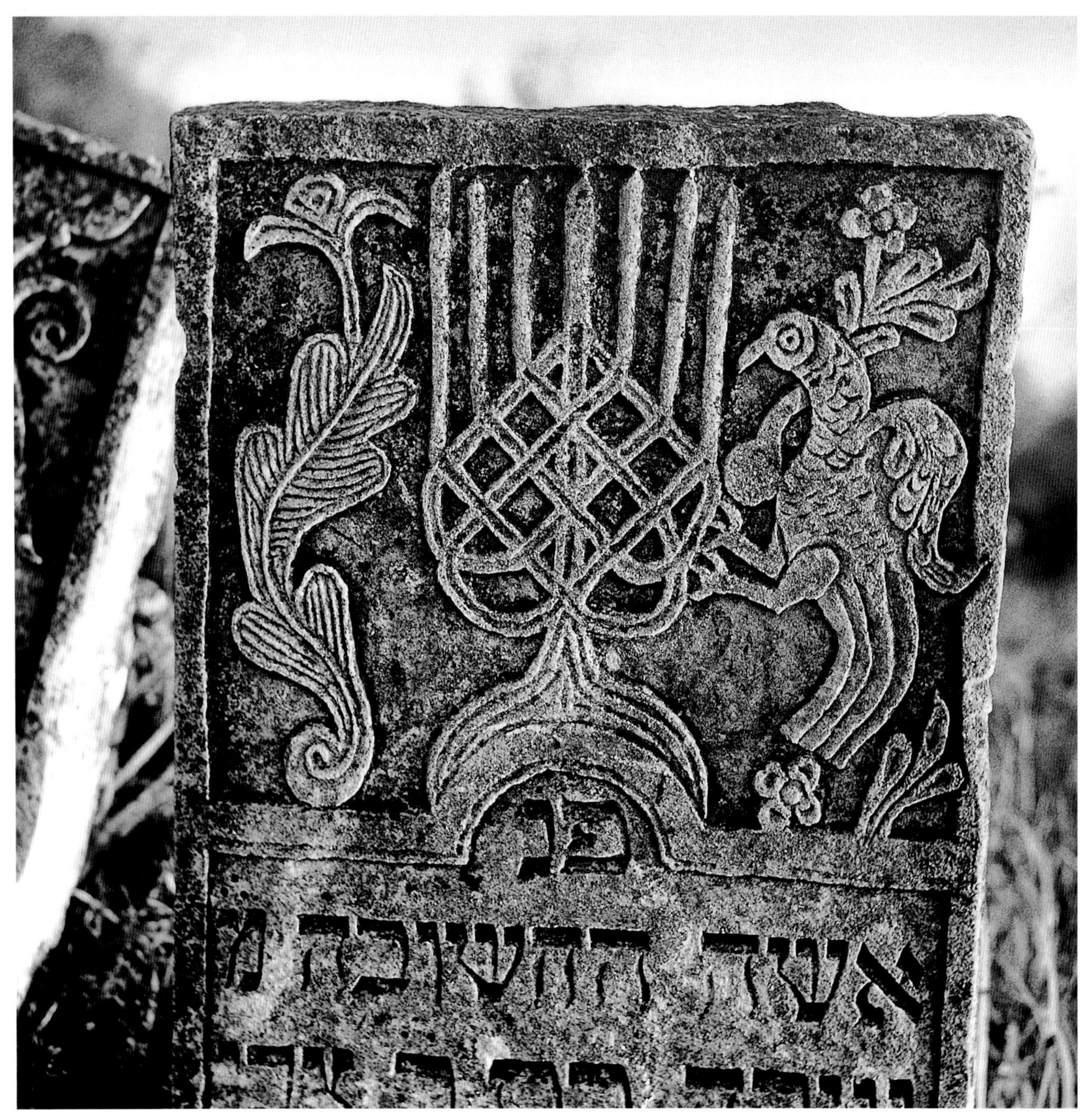

Khotin. Between 1850 and 1900.

A seven-branched menorah flanked by a peacock and flowers.

A worthy woman. Sarah daughter of Zvi.

Opposite:

Khotin. Between 1850 and 1900.

Seven-branched lighted menorah in the shape of a crown.

The worthy woman, Miriam Rifka, daughter of Jacob.

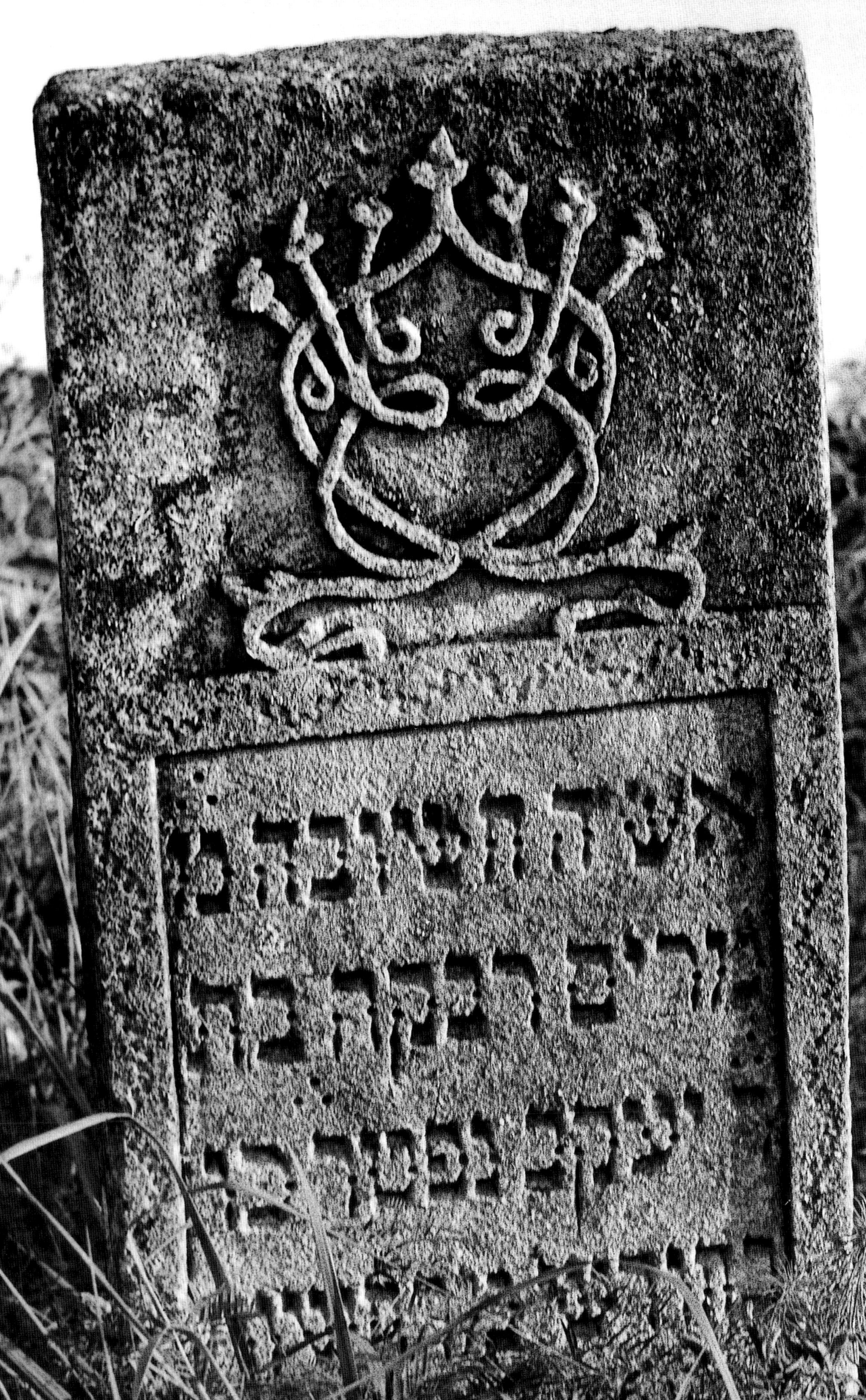

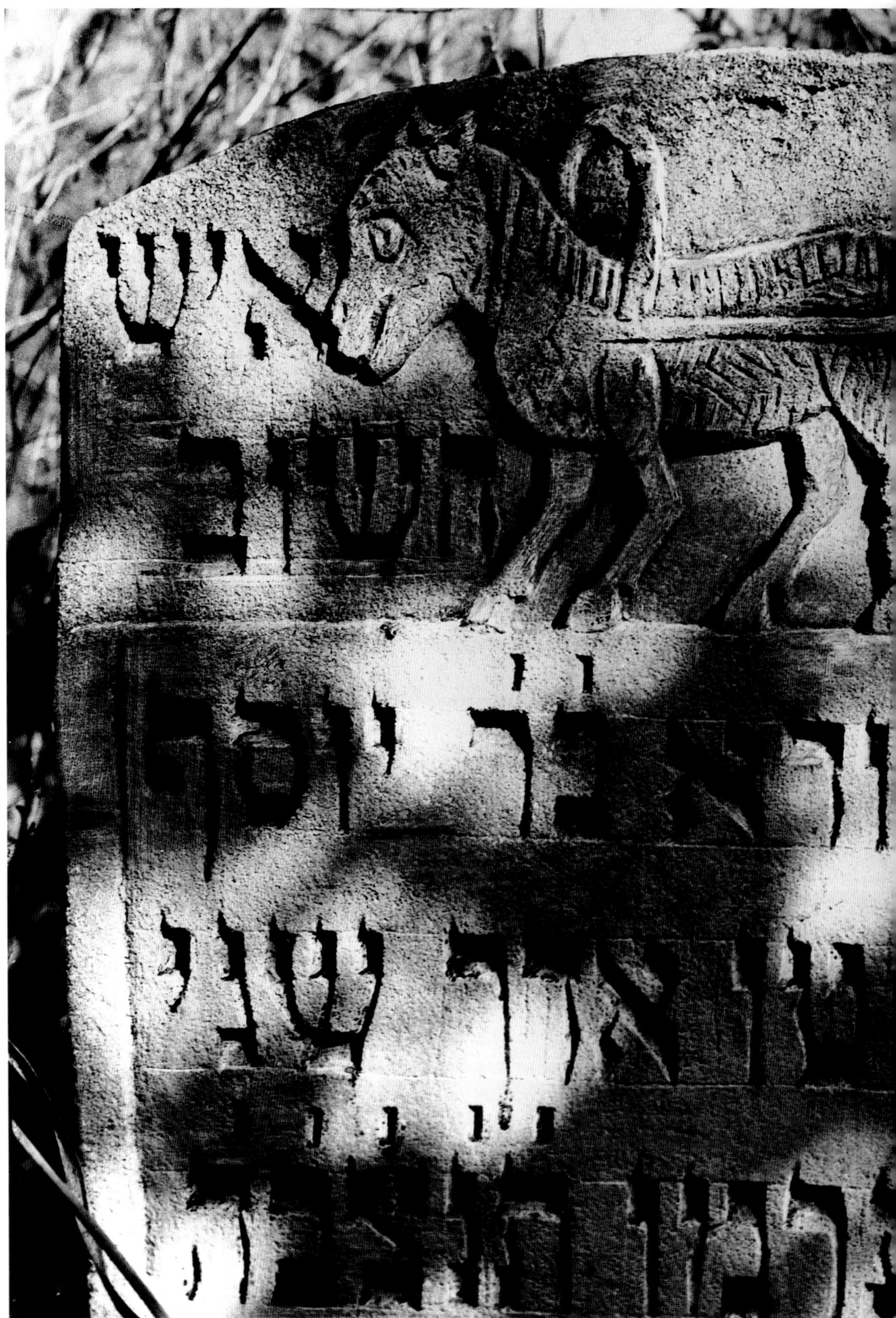

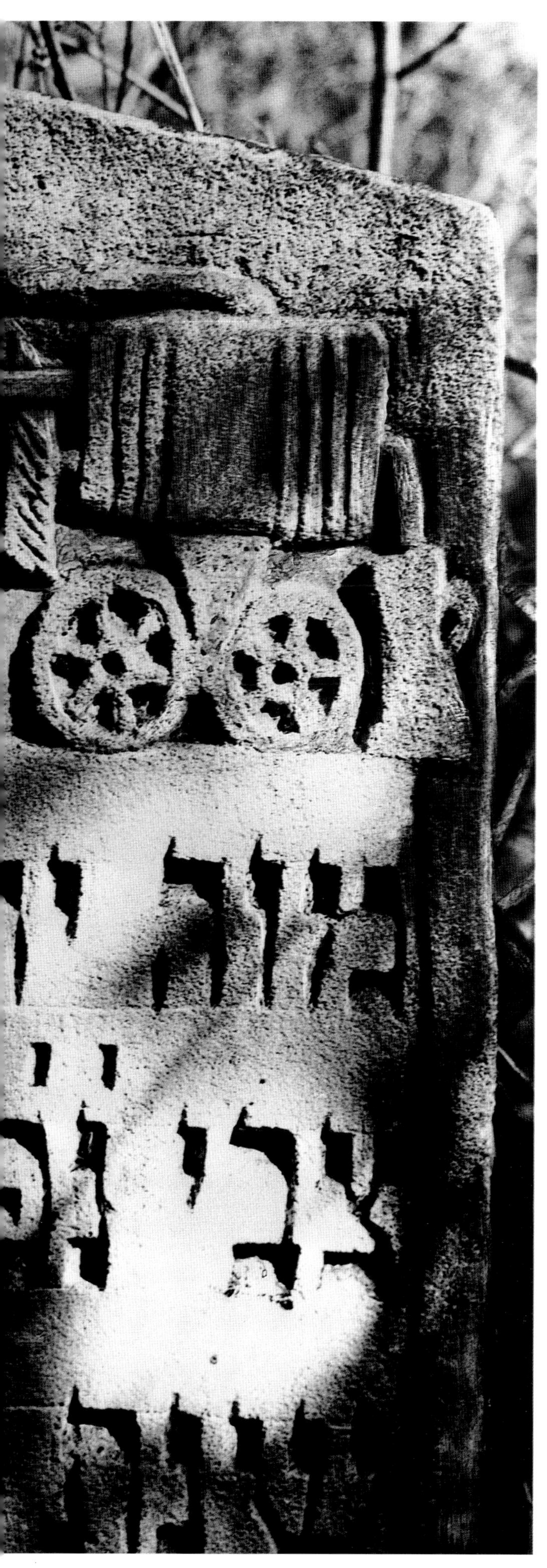

Khotin. 1886.

A horse-drawn wagon with liquid or grain being poured into a container at the rear of the cart. Possibly a water carrier, milk vendor, or grain merchant. *A prominent man. Yehuda Baer, son of Joseph Zvi. Died on the fifteenth day of Adar in 5646.*

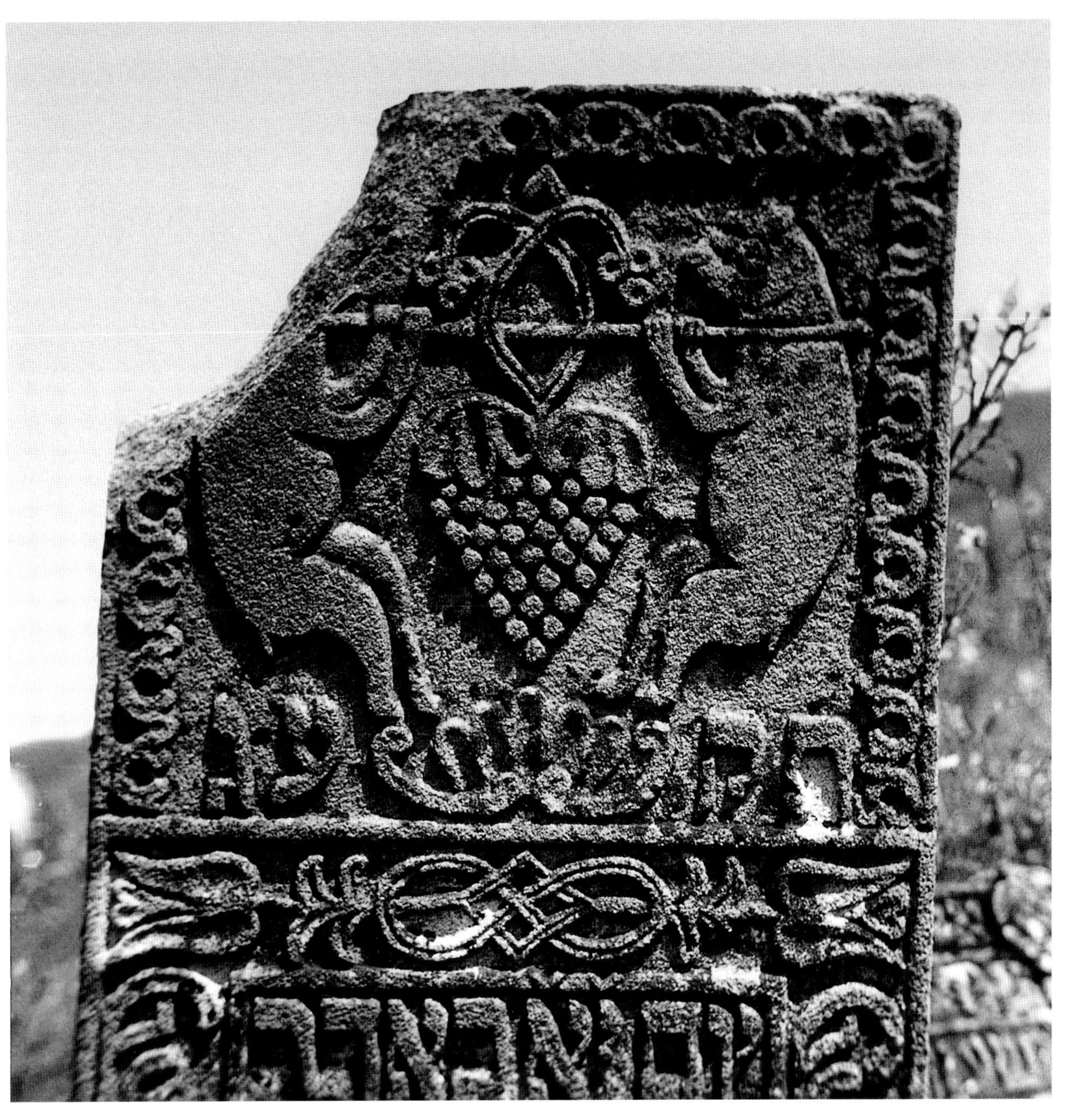

Sadgora. 1813.

Bears carrying grapes on a staff. The deceased died eleven days into the month of Adar, which is just before the holiday of Purim. It is possible that the grapes signify the drinking of wine, which is traditional at Purim. However, it is more likely that the carrying of grapes on a staff is symbolic of a story in the Torah. During the period of wandering in the desert, Moses sent spies on a reconnaissance mission to the Promised Land. They returned carrying grapes on a staff, representing the potential abundance to come.

Opposite:
Sadgora. 1789.

A Hebrew inscription in raised relief surrounded by an ornamental border.

A righteous man. Avram [Abraham] son of Aaron. Died ten days into the month of Teves in 5549. Here is buried a pure and wholesome man.

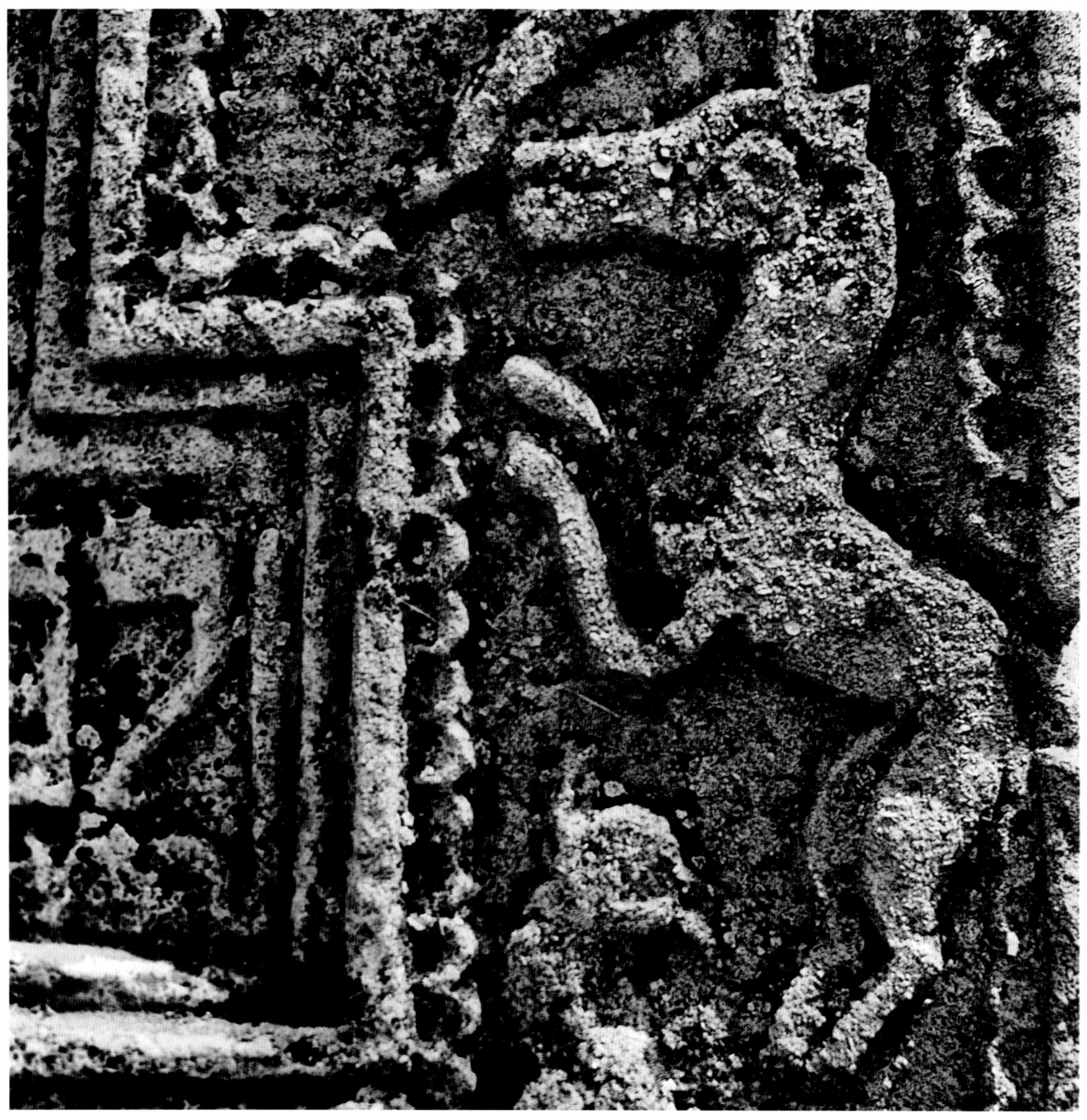

Sadgora. 1819.

Detail of a unicorn. The unicorn was said to live high in the mountains, thus embodying the loftiness of the human spirit.

Opposite:

Sadgora. 1819.

Griffins, unicorns, and birds.

An important woman, the rabbi's wife. Deborah, daughter of Shimshon, who was our teacher and rabbi.

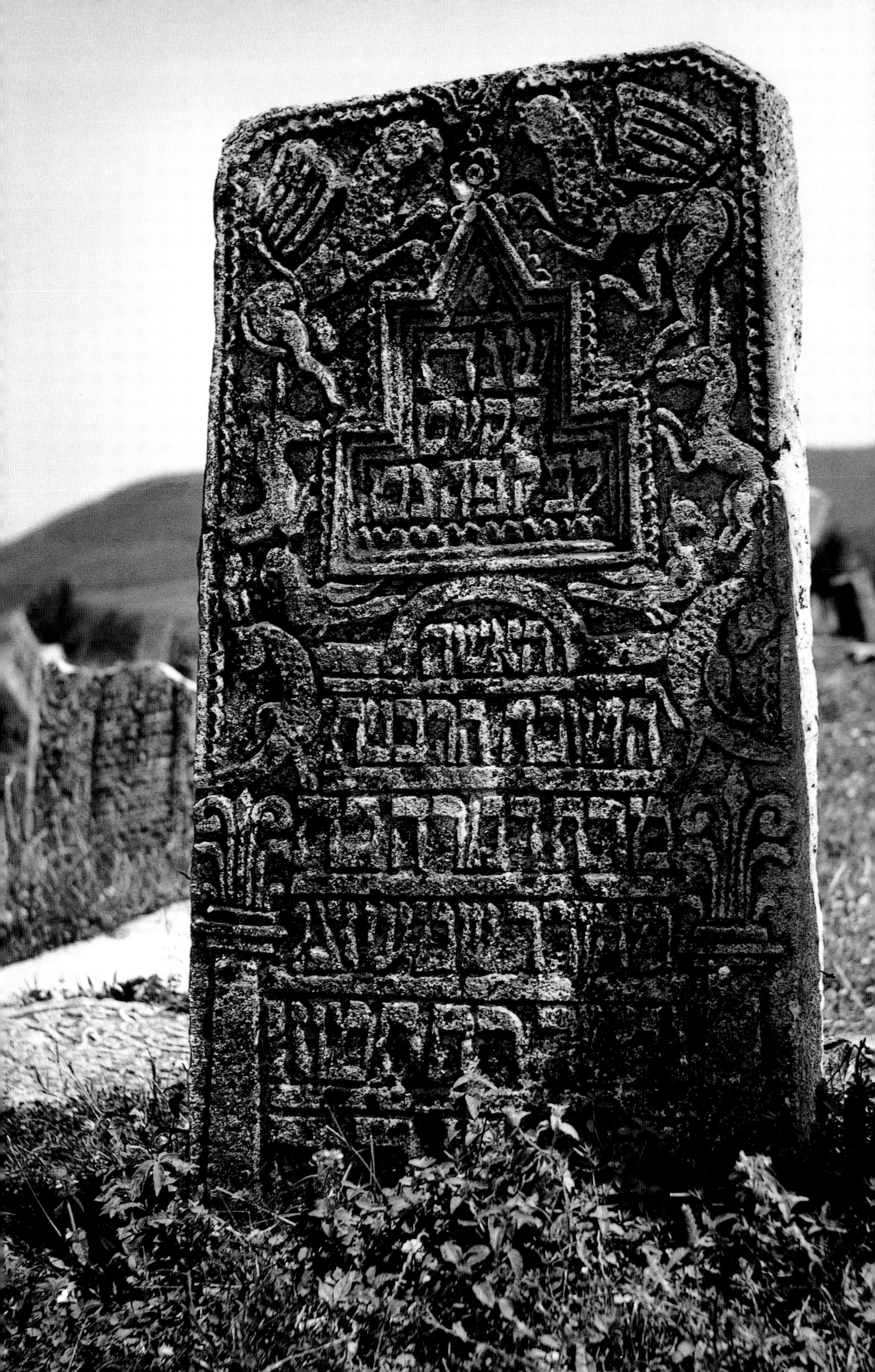
האשה

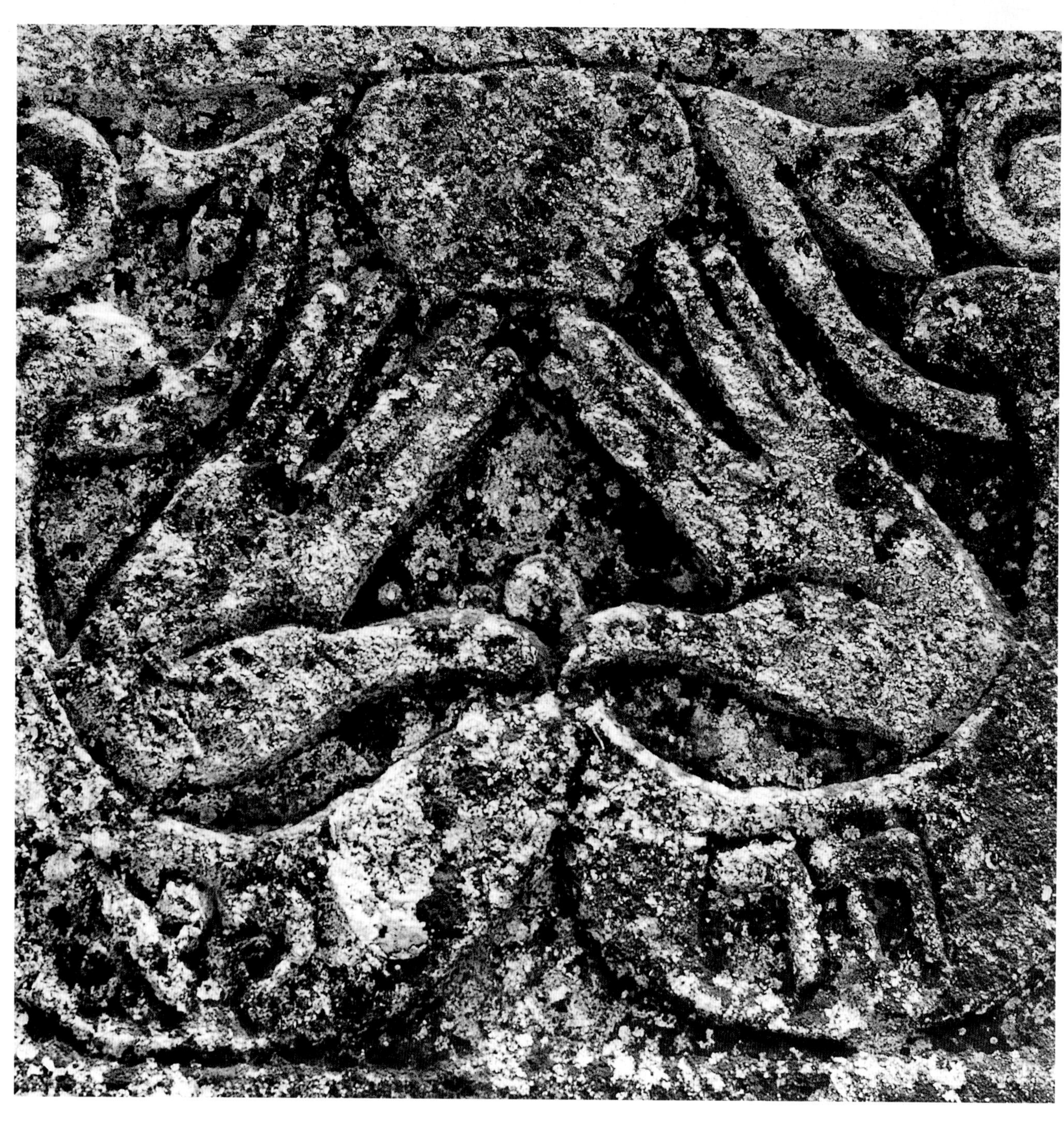

Sadgora. Between 1850 and 1900.
Praying hands of a Cohain (priest), topped by a crown.

Opposite:
Sadgora. 1824.
A lemon tree.

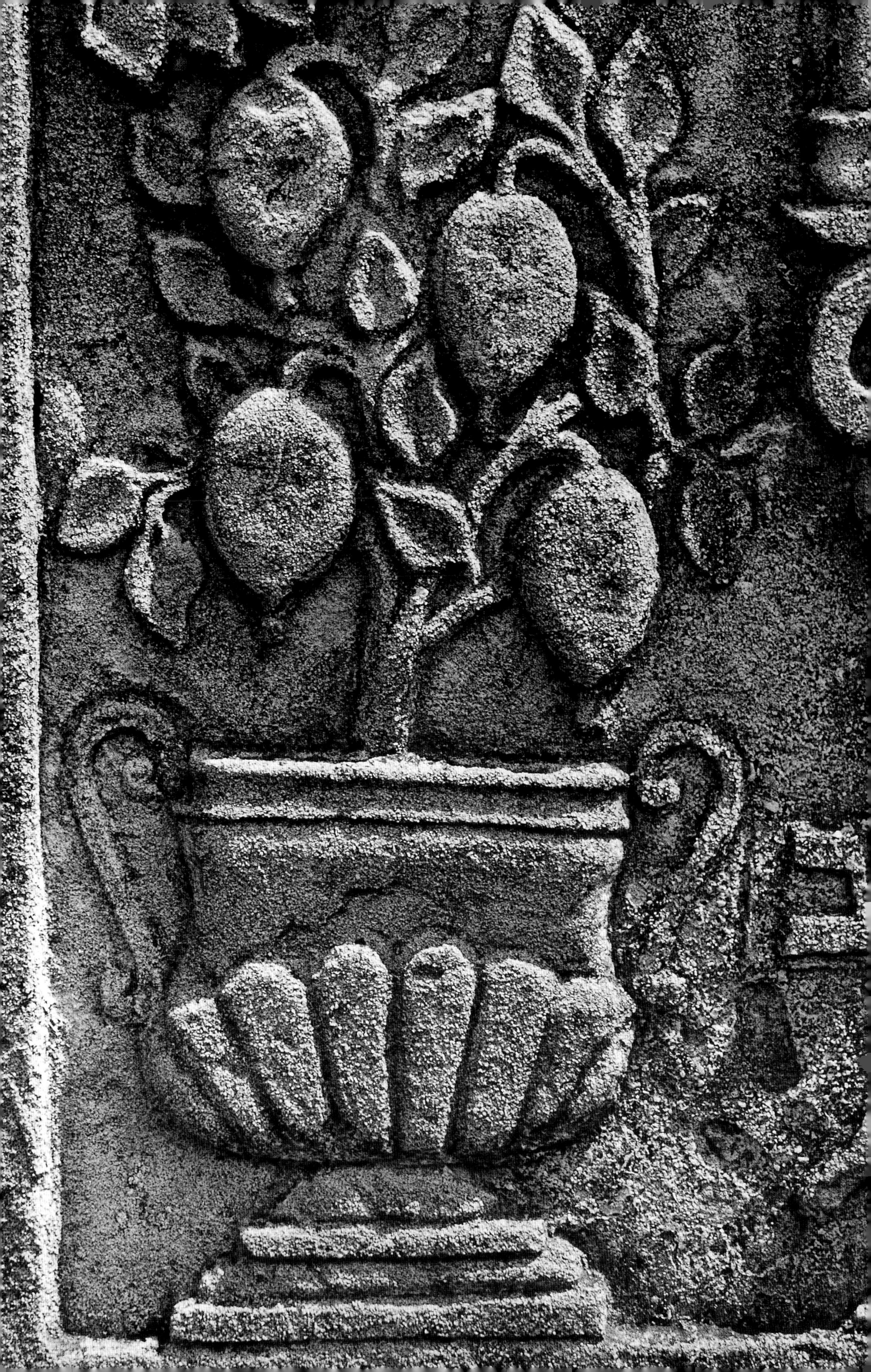

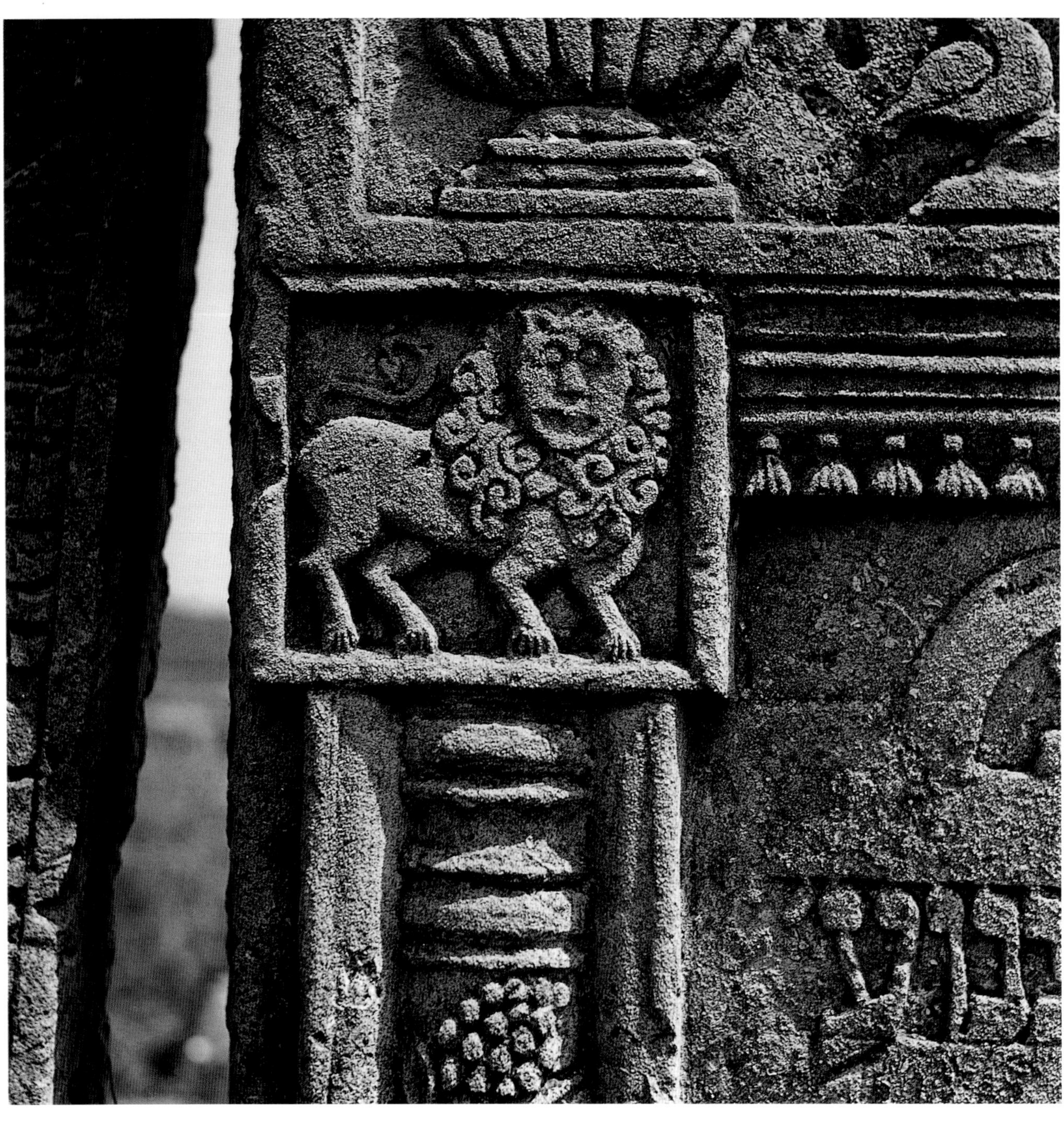

Sadgora. Between 1800 and 1850.
A lion with a stylized mane.

Opposite:
Sadgora Cemetery.

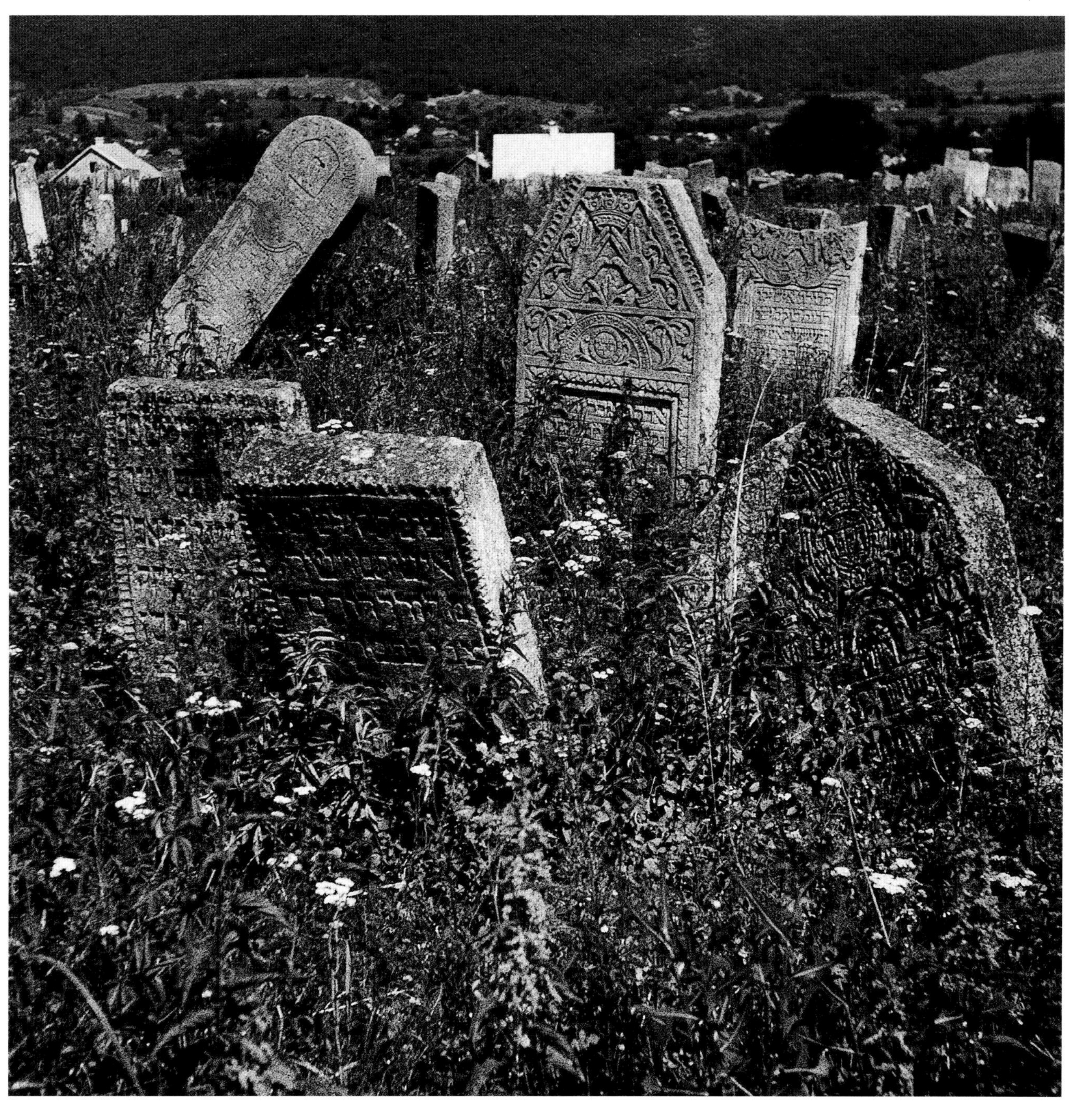

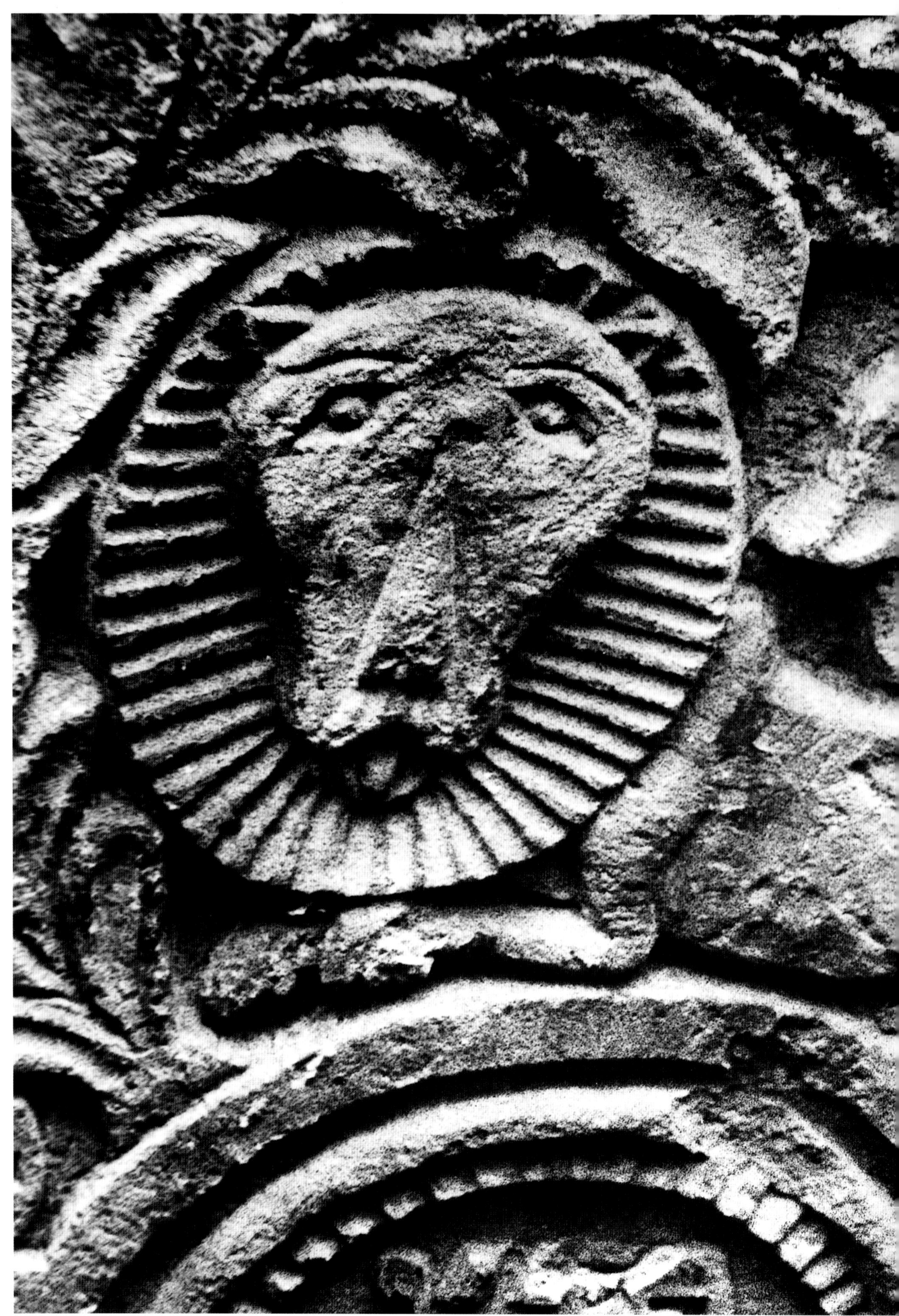

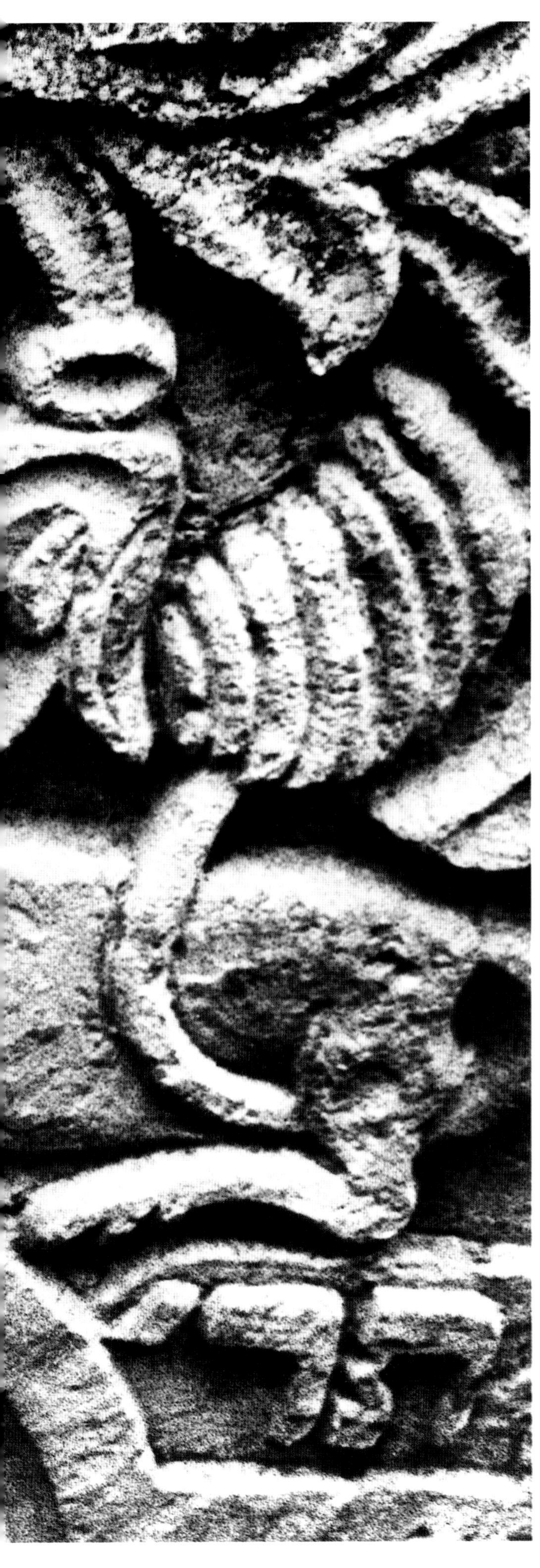

Chernovtsy. 1800s.

A sad-eyed lion as a guardian, with a flower drooping over him.

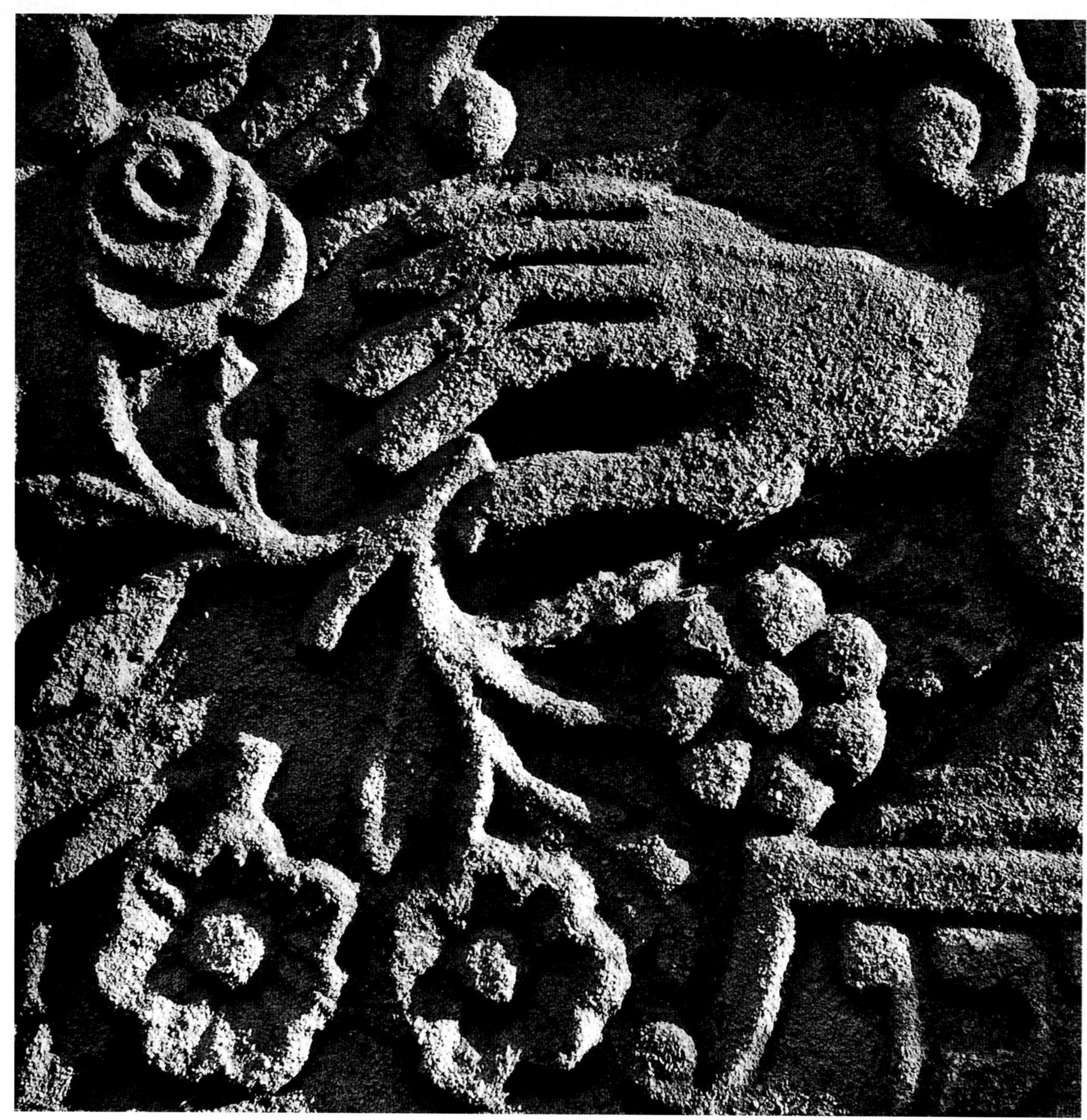

Chernovtsy. 1866.

A branch in bloom broken, a reference to a passage in the Song of Songs, "God's hand went down and plucked a flower."

Opposite:

Chernovtsy. Between 1850 and 1900.

A dove with leaves in its beak.

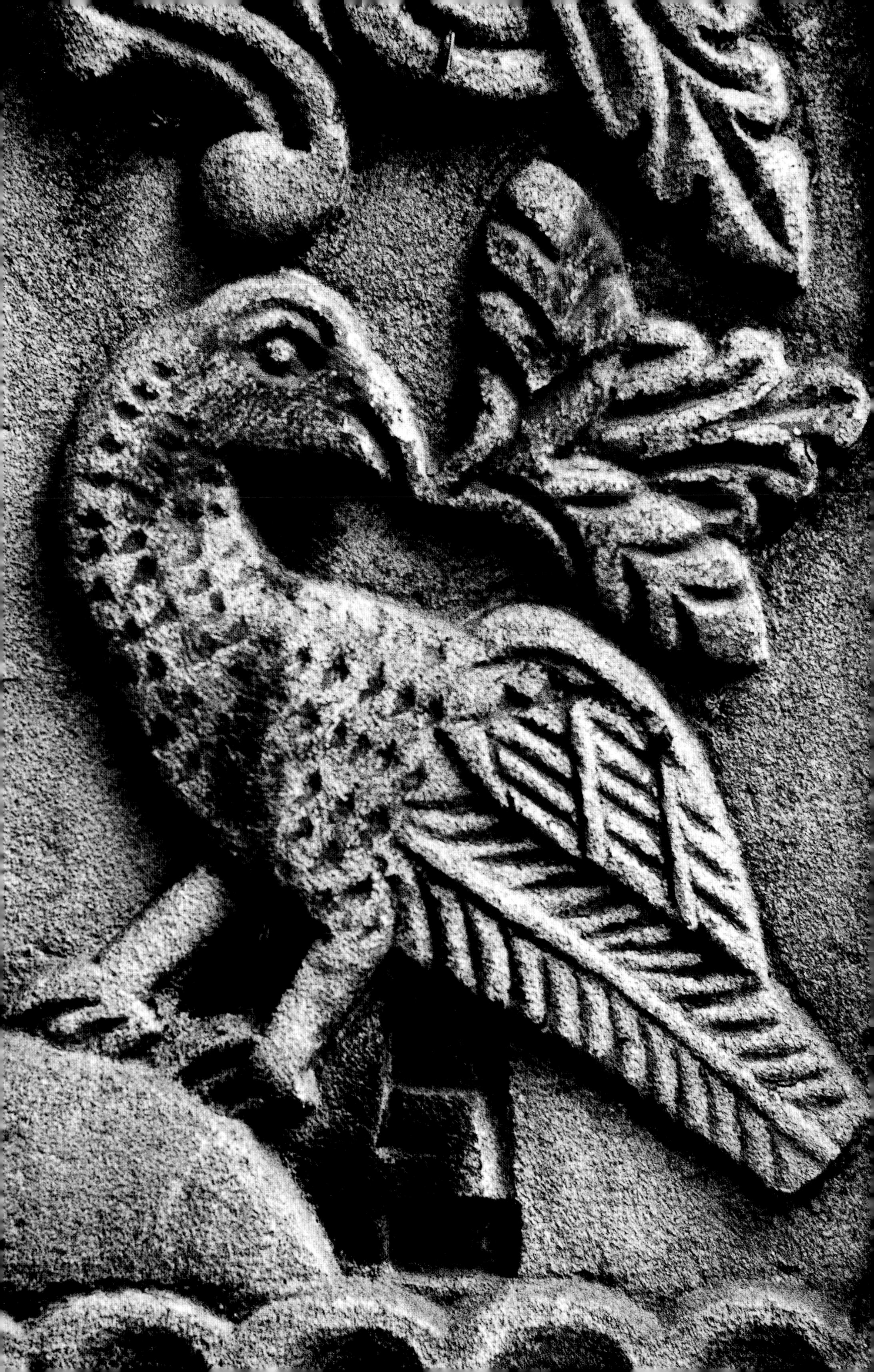

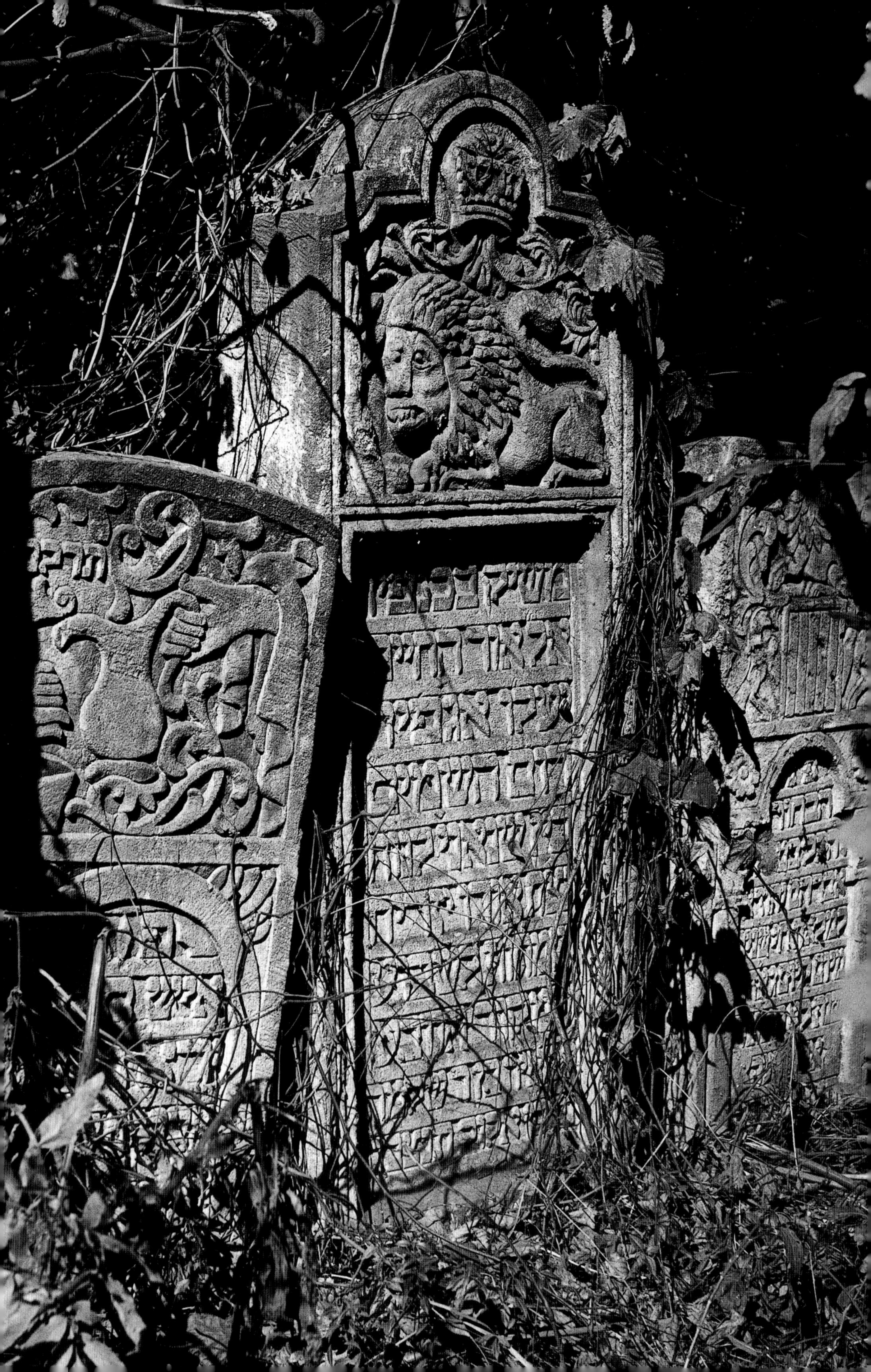

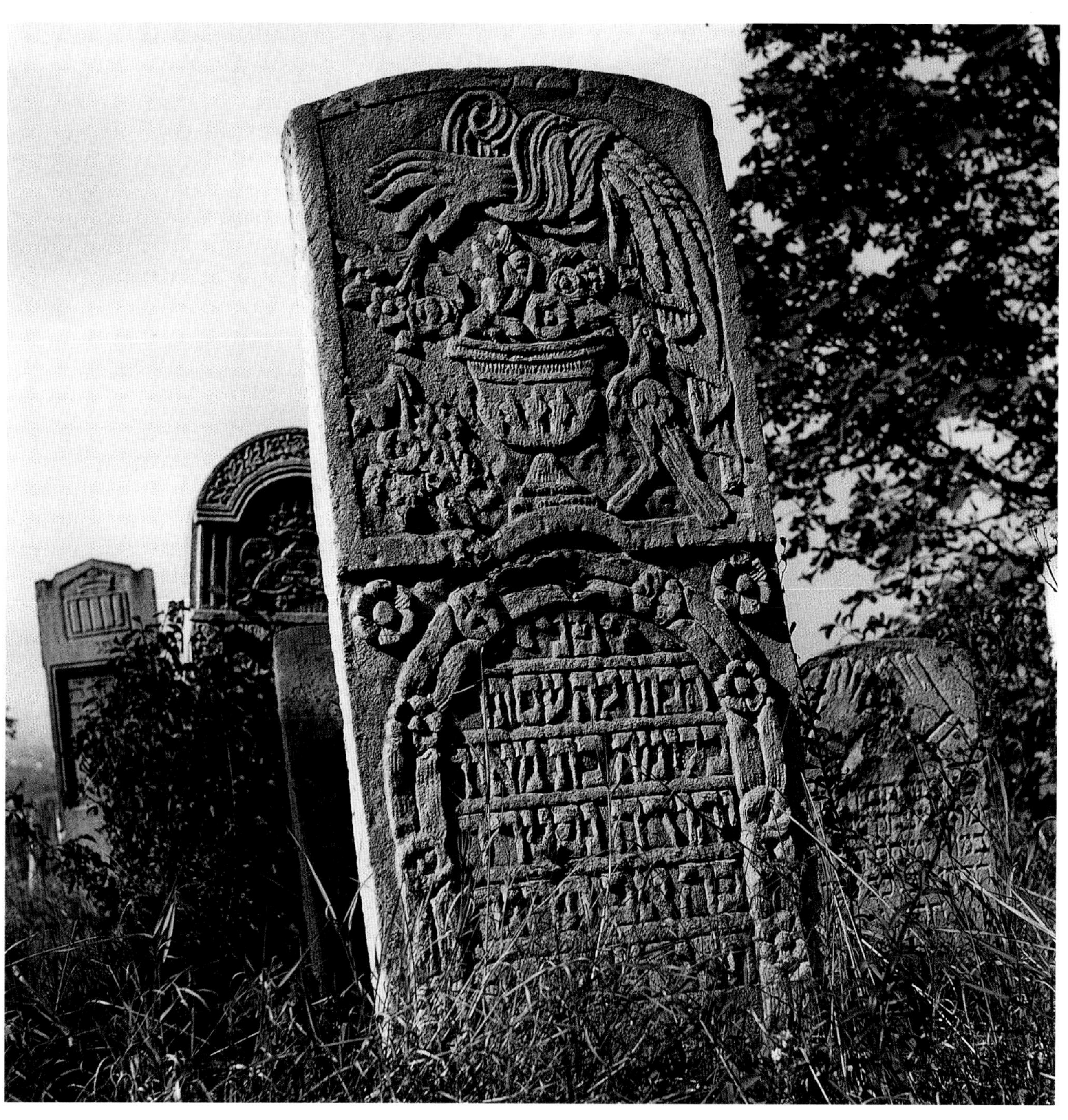

Chernovtsy. 1884.

The hand of God from Song of Songs, plucking a flower, with a vase and a bird.

The young woman (maiden) Esther Bluma, daughter of Meir Yehuda.

Opposite:

Chernovtsy. 1876

A crown above a lion with a human face.

Waving his wings to the light of life.

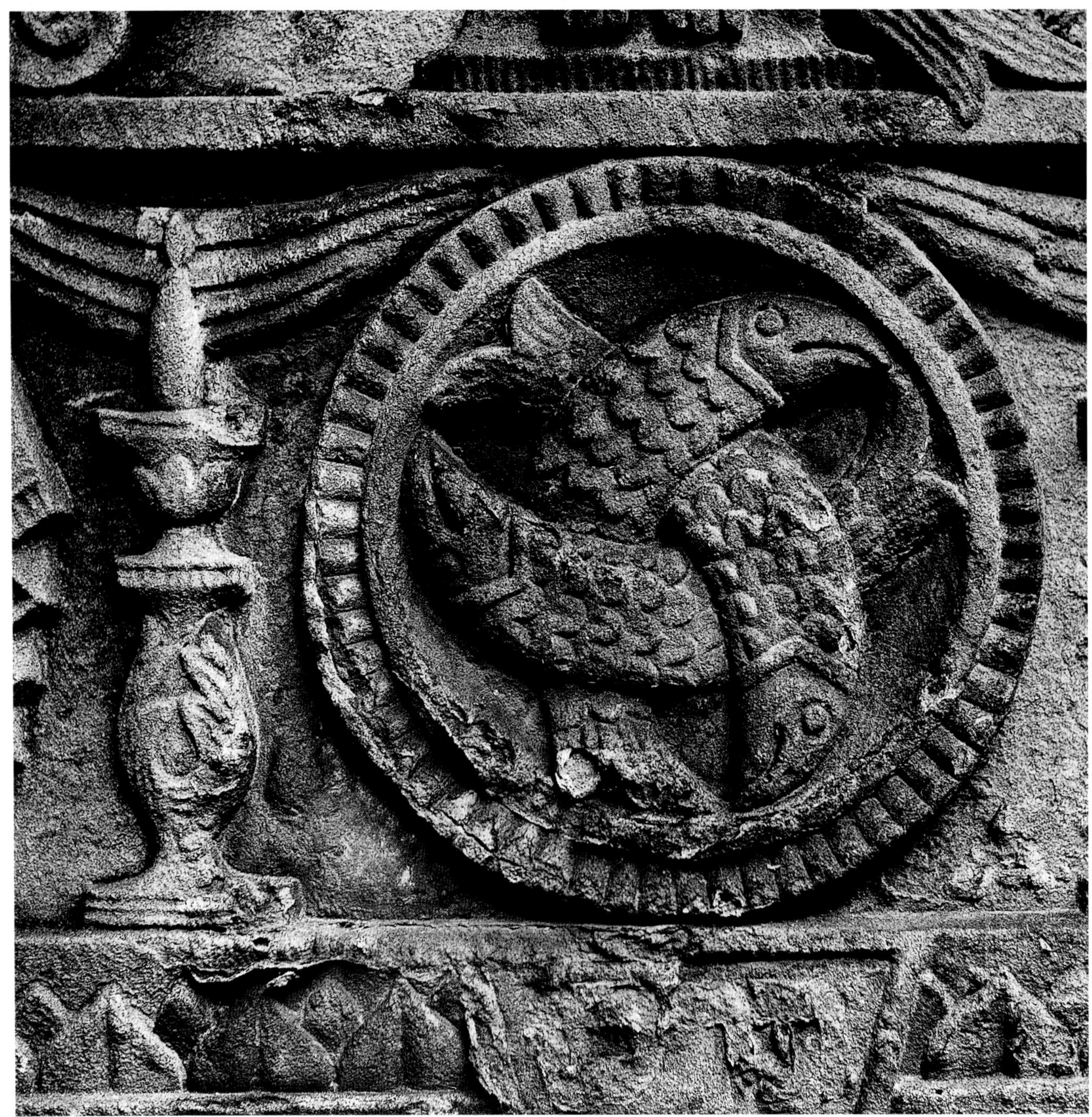

Chernovtsy. 1876.
Three fish on a plate and a candlestick.

Opposite:
Chernovtsy. 1866
A majestic lion, bitten by a snake, is about to die. The cornucopia beneath the lion's forepaws is overflowing, to signify a life filled with blessings.

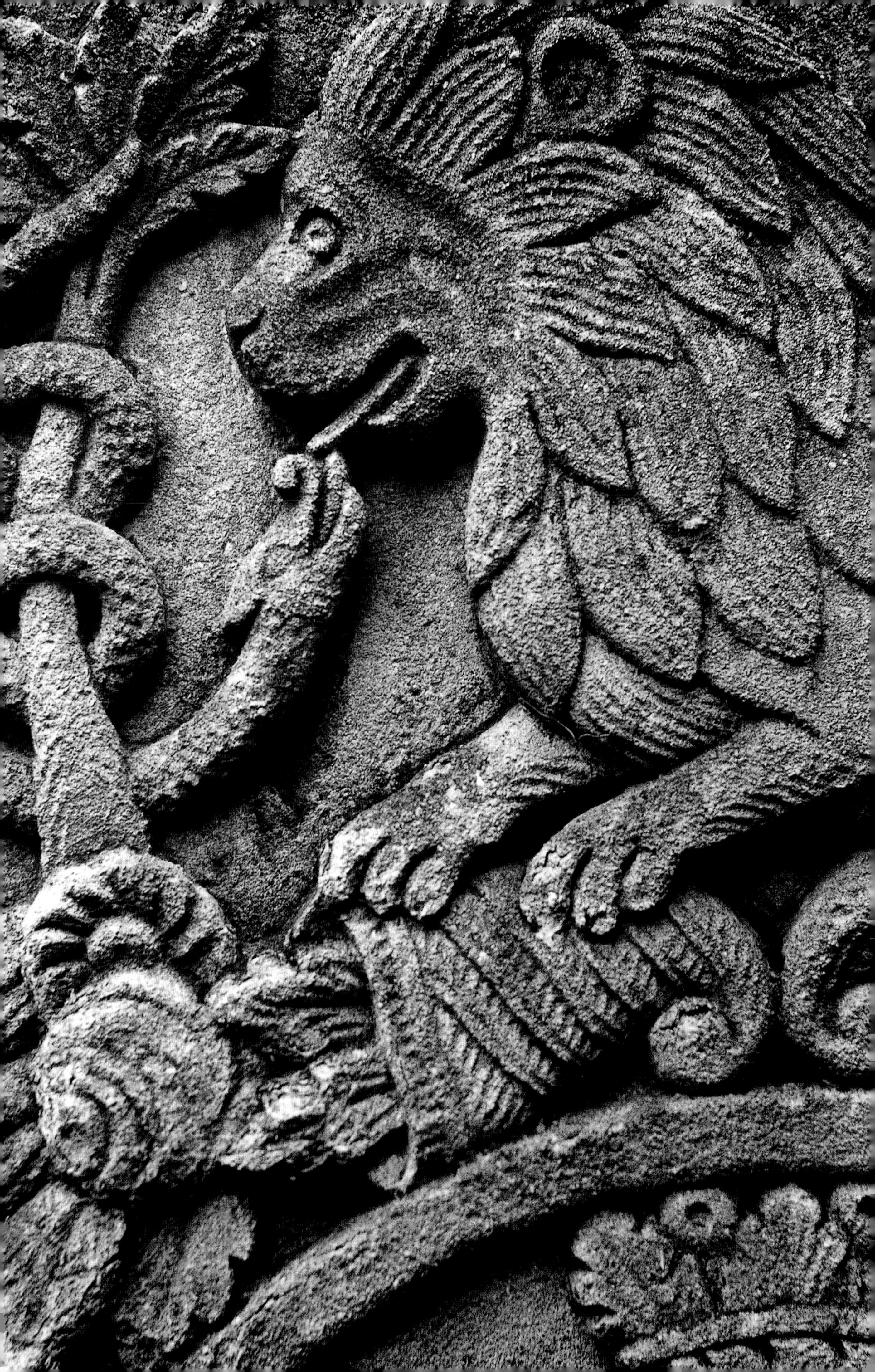

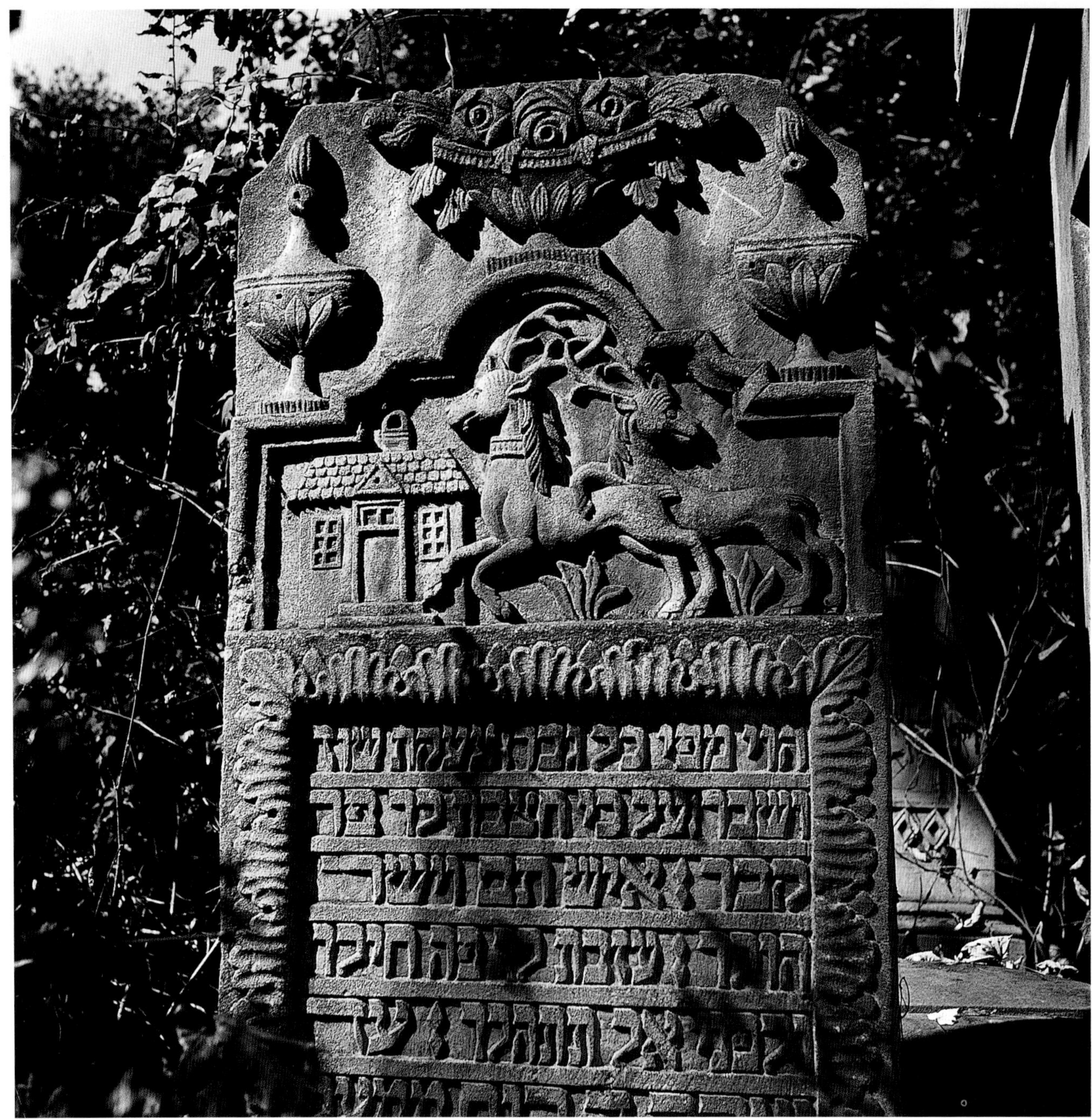

Chernovtsy. Between 1850 and 1900.

Two deer by a deserted house, one looking forward, the other back. Two lamps and a shallow bowl with roses are set above the frame of the composition. *Hoy [a cry of sorrow] from the mouth of every man. The house is robbed and shattered. Here lies a strong and honest man who walked before the Lord.*

Opposite:

Chernovtsy. 1868.

The pitcher signifies a Levite performing the ritual washing of hands. A bird plucks a leaf from a tree with a broken branch.

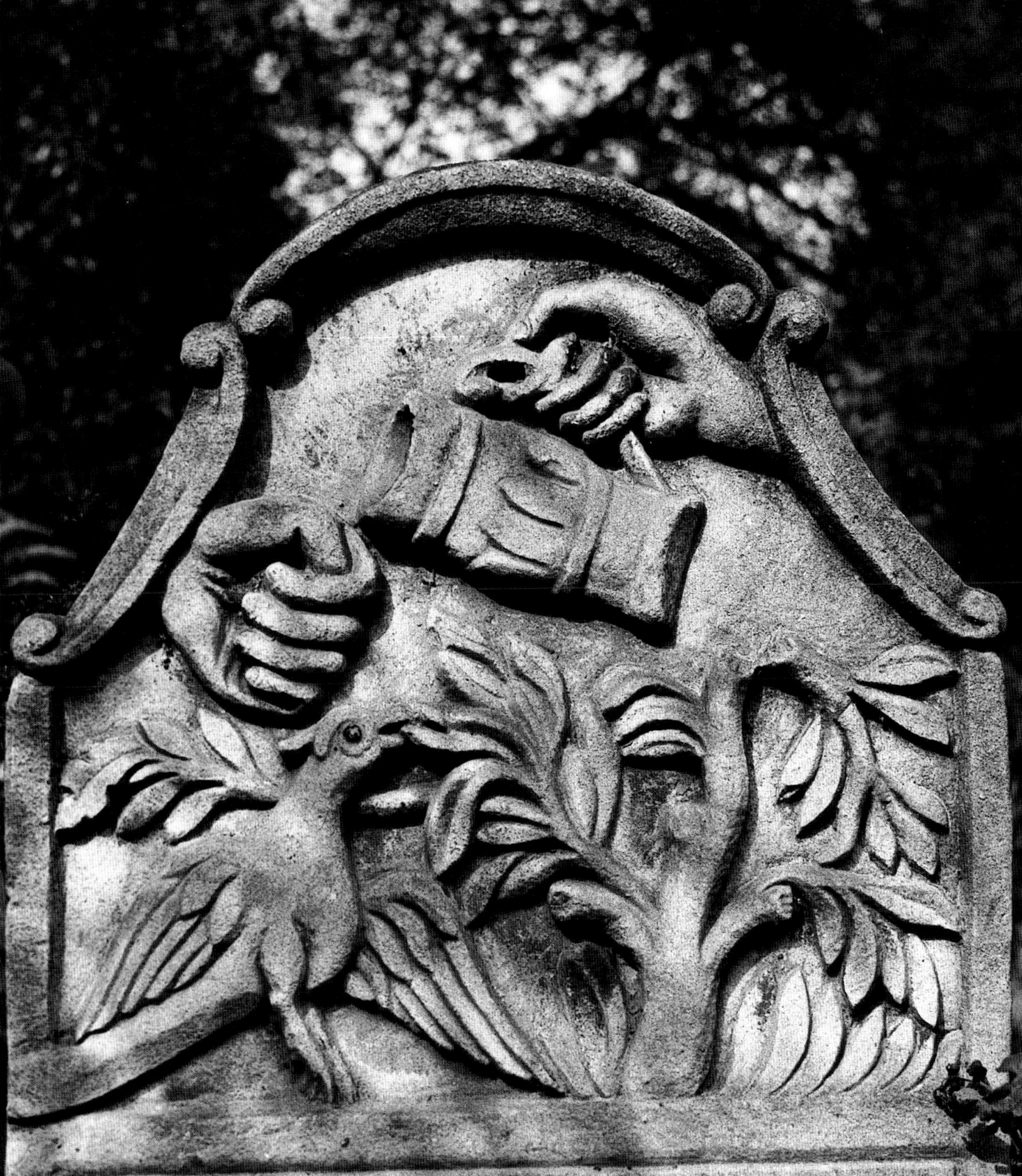
הרבח׳ בג״
איש תם וישר

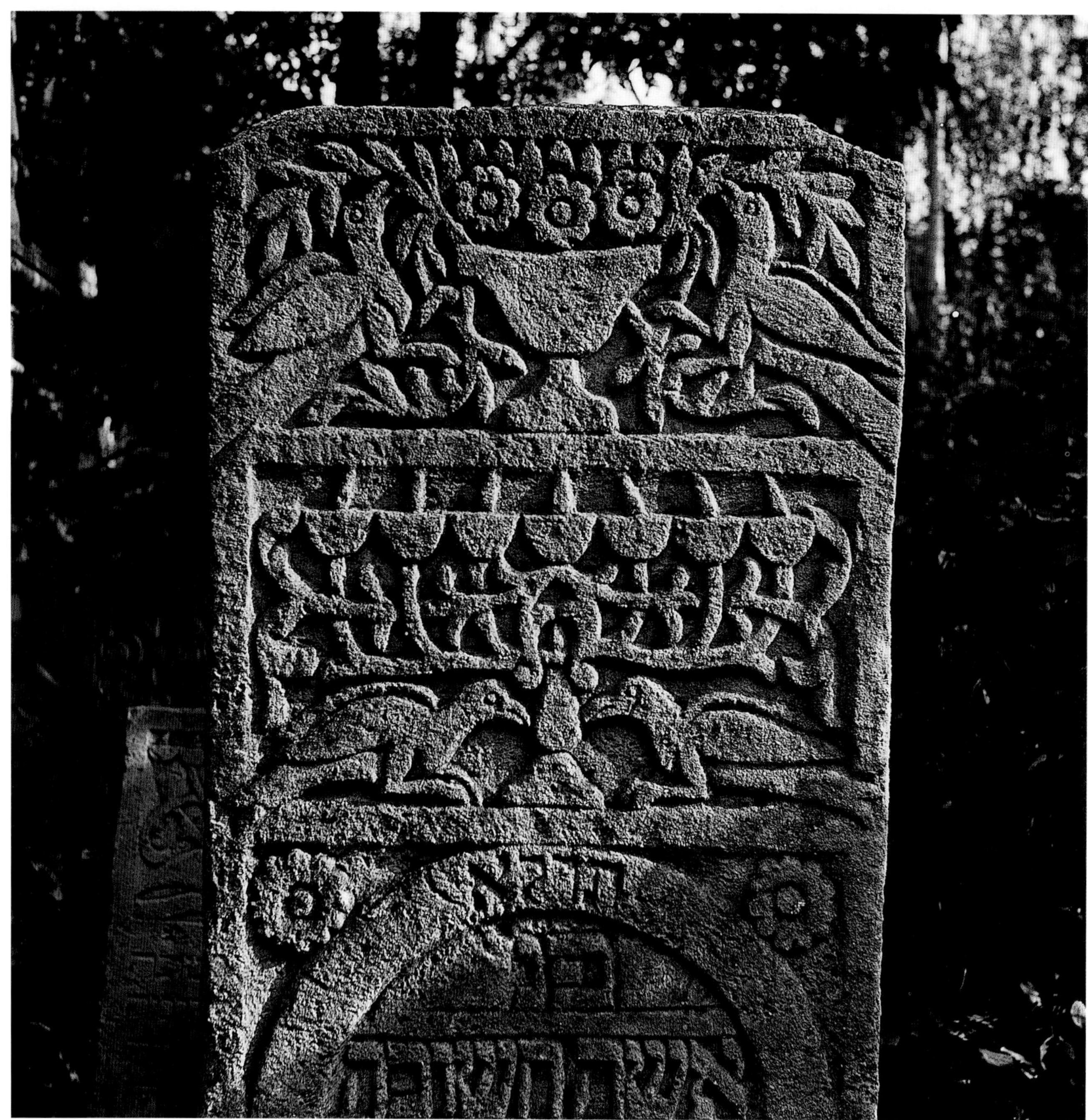

Chernovtsy. 1871.

A bowl with flowers, birds, and a menorah.

An important woman.

Opposite:

Chernovtsy. Between 1850 and 1900.

The hand of God severing a flower, a reference to the Song of Songs: “God’s hand went down and plucked a flower.”

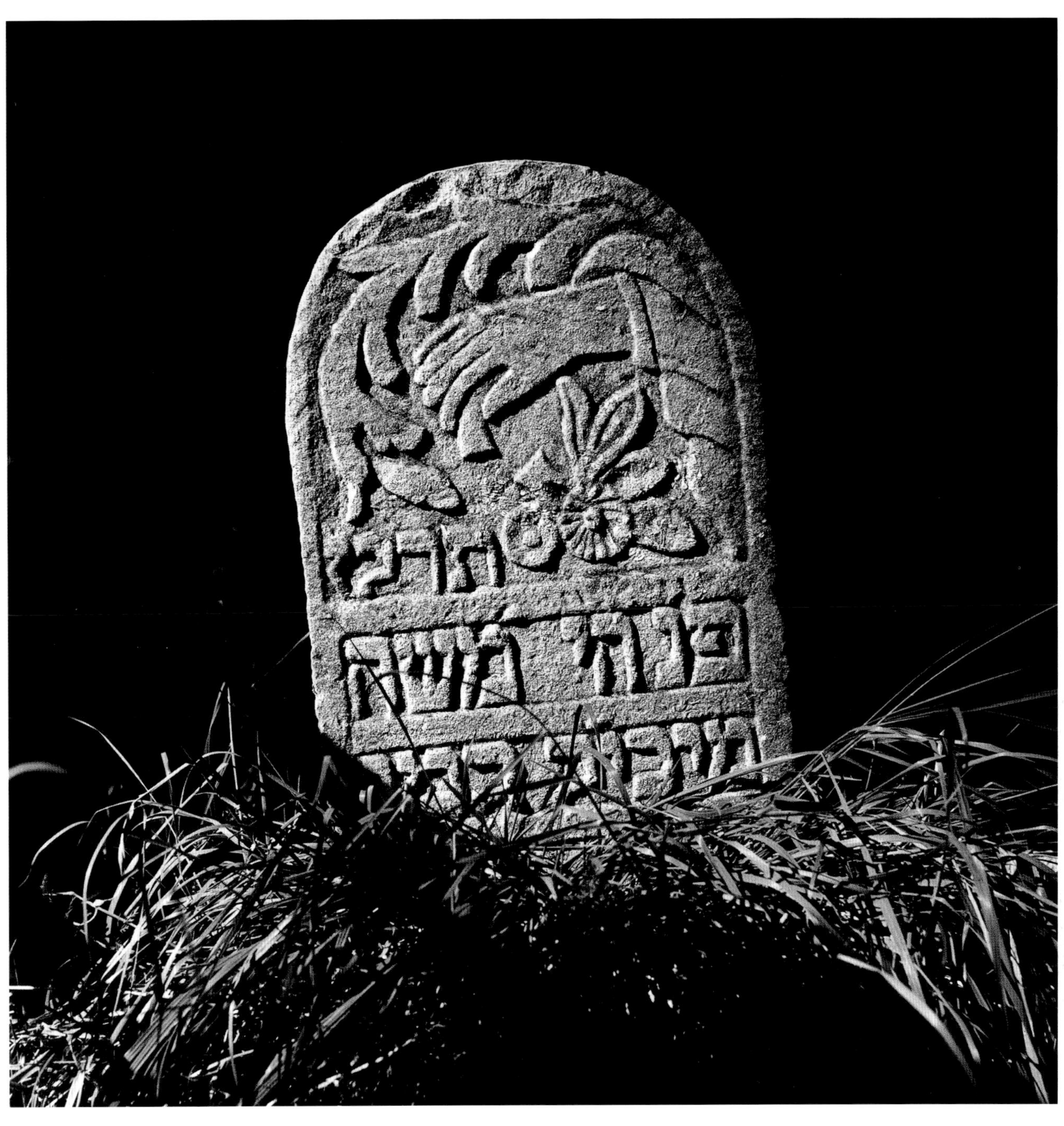

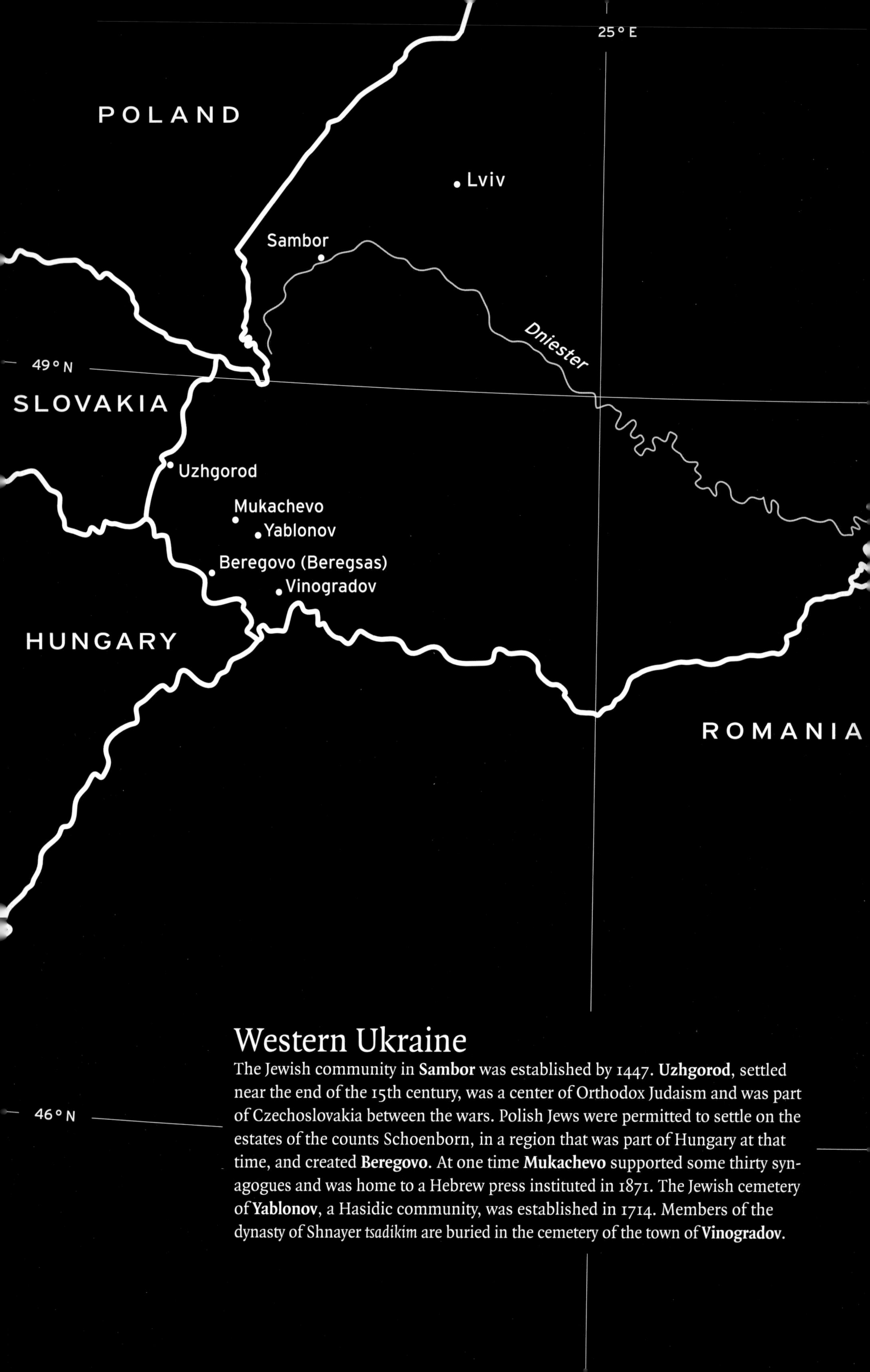

25° E

POLAND

Lviv

Sambor

Dniester

49° N

SLOVAKIA

Uzhgorod

Mukachevo

Yablonov

Beregovo (Beregsas)

Vinogradov

HUNGARY

ROMANIA

46° N

Western Ukraine

The Jewish community in **Sambor** was established by 1447. **Uzhgorod**, settled near the end of the 15th century, was a center of Orthodox Judaism and was part of Czechoslovakia between the wars. Polish Jews were permitted to settle on the estates of the counts Schoenborn, in a region that was part of Hungary at that time, and created **Beregovo**. At one time **Mukachevo** supported some thirty synagogues and was home to a Hebrew press instituted in 1871. The Jewish cemetery of **Yablonov**, a Hasidic community, was established in 1714. Members of the dynasty of Shnayer *tsadikim* are buried in the cemetery of the town of **Vinogradov**.

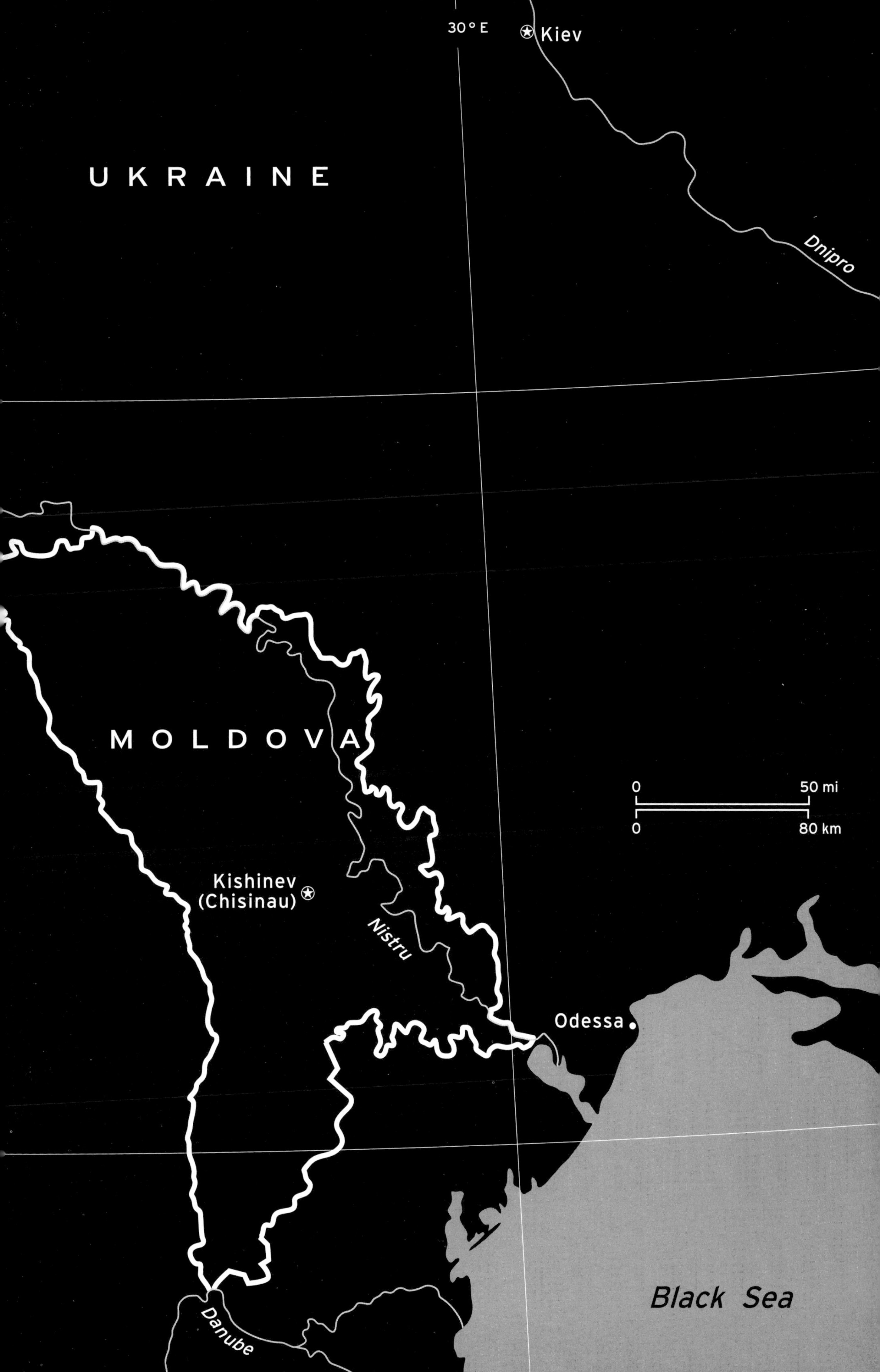
30° E
Kiev
UKRAINE
Dnipro
MOLDOVA
0
50 mi
0
80 km
Kishinev
(Chisinau)
Nistru
Odessa
Danube
Black Sea

Uzhgorod. 1816.

Ephraim son of Ber. A righteous and honest person. Ephraim, who went the way of all earth, died on the twenty-eighth day of the month of Nissan.

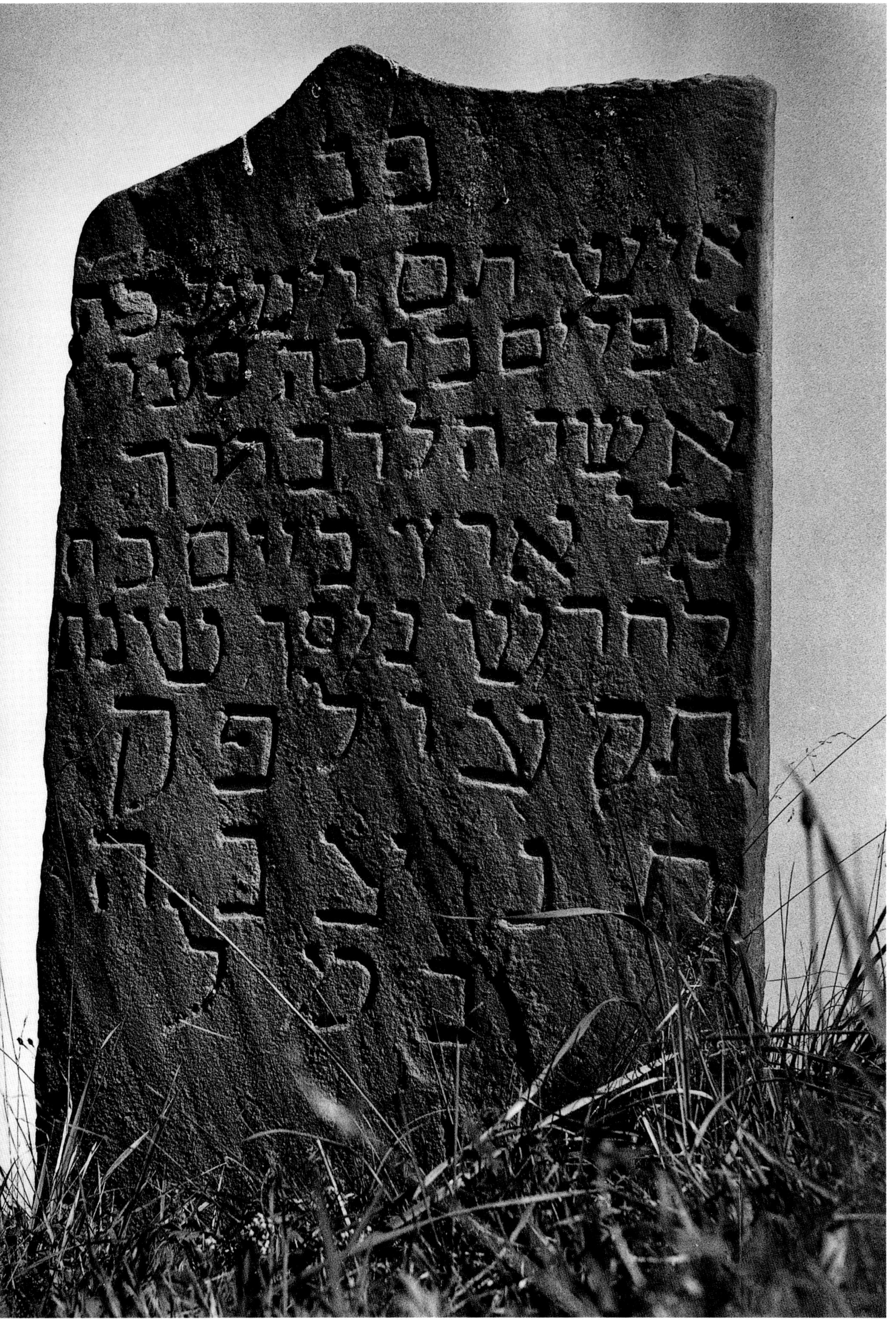
פנ

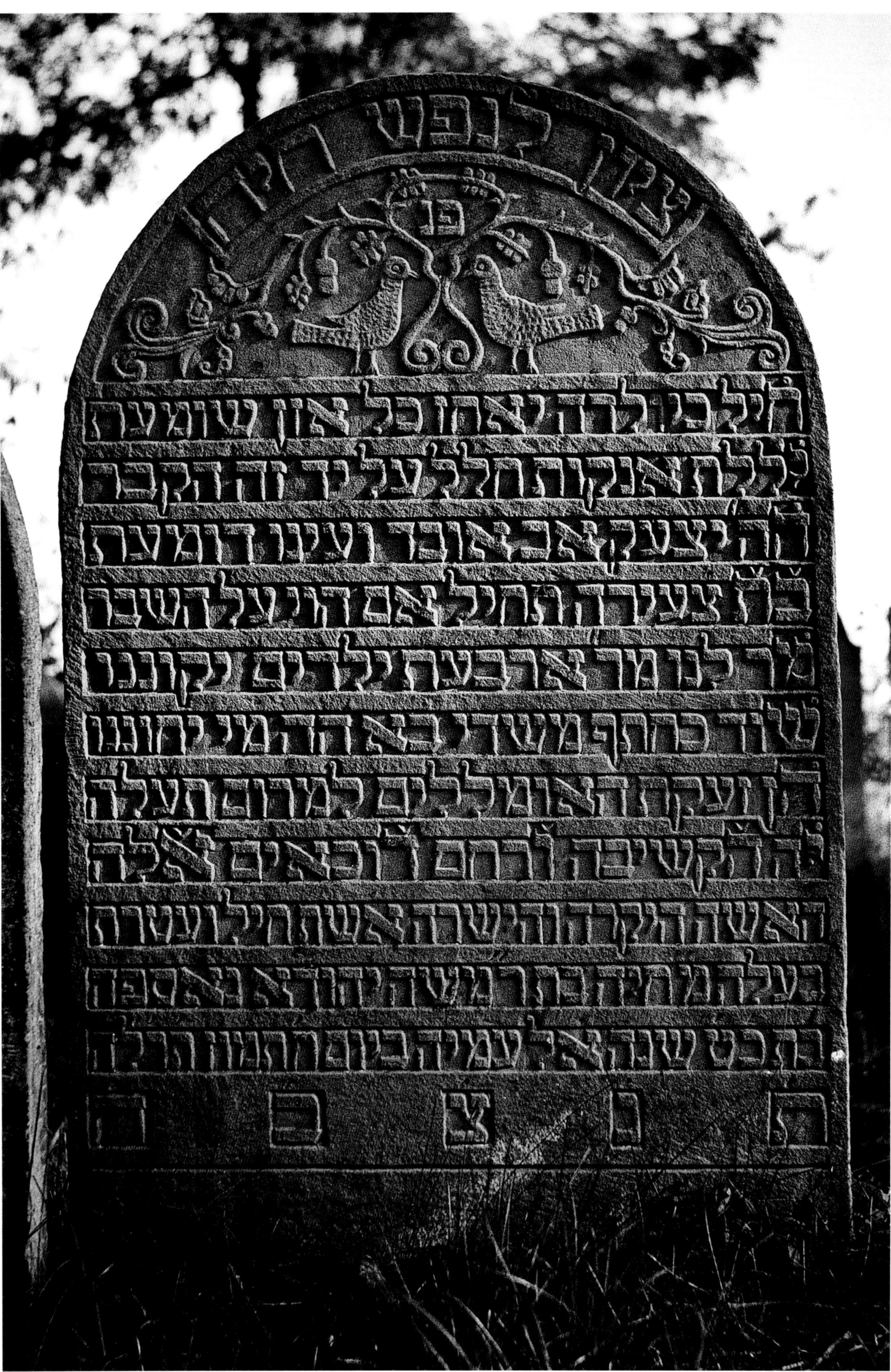
פנ
ת נ צ ב ה

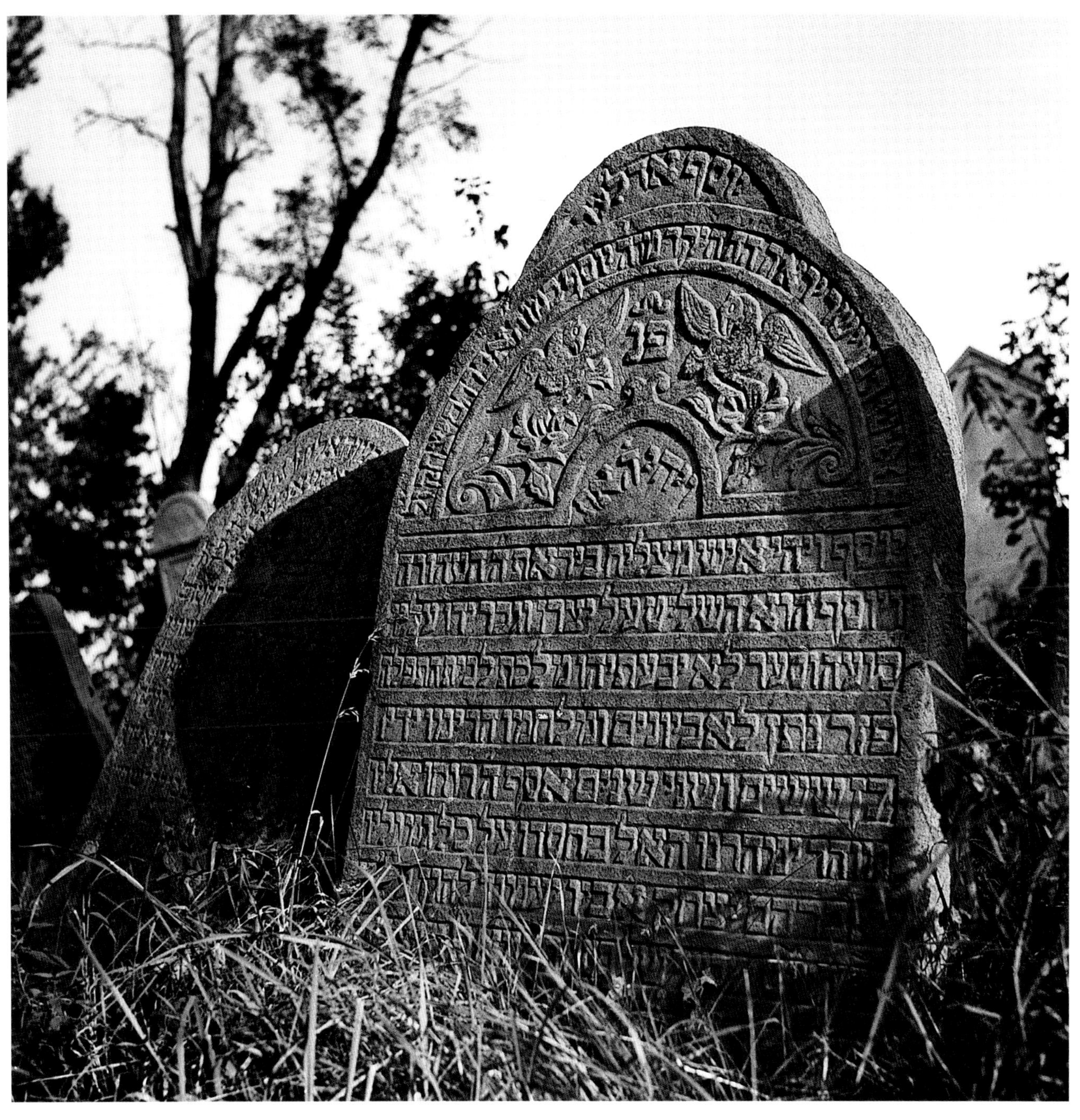

Uzhgorod. 1870.
Decorated with flying eagles.

Joseph Adler, a charitable man, son of Abraham Yitsak. A successful man in pure obedience to the Lord. He is in control of his inclinations (or desires) and will suppress them. [This may be an allusion to the story of Joseph and Potiphar's wife]. *A* [illegible] *and storm will not frighten him from going to the House of Prayer. He shared his bread with the poor* [illegible], *for sixty-two years.*

Opposite:
Uzhgorod. 1870.

The arch above the birds reads: *A memorial to the soul of Chaya.* Below: *Fear and trembling will hold each ear which will hear wailing near this grave. A lost father will cry and his eye will fill with tears.*
A young daughter.... Hoy on the destruction! It is bitter for us. It is bitter. Four children will mourn. Violence came suddenly from the lord, He who will have mercy on us. Indeed the cry of the unfortunates will rise toward heaven. God listen and have pity. The dear and honest woman, a woman of valor and her husband's crown, Chaya, daughter of Moshe Yehuda, was gathered to her people at twenty-nine years.

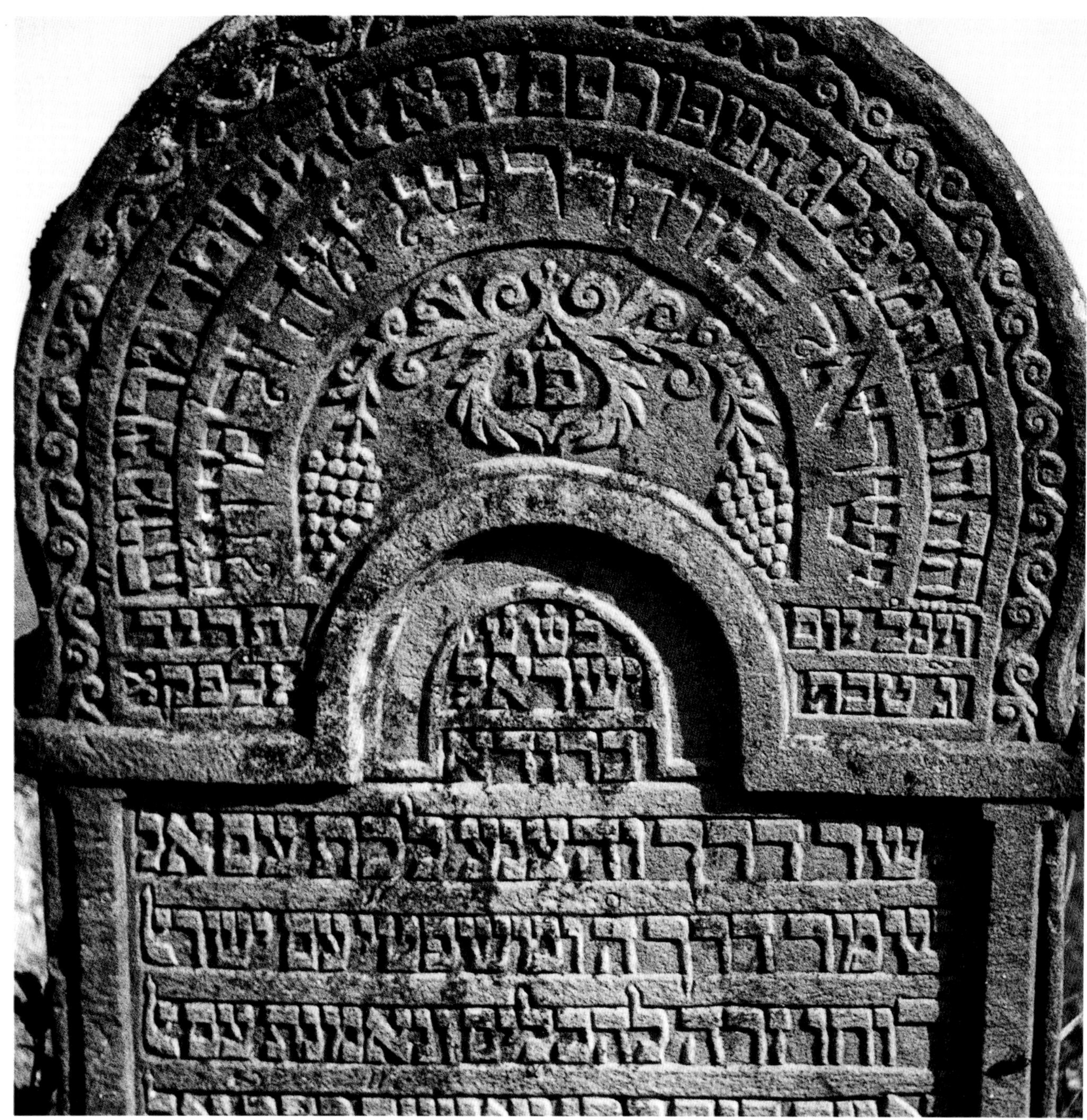

Uzhgorod. 1854.

A famous rabbi, Yisroel Brody, son of Shlomo Zalmon.
He walked modestly on a just path and followed the laws of Israel. His spiritual aspect was stronger than the physical. He is faithful with God.

Opposite:

Uzhgorod. 1872.

Two stags flank an unusual multi-circled design.
In the year 5632 an honest man passed on. He was clear and honorable, and did right in the eyes of God and man. Eleazar Yitsak, son of Israel Chaim.

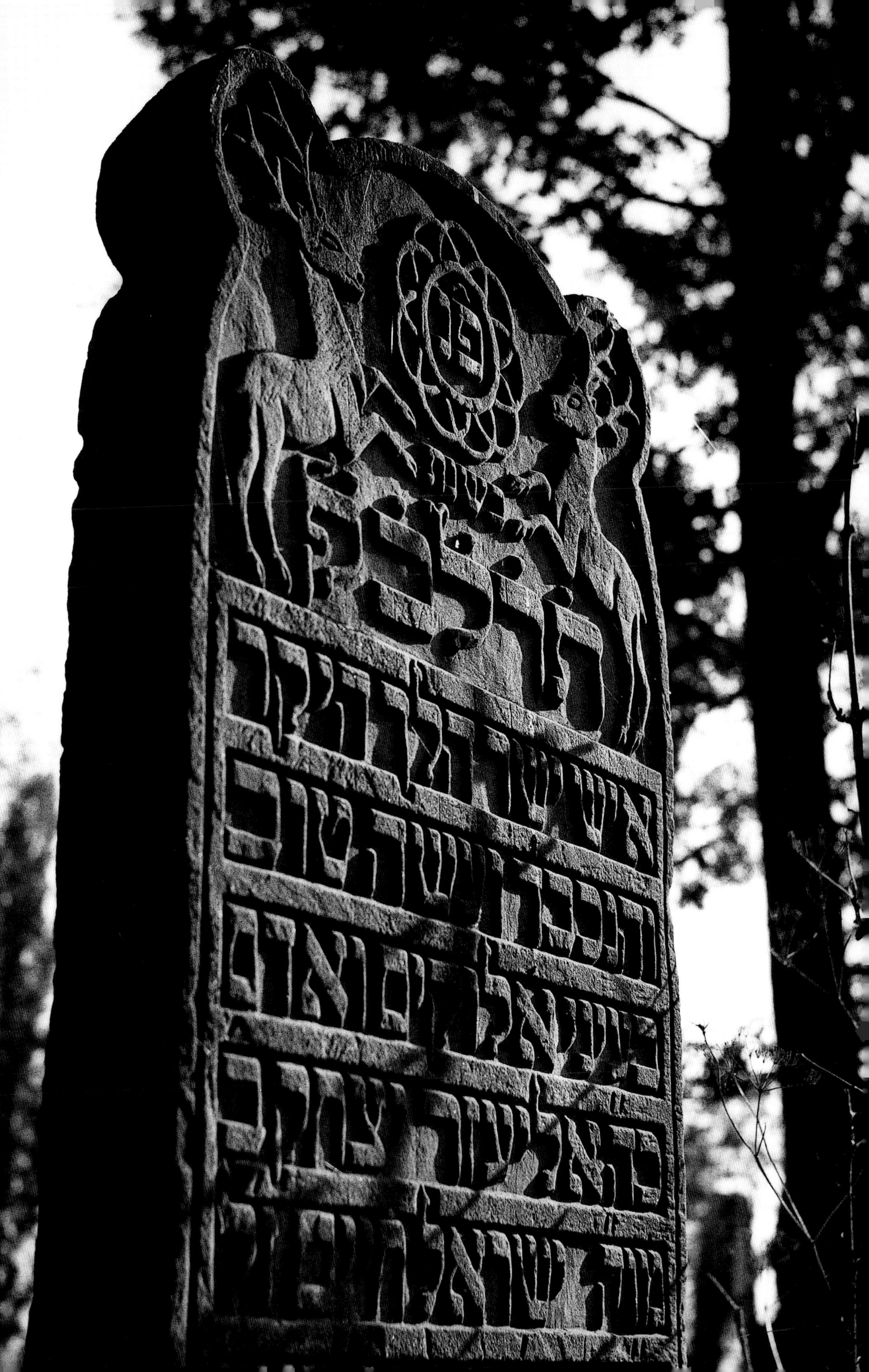

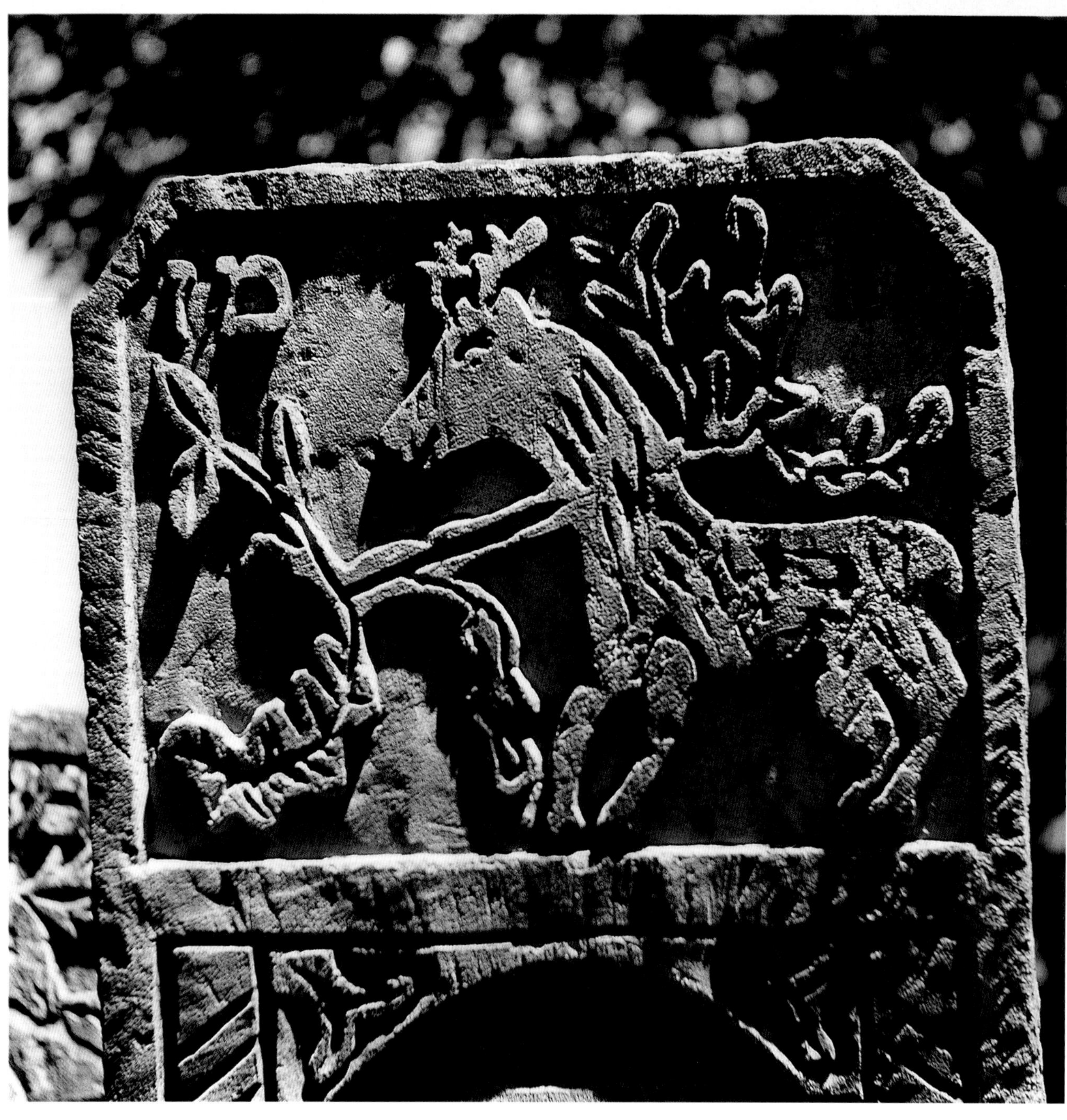

Uzhgorod. Undated.
A deer surrounded by the tree of life.

Opposite:
Uzhgorod. Late 1800s.
A pitcher.

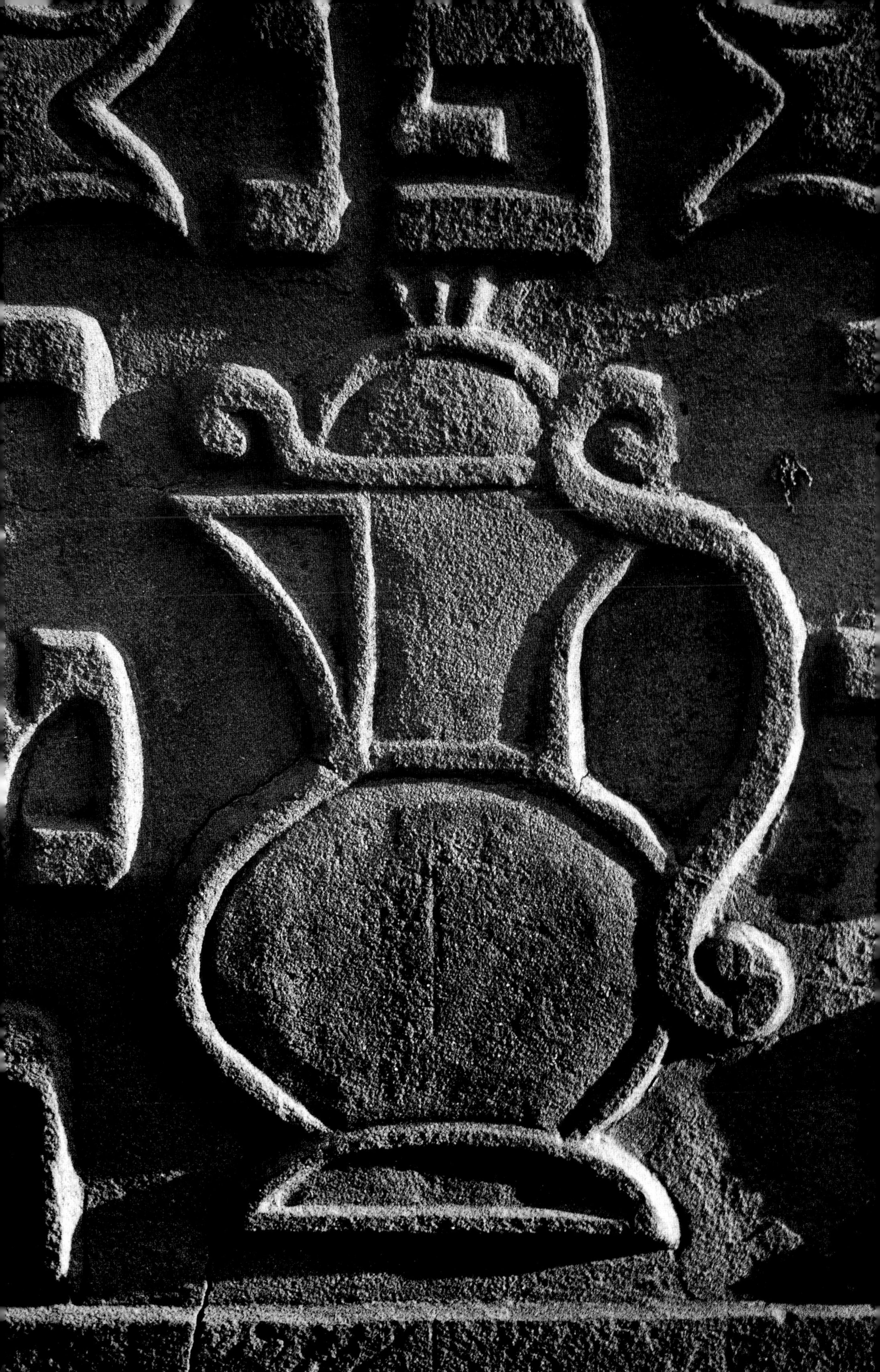

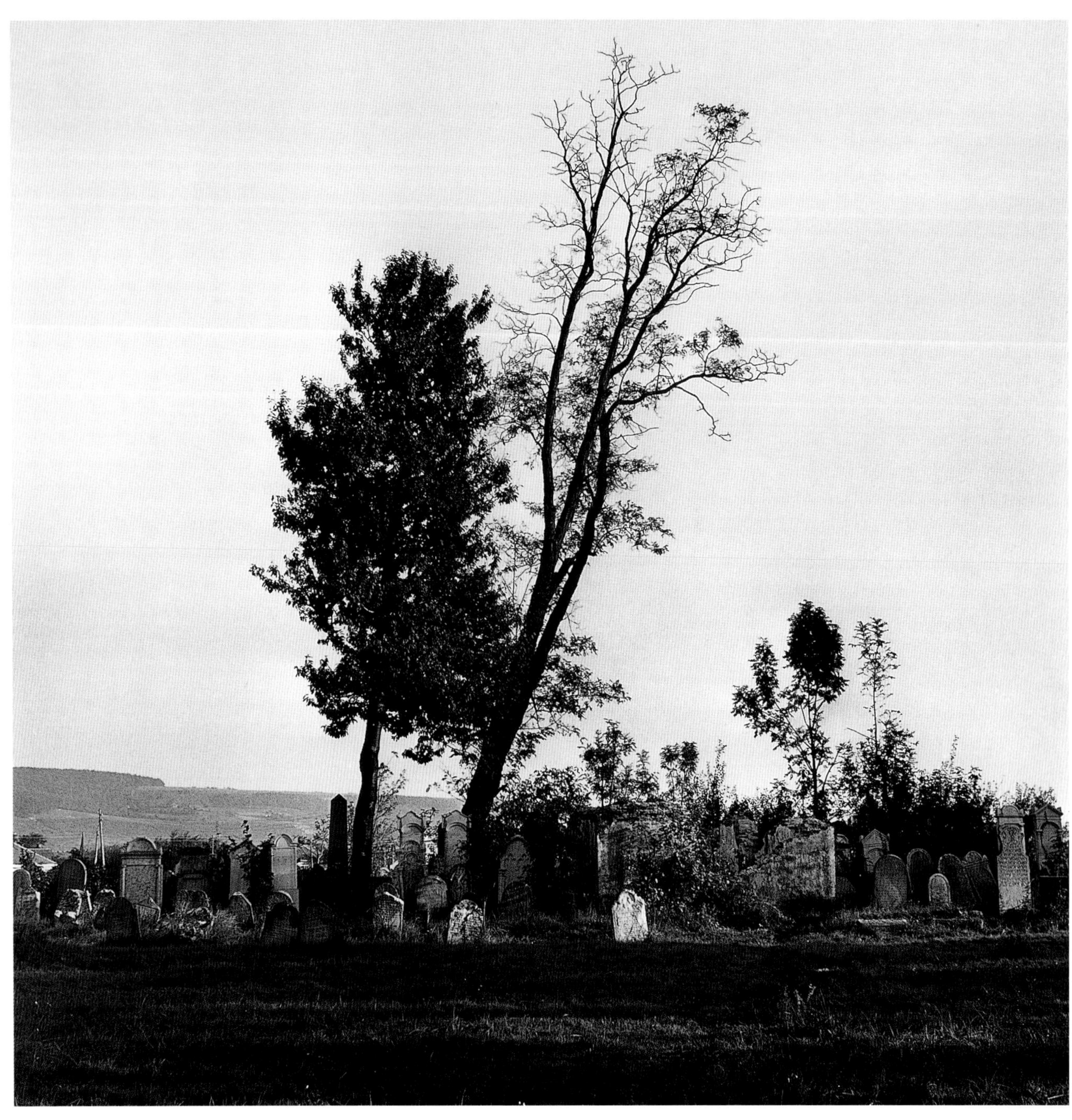

Uzhgorod Cemetery.

Opposite:
Beregovo. Mid-1800s.
A lion sleeping on an altar.

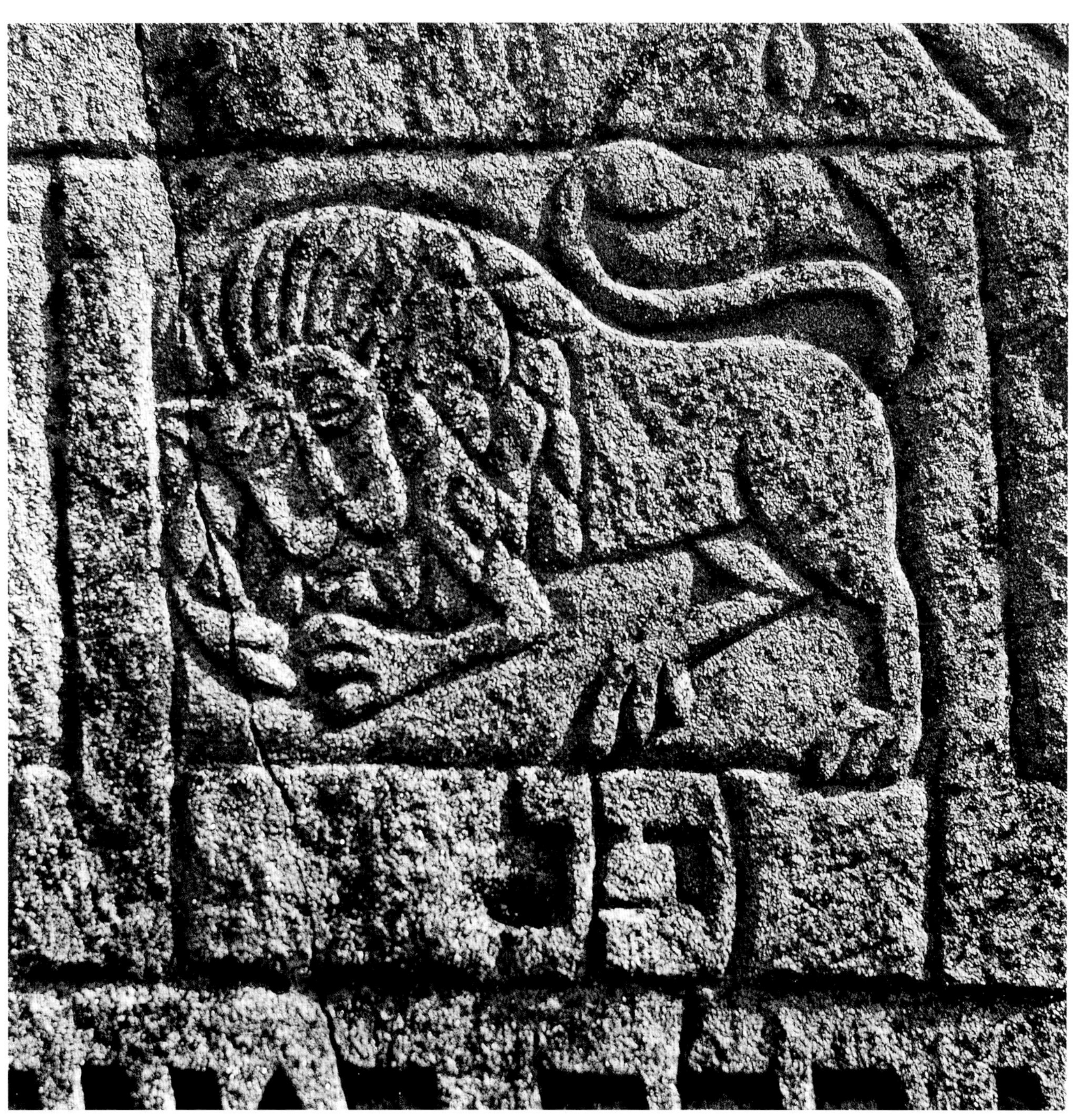

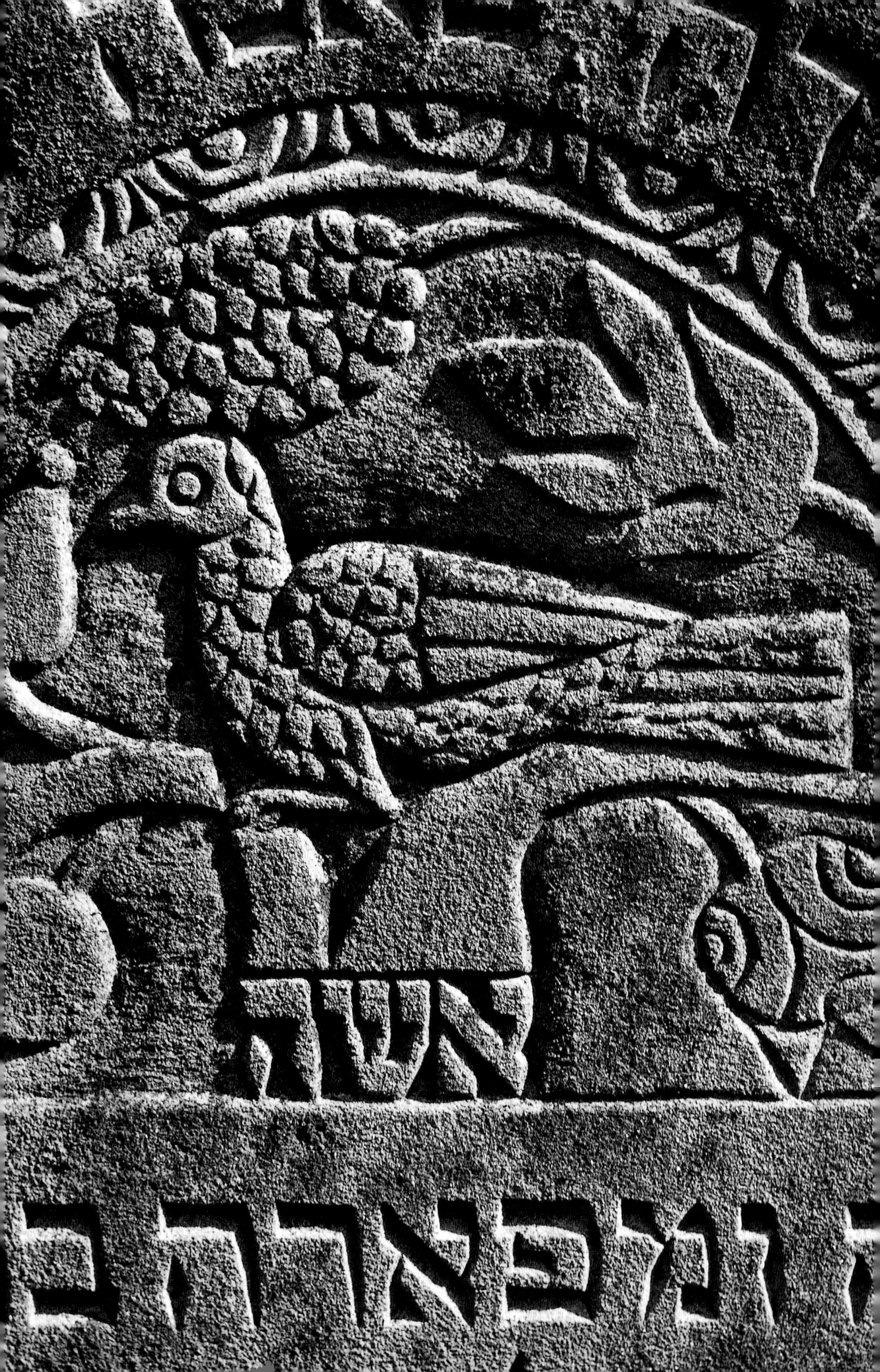
אשה

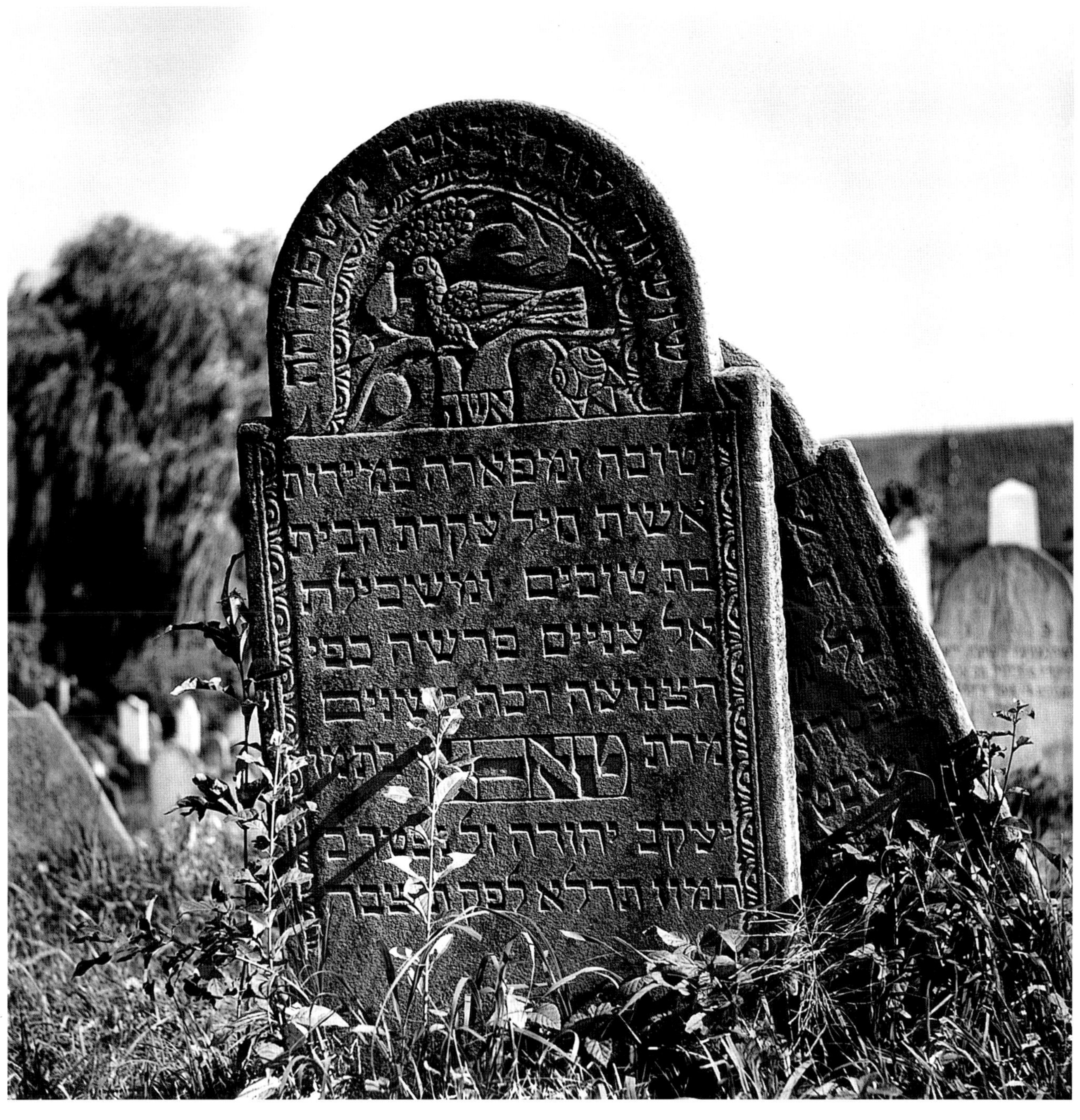

Beregovo. 1871.

A bird on the trunk of a tree beside a severed branch. The Hebrew name of the deceased, Shoshana Sara, and the secular name, Tova, are both inscribed. Tova appears in large letters in the center.

Shoshana Sara. Cut away in a time of fruitfulness. A good woman, glorious in her attributes. A woman of valor. The mainstay of her home. The daughter of a wonderful family and wise in her dealings with the poor, to whom she stretched out her hand. Her name was Tovah and she died twenty days into Tammuz, 5631. She is the daughter of Jacob Yehuda.

Opposite:
Beregovo. 1871.

Detail.

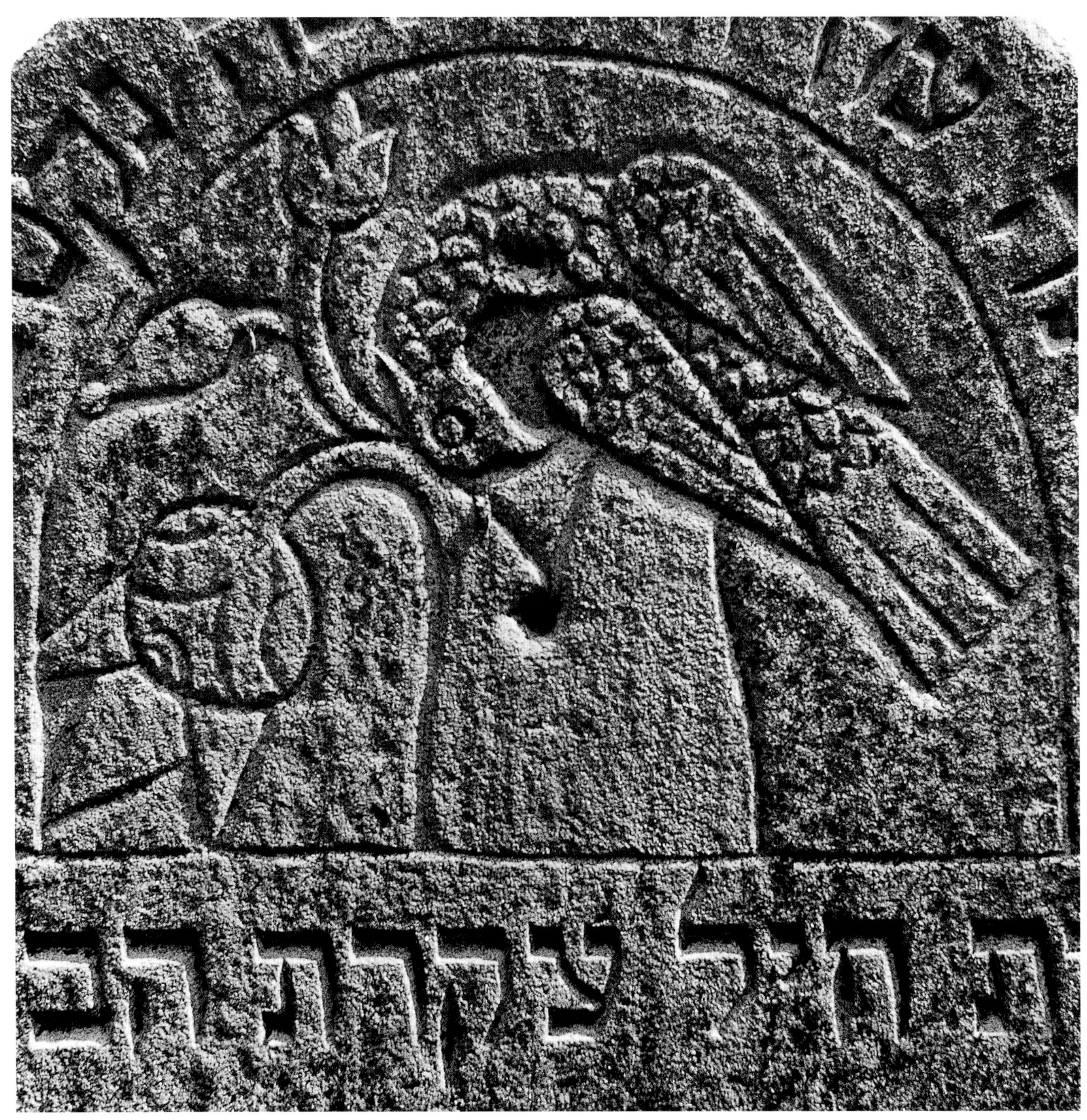

Beregovo. Undated.

A bird in a tree bowing its head against a dying flower. Birds often represent a deceased woman and may sometimes symbolize the name Feigele ("little bird" in Yiddish).

Opposite:

Beregovo. Undated.

Bird perched on a tree, which has a severed blossom. The daughter predeceased her father.

Miriam, with the good in her hand, a woman of valor, married, young, daughter of the Cohain David. Let his light shine.

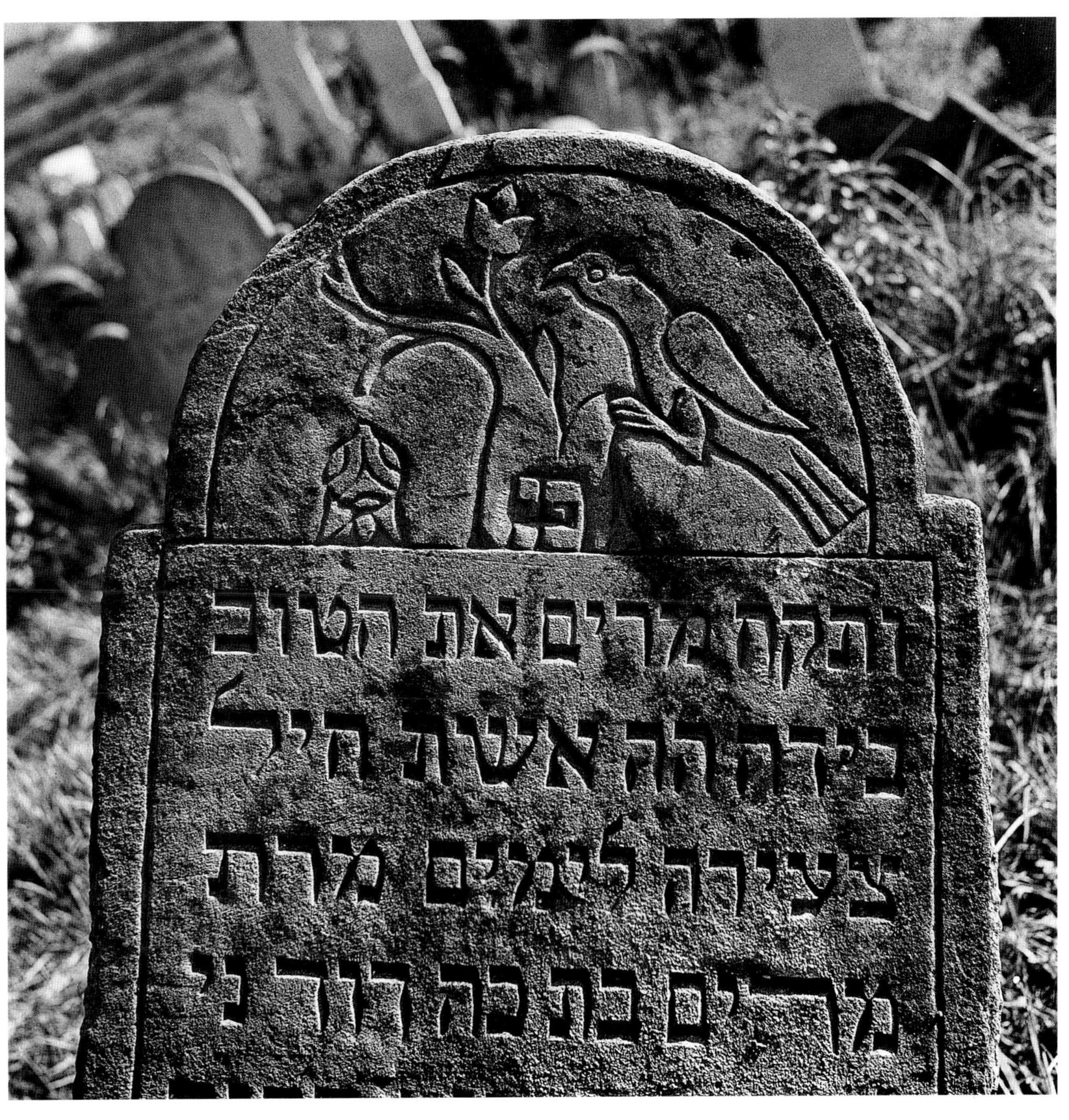

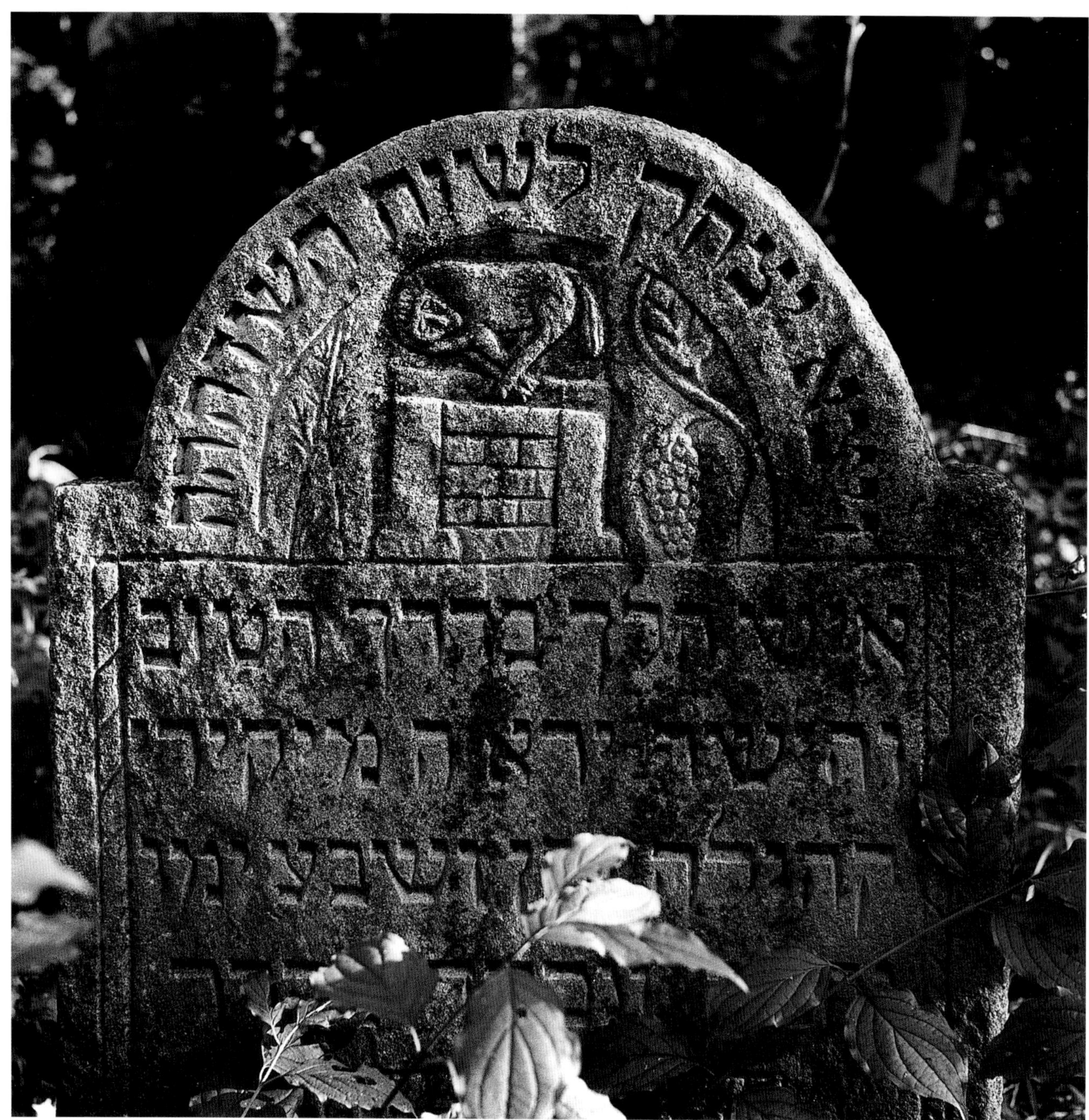

Beregovo. Between 1850 and 1900.

Sleeping lion on an altar, with a date tree or grape vine. The epitaph alludes to a verse in Genesis in which Isaac went out to walk in a field. The lion depicted on an altar may also refer Abraham's offering Isaac as a sacrifice to God.

He took the good and honest road, was one of the precious members of the community, was sated with years, and was God fearing.

Opposite:

Beregovo. 1860.

Lion beside a date tree or grape vine.

On the death of this pious man who followed the path of righteousness. Honest and straight, he gave to charity.

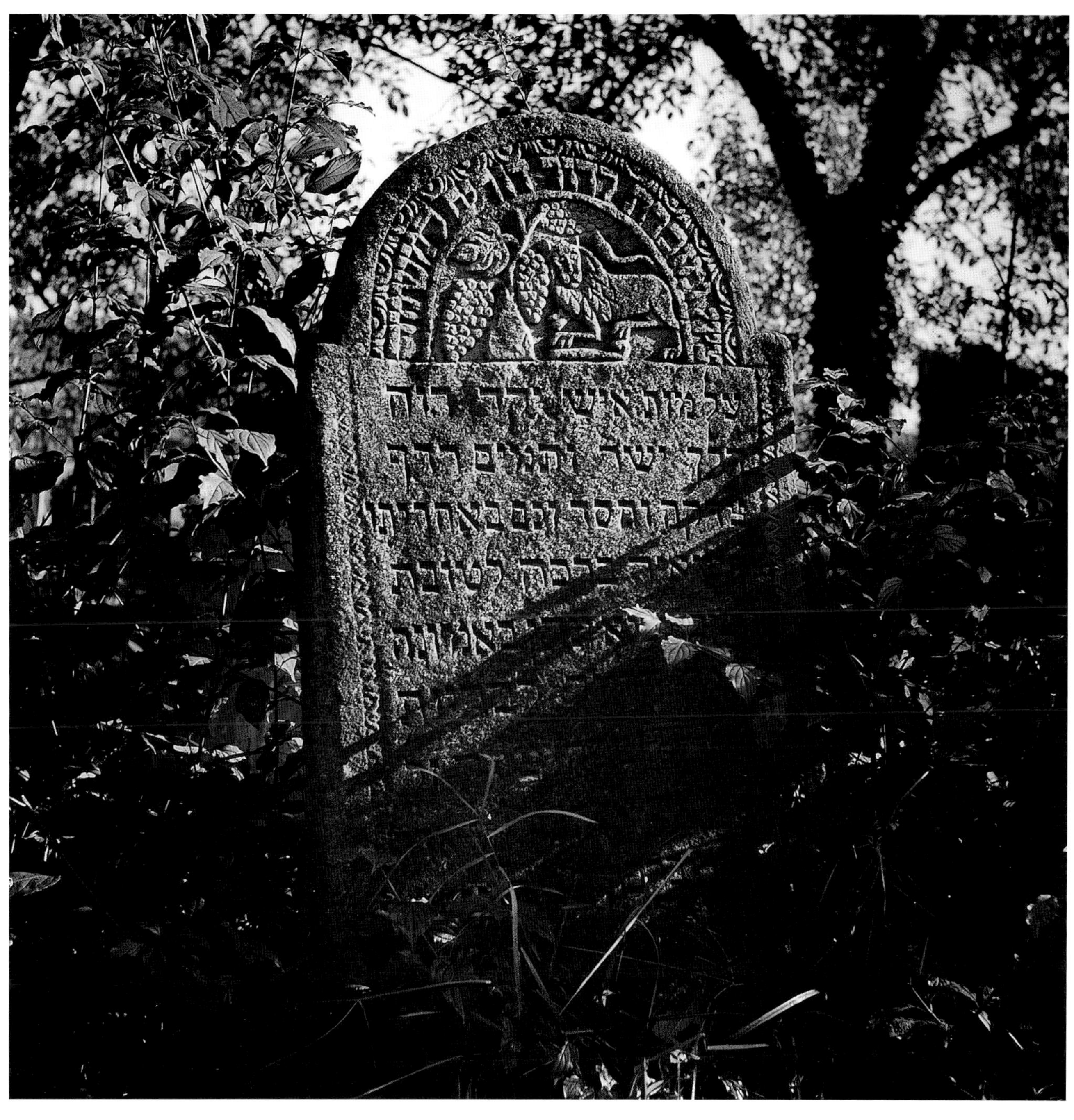

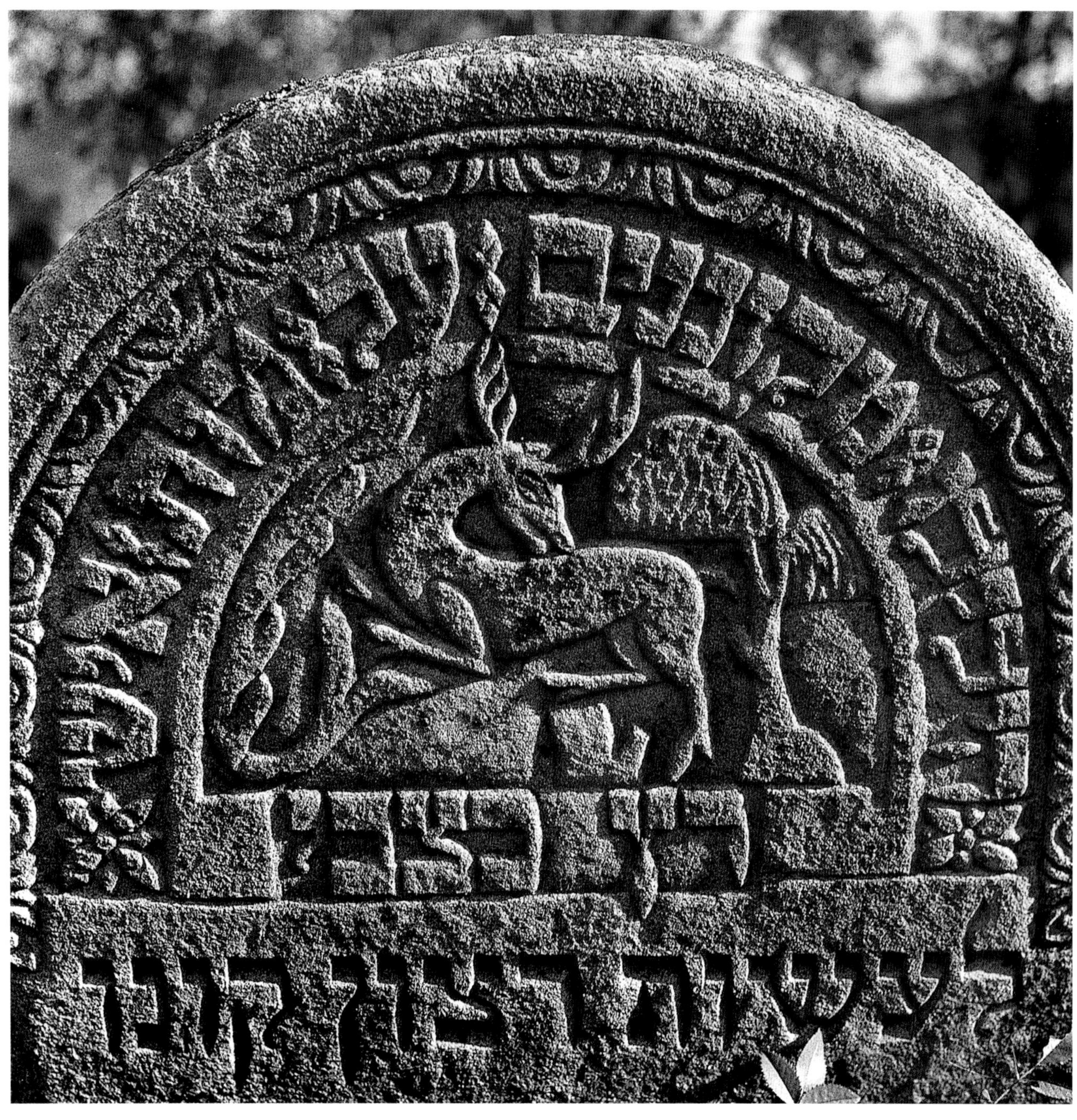

Beregovo. Between 1850 and 1900.

A running stag looking backward.

Zvi [meaning "deer" or "stag"], *son of Jacob.*

Above the image: *They wailed for the death of a man.*
He ran like a deer to do the will of his Creator.

Opposite:

Beregovo. 1869.

A house of prayer with hands in the traditional Cohain or priestly blessing.

The Cohain Shlomo Yehuda, son of Isaiah, Cohain. A man went [passed on], pure, God-fearing, and a solace for people.

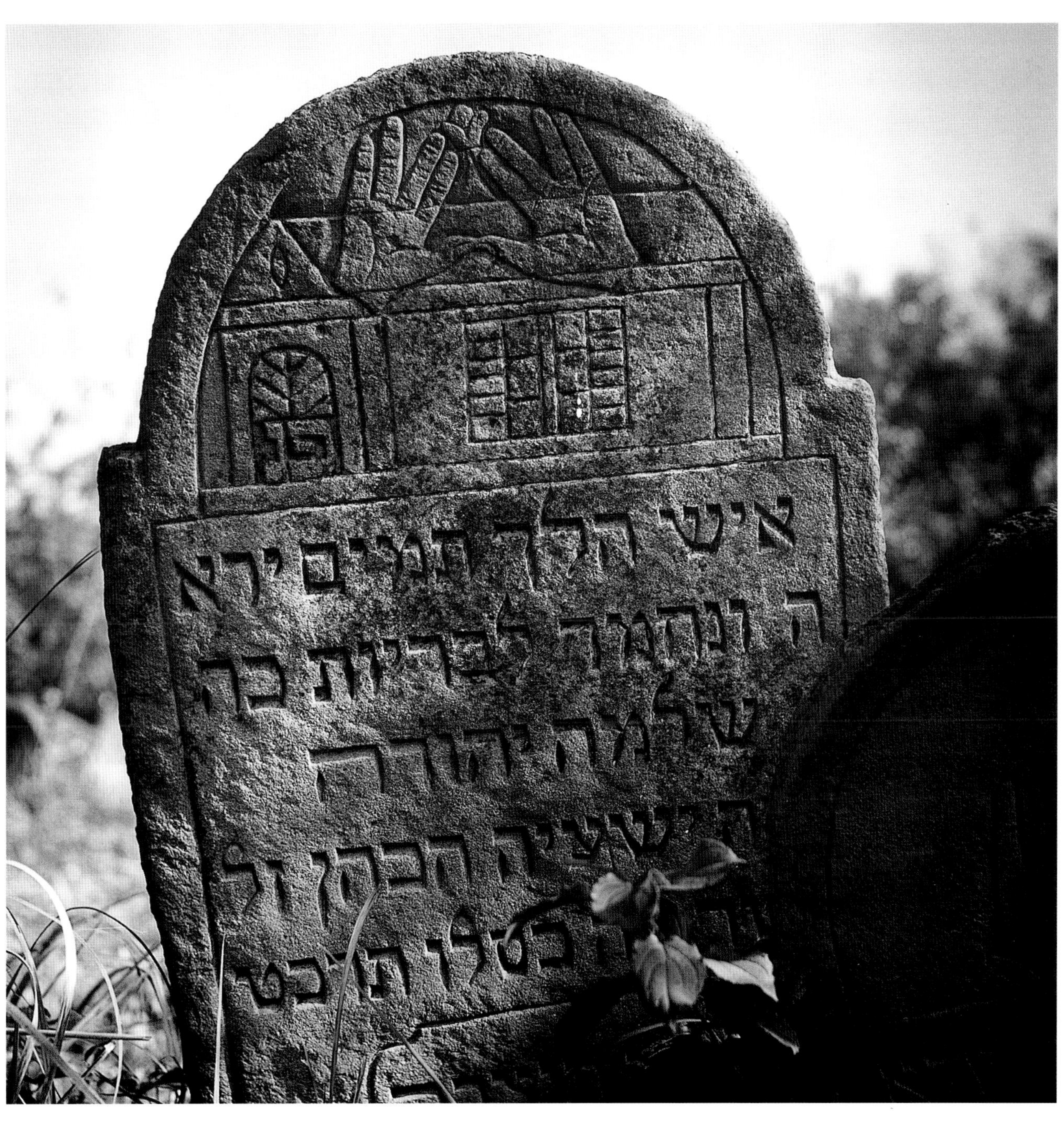

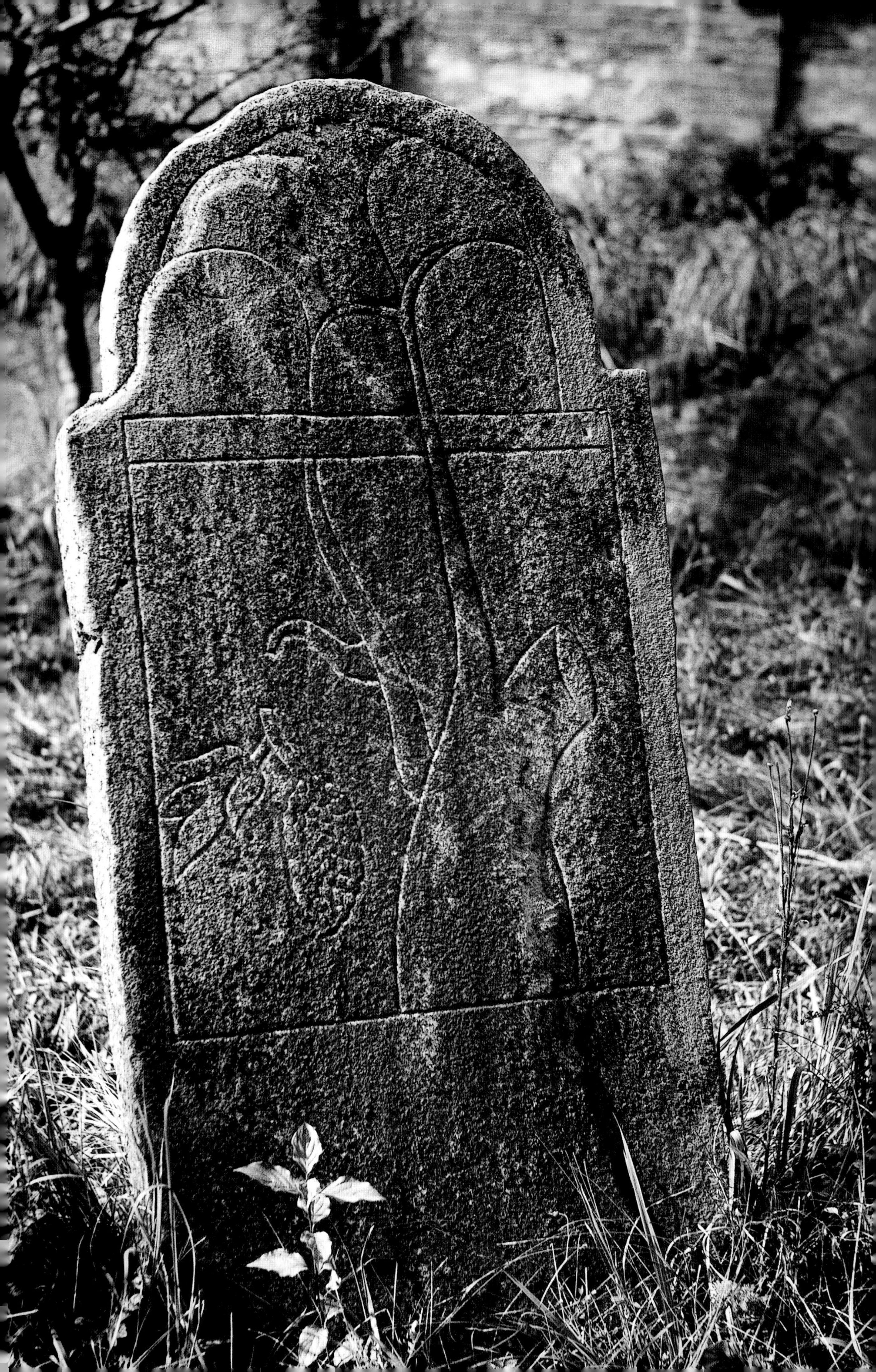

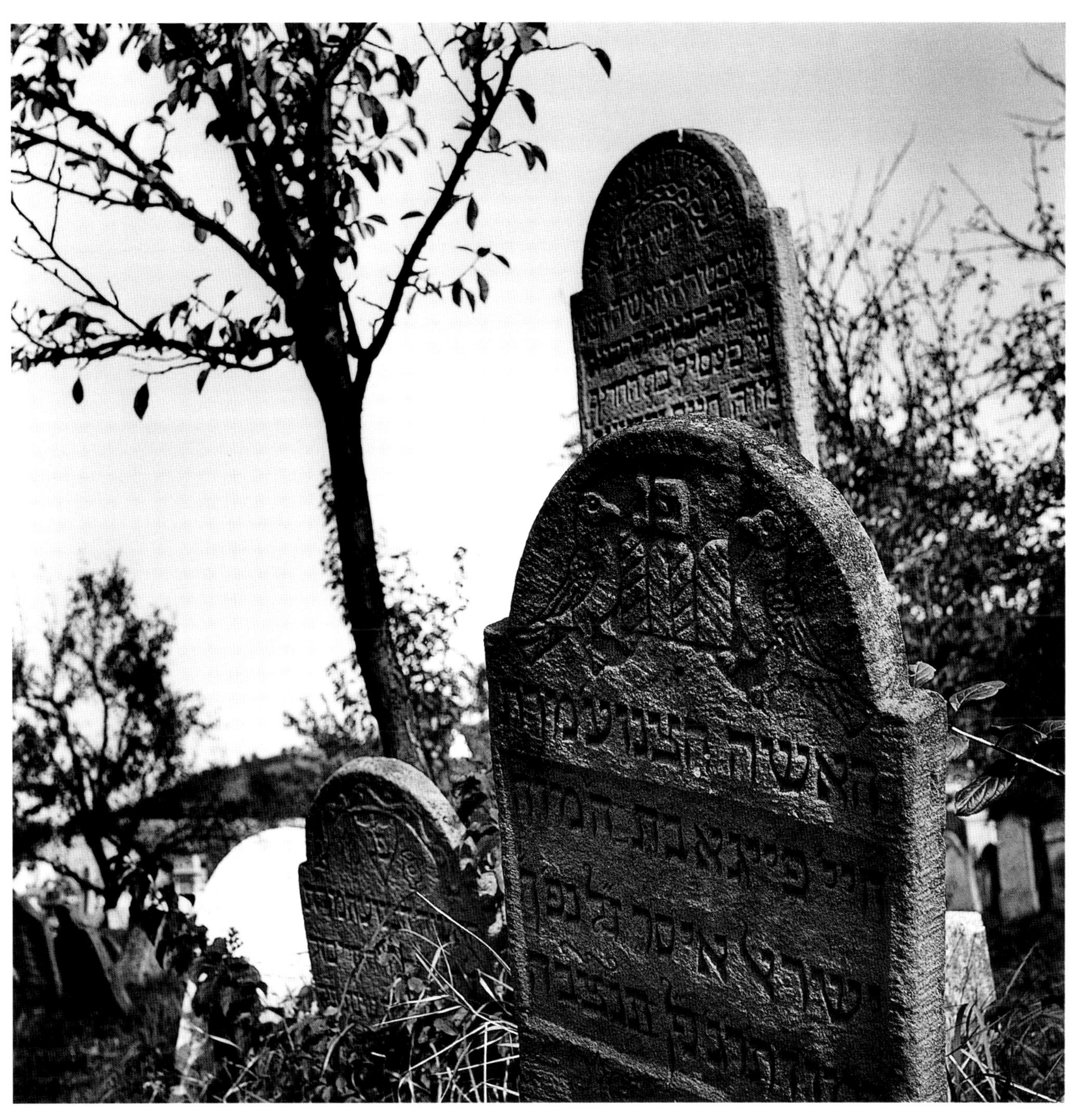

Beregovo. Mid 1800s.

Two birds flanking a design that may allude to the doors of an ark.

Sarah, daughter of Abraham Jacob. A modest woman.

Opposite:

Beregovo. Between 1850 and 1900.

Line drawing of a date tree with the fruit broken off the branch. Symbolic of Psalm 92, signifying a righteous man who has fallen. Probably the rear side of the tombstone.

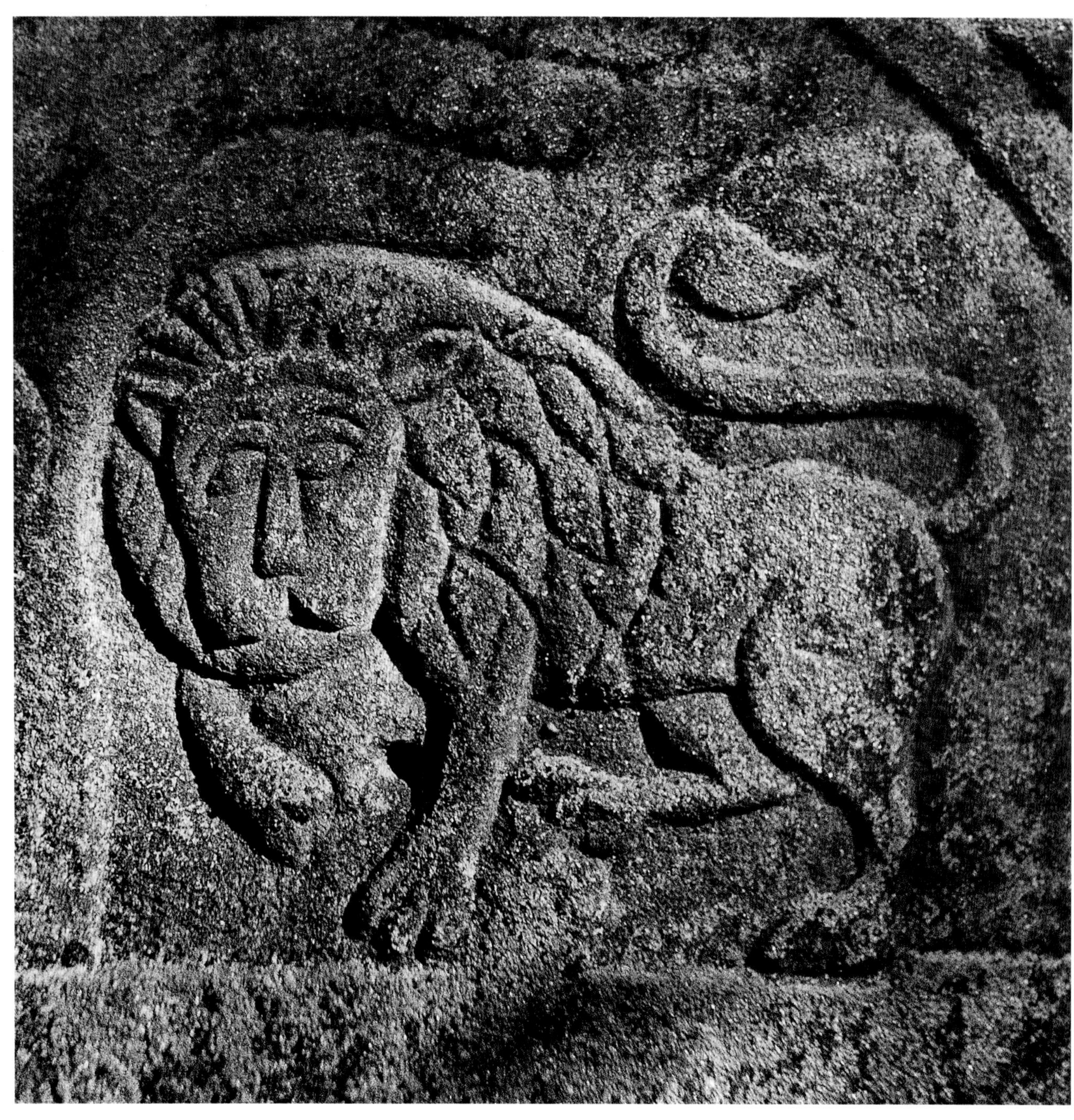

Mukachevo. Between 1850 and 1900.
A sleeping lion on an altar.

Opposite:
Mukachevo. 1800s.
A lion within an altar.
The lion is surrounded by a verse which begins:
All those who love ...

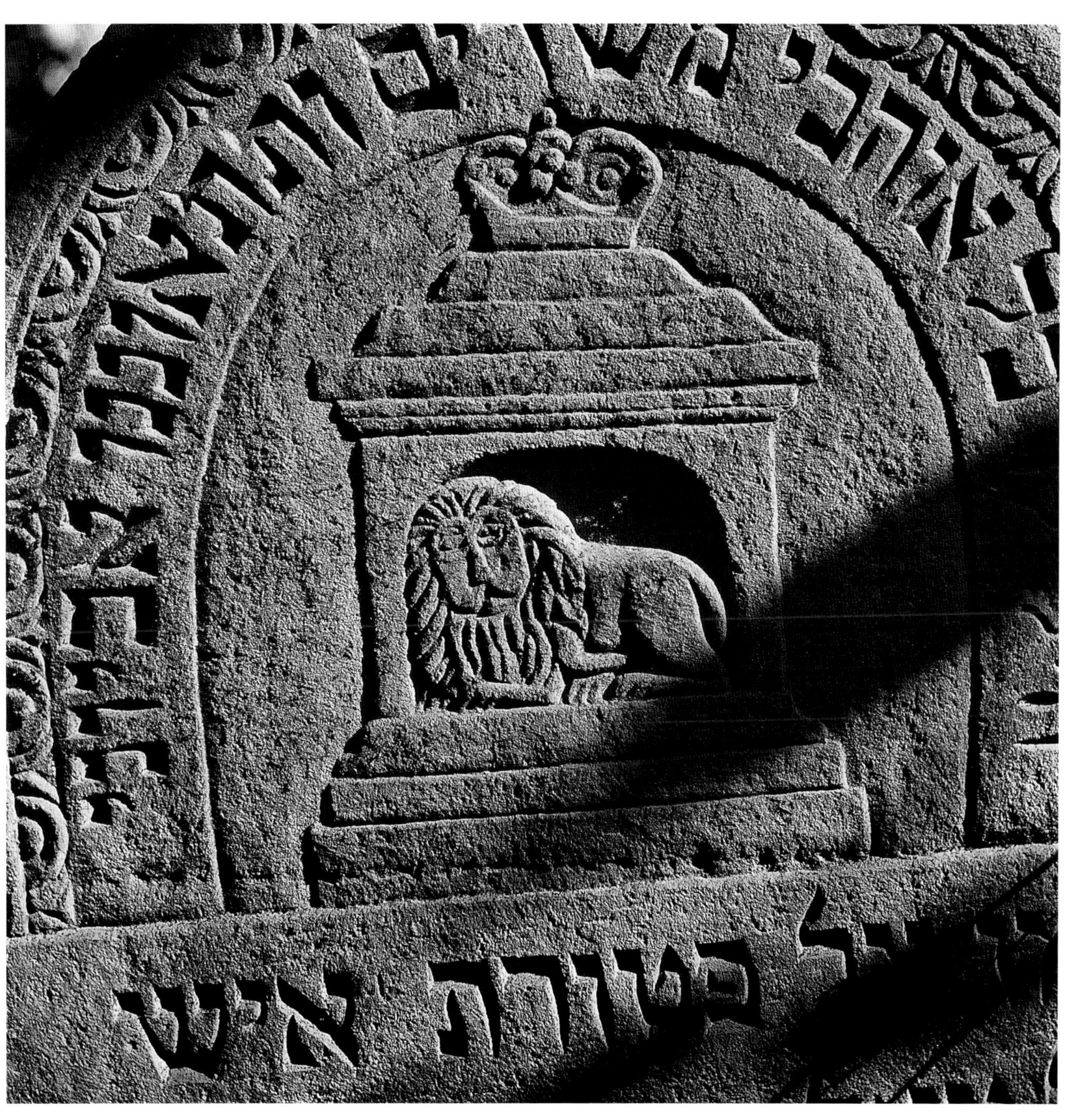

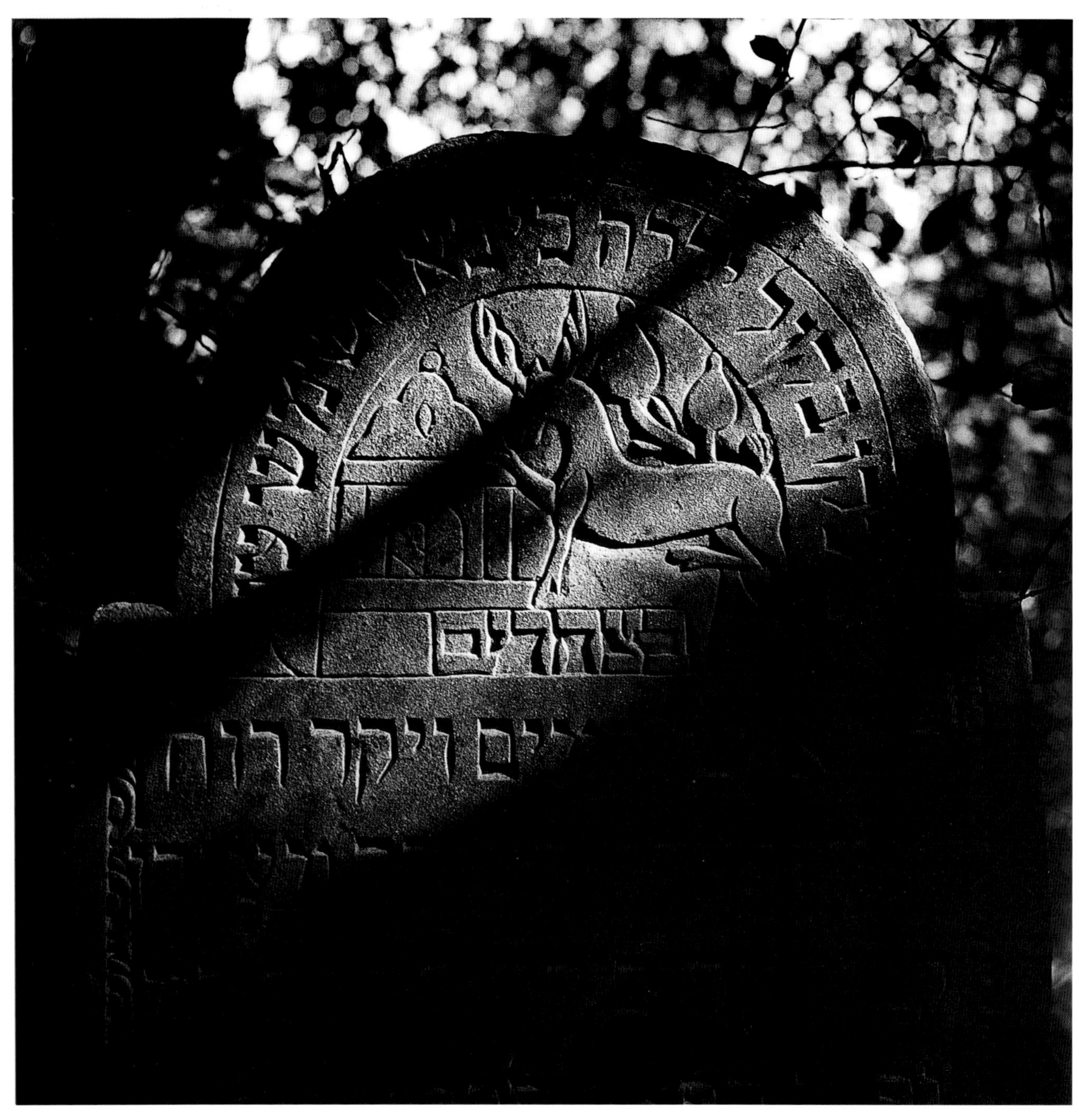

Mukachevo. Between 1850 and 1900.
A stag running by a house of prayer.
The sun set in midday. A young man. The beloved. Noble of spirit.

Opposite:
Mukachevo. Between 1850 and 1900.
On the back side of a monument, a house of prayer with clouds above.

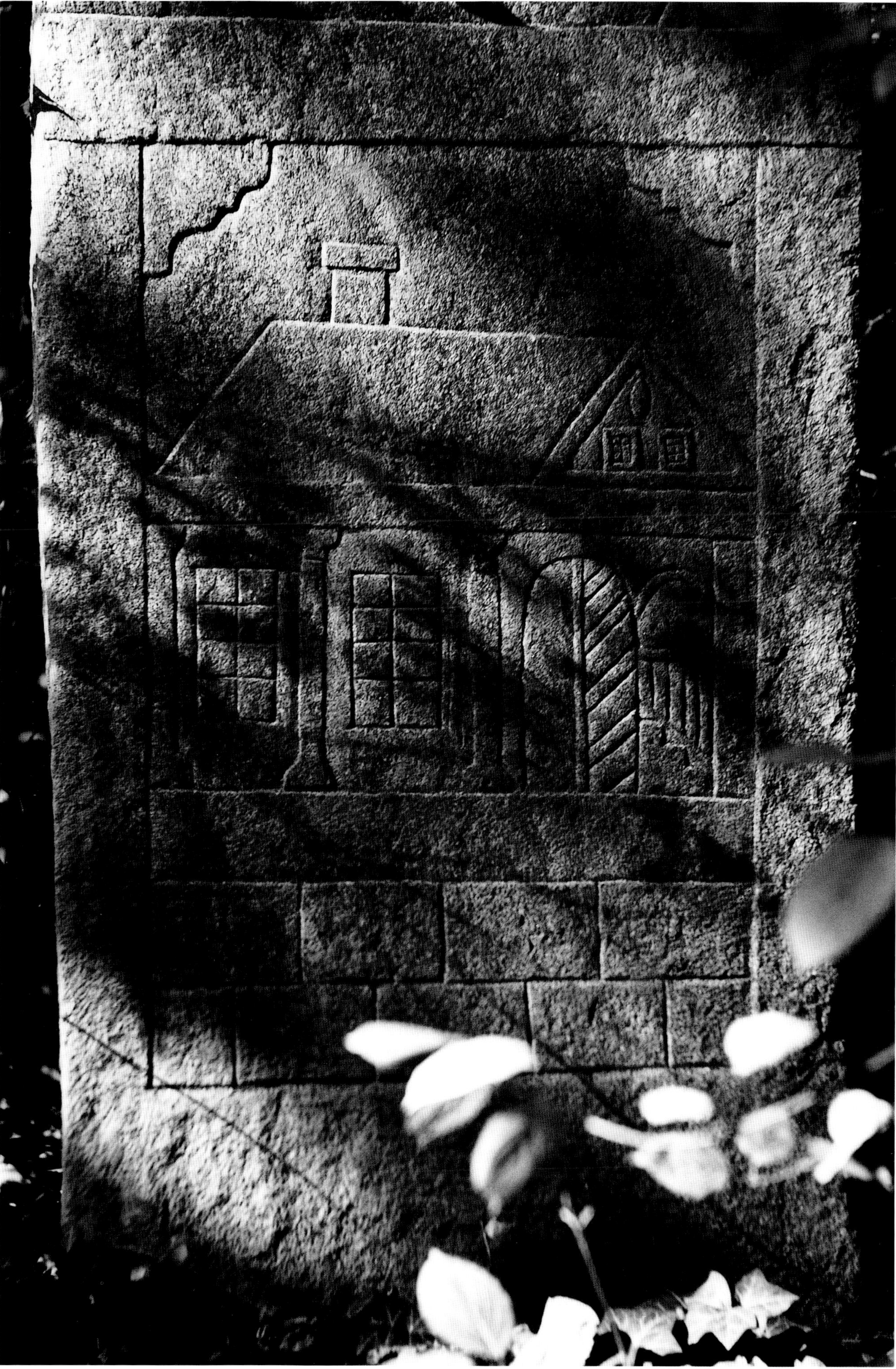

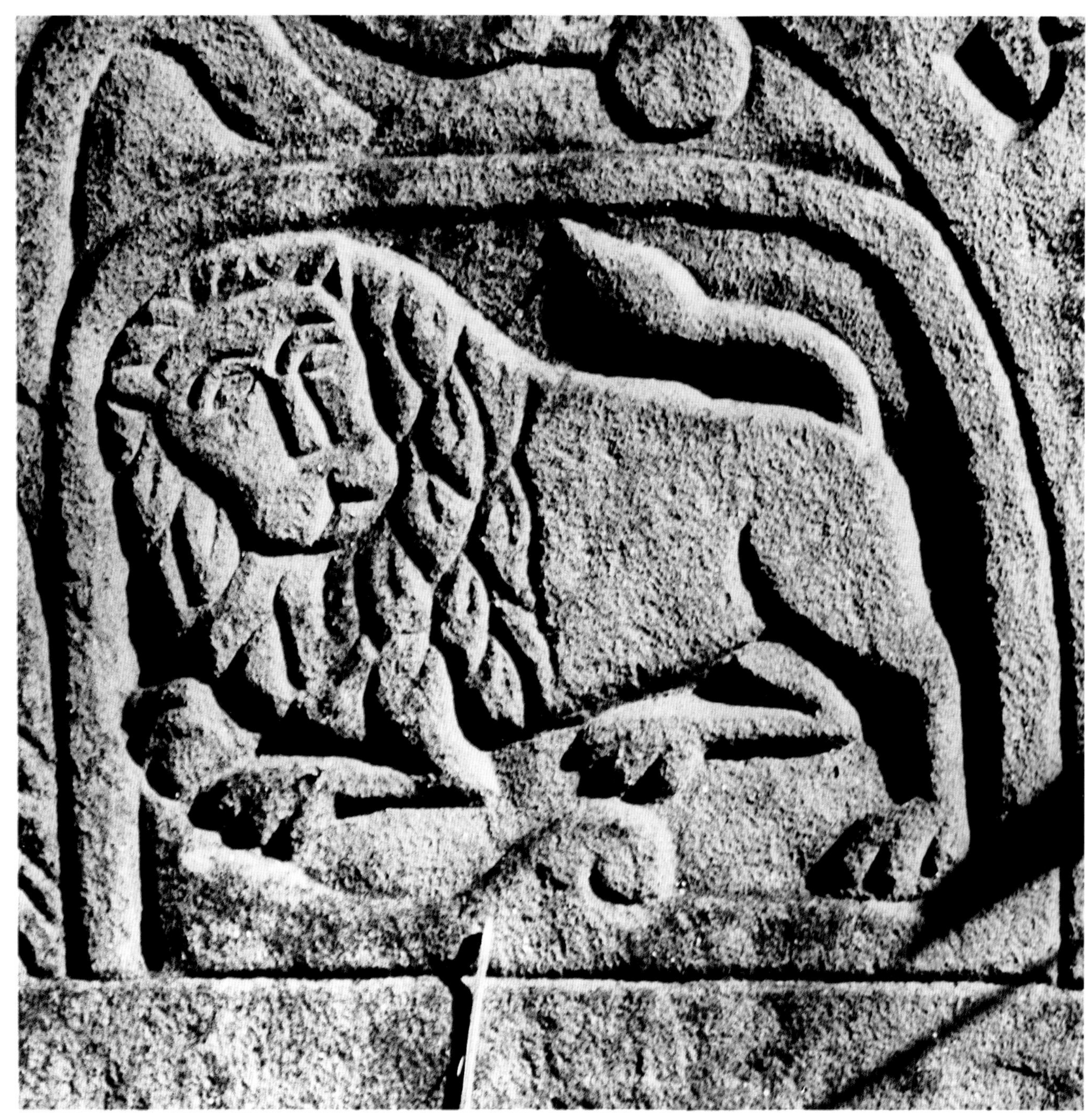

Vinogradov. Between 1850 and 1900.
A sleeping lion on an altar.

Opposite:
Yablonov. Late 1700s.
Two flying griffins, above, and reclining deer or stags below.
Here lies a righteous and honest person.

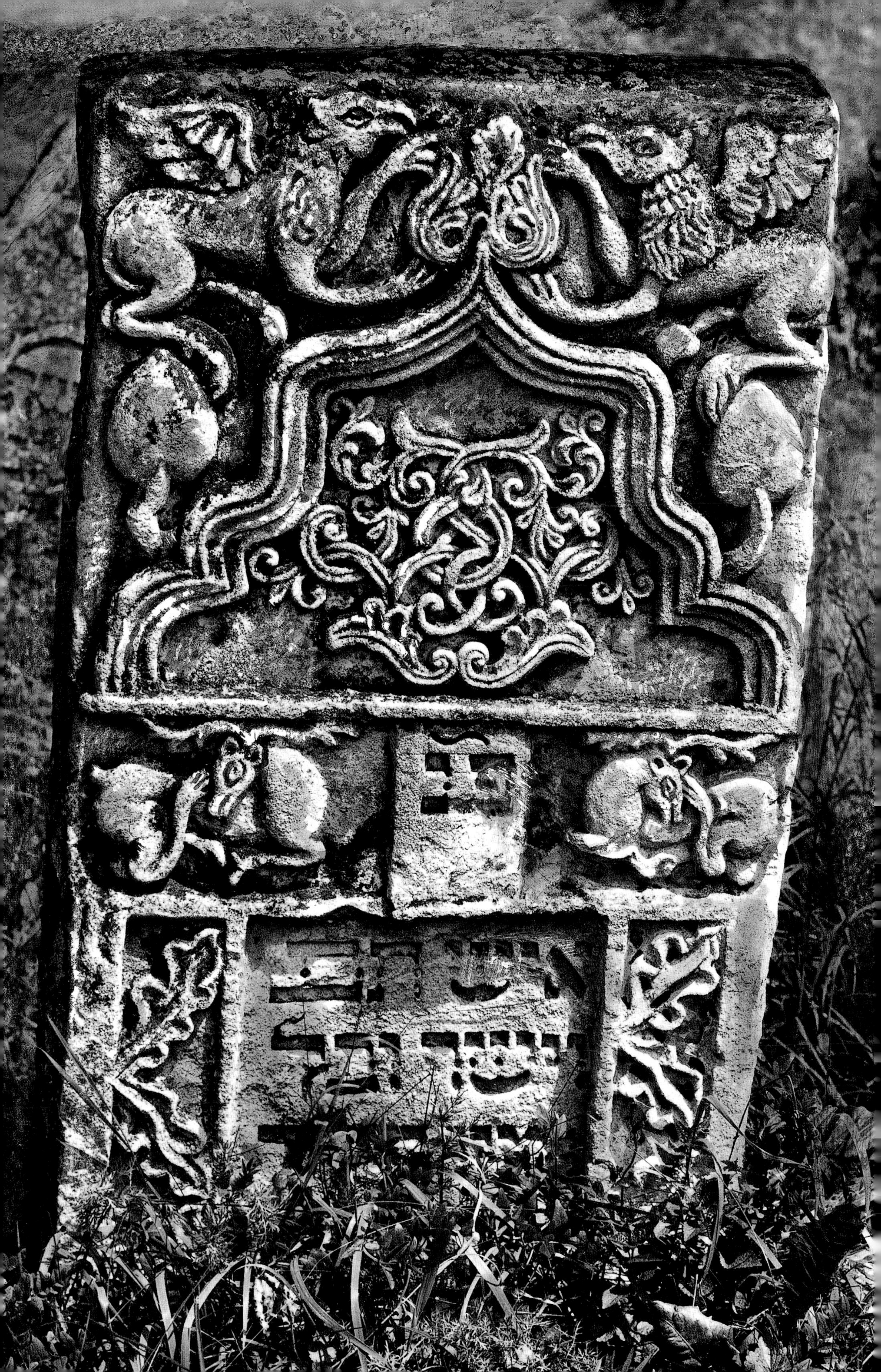

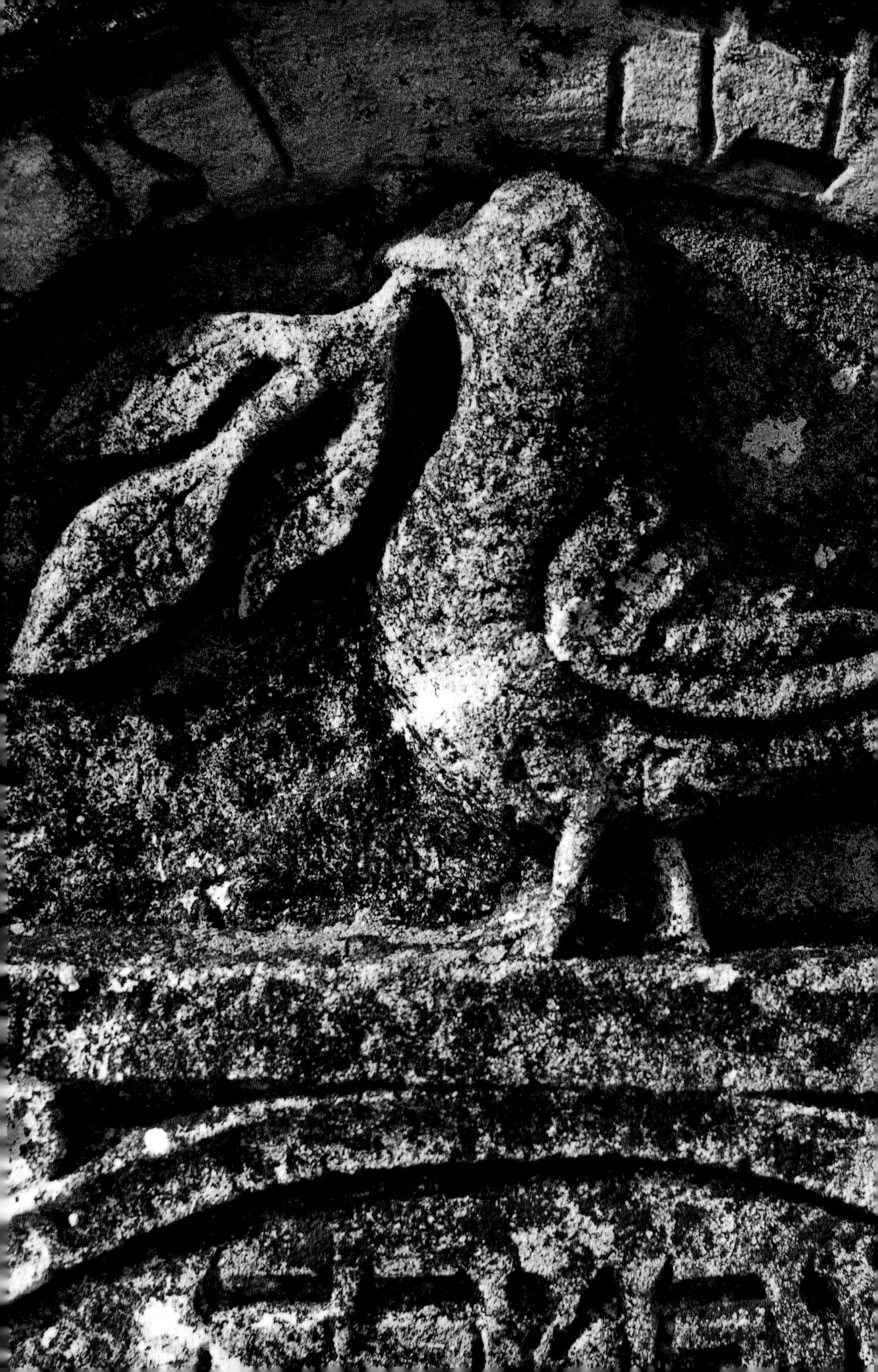

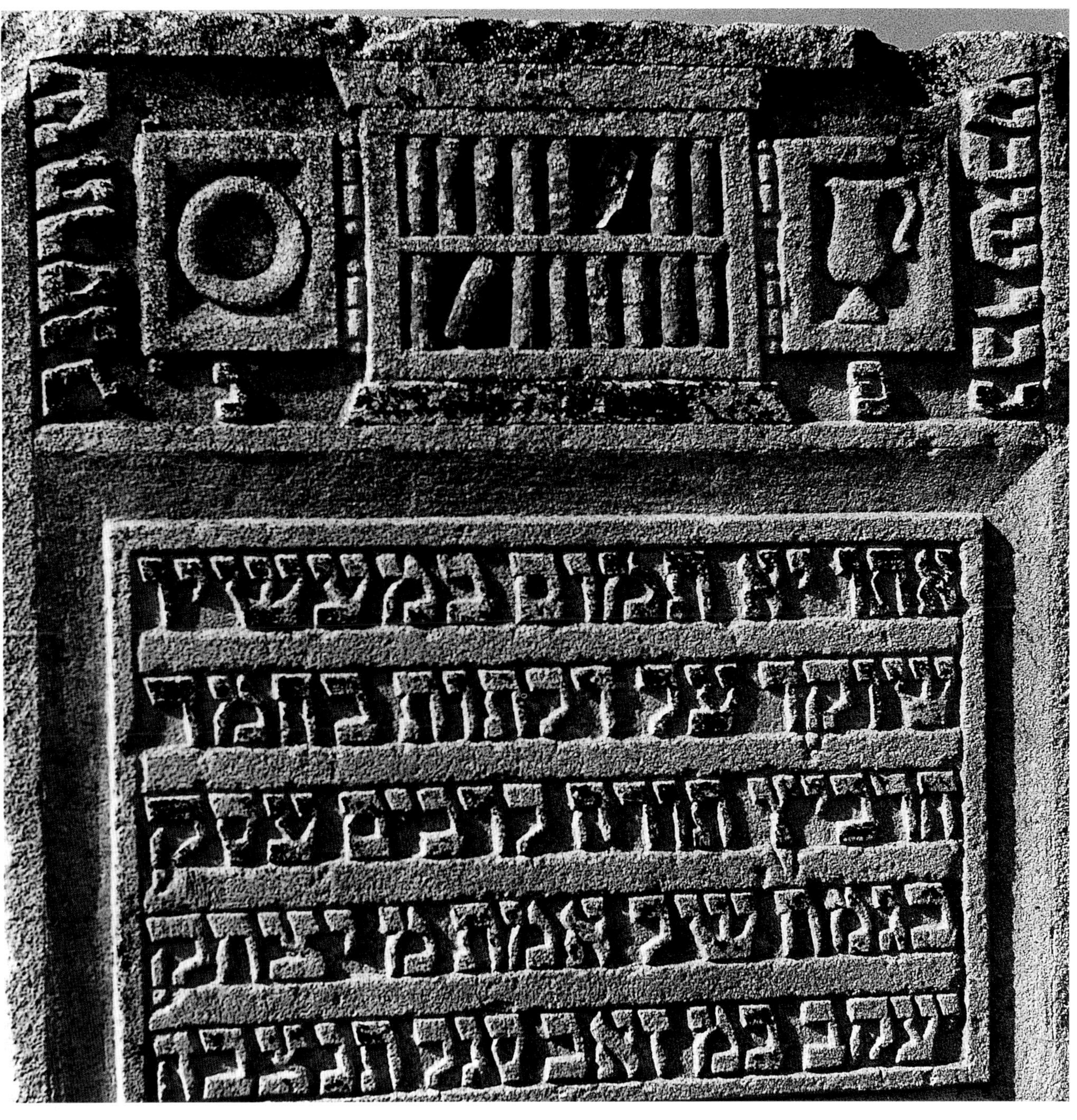

Sambor. 1903.

A bookcase with the books of the Bible, proclaiming the deceased's intelligence and stature as a learned and respected person. On the bookcase are depicted a pitcher and a bowl, indicating that he was a Levite. *Issac Jacob son of Zeyev Siegel. He spread Torah to many, He gave charity, kindness, and truth. He was complete in his acts.*

Opposite:

Sambor. 1882.

A dove carrying a branch in its beak. This is the tombstone of a woman.

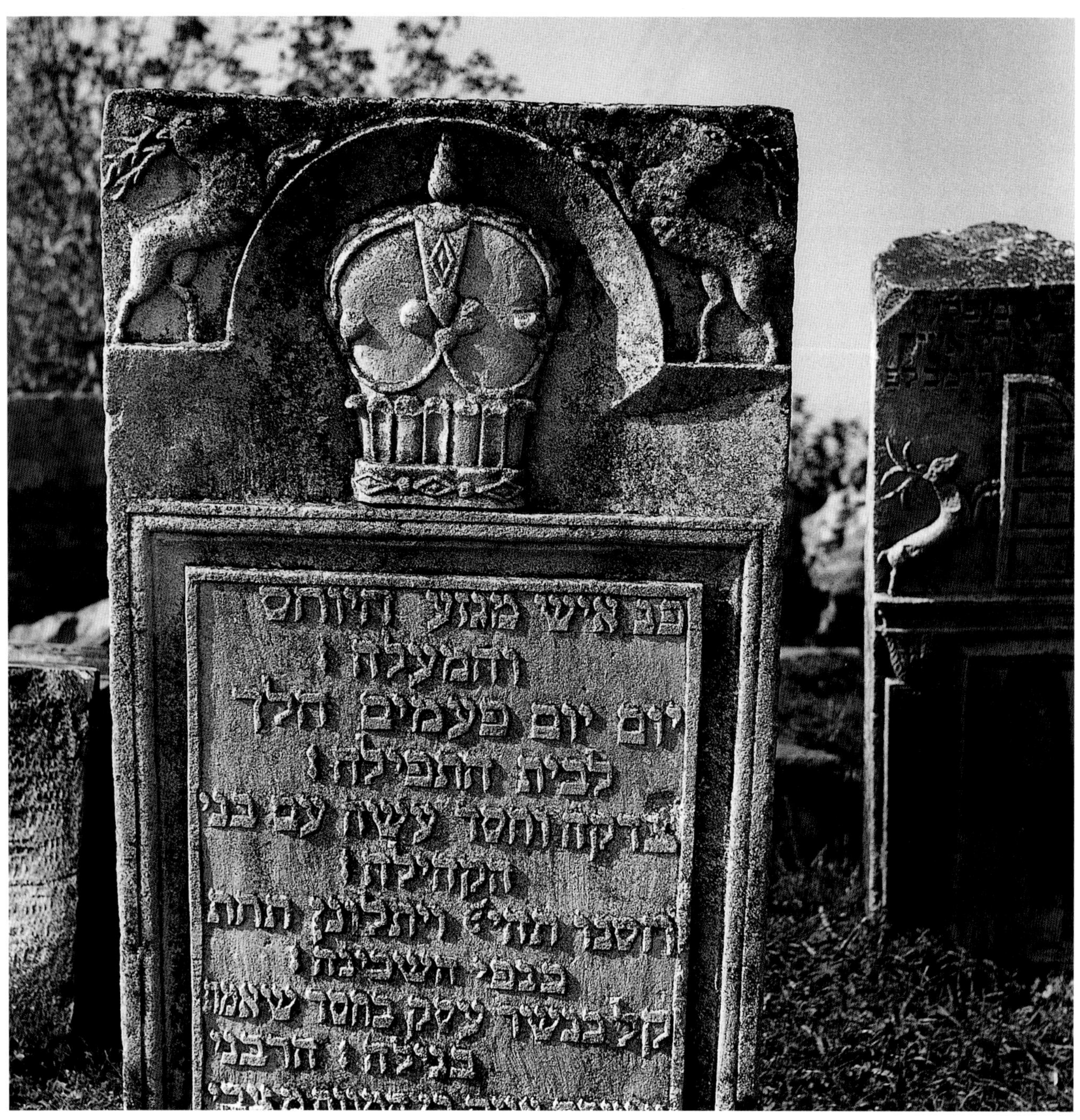

Sambor. 1850s.

An elaborate Cohain crown flanked by deer or stags. The epitaph paraphrases a verse from Psalms.

Yitzhak Issac son of the deceased Zvi. He came from noble seed and from the elite. Every day he went twice to the synagogue. He was charitable and kind to the community and he will rest under the wings of the Shekhina. He dealt with compassion and truth as swiftly as an eagle.

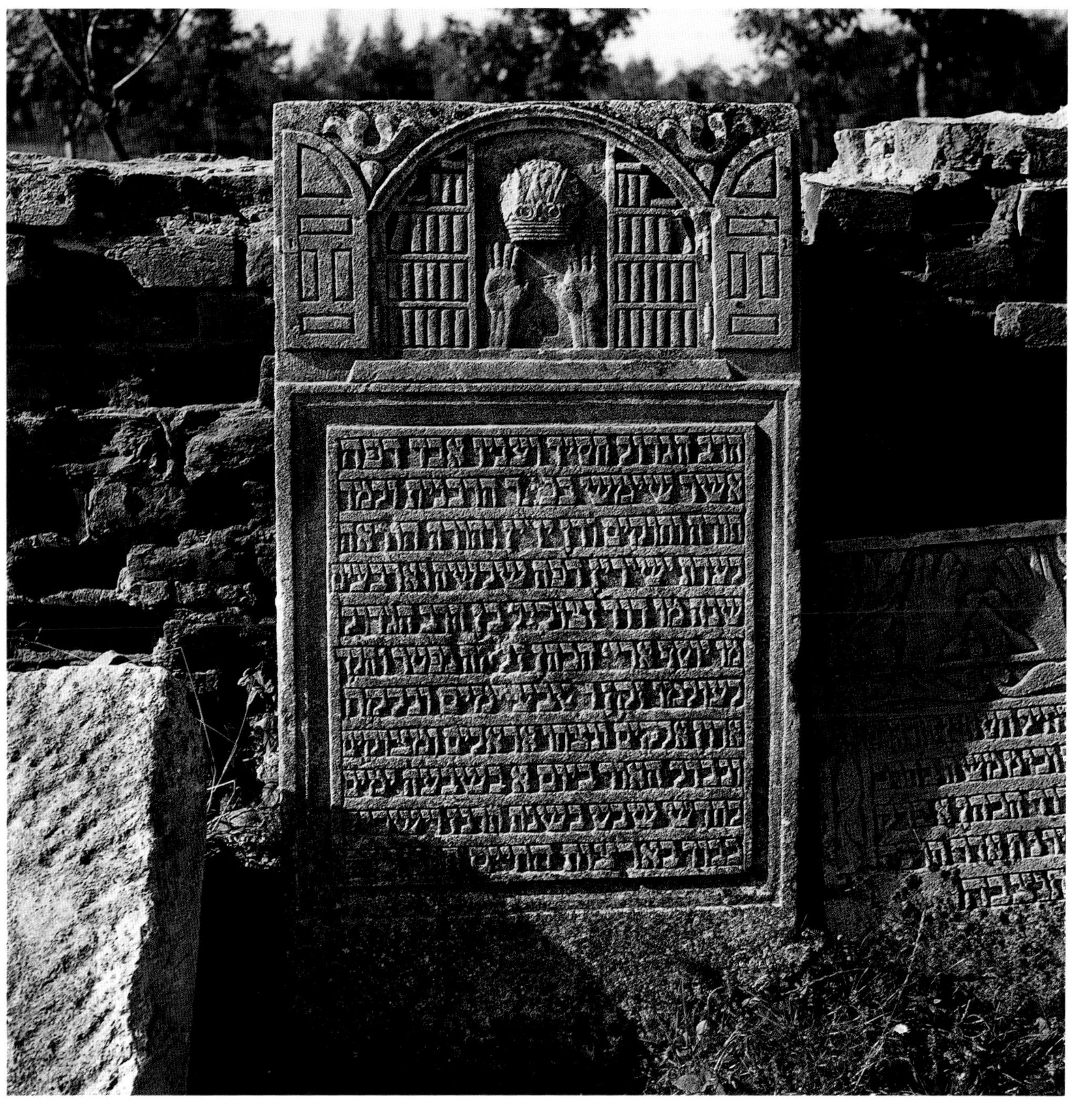

Sambor. 1897.

An open bookcase containing the Bible. In the center, Cohain hands in prayer below a Cohain crown.

He was the Chief Justice [or Chief Rabbi] of the local court. He served the crown of the Rabbinate. He taught Torah and laws, he judged and he made Halakhic rulings. He made rulings to the community of Israel for forty-three years. David, son of a rabbi, who was Joseph Arie, a Cohain, died and went into the eternal world. He was old and satisfied in his days. He was taken and the ark of God was taken—the angels of death triumphed over the angels of life. And the light was separated. Died on a Sunday, the seventh of Shevat, 5657. May his honor rest in the land of the living.

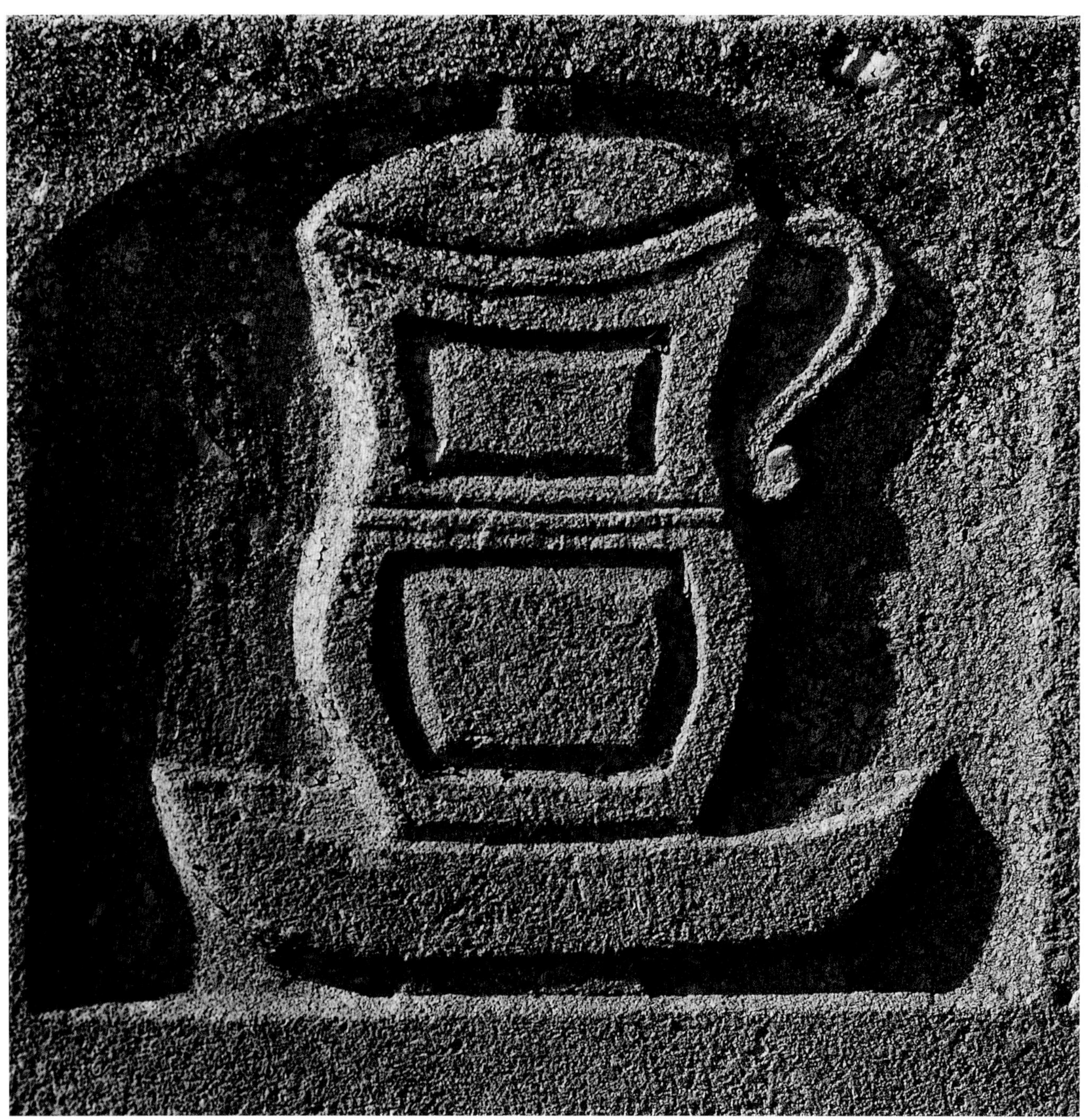

Sambor. 1926.
A pitcher carved in a modernist style, on the tombstone of a Levite.

Opposite:
Sambor Cemetery.

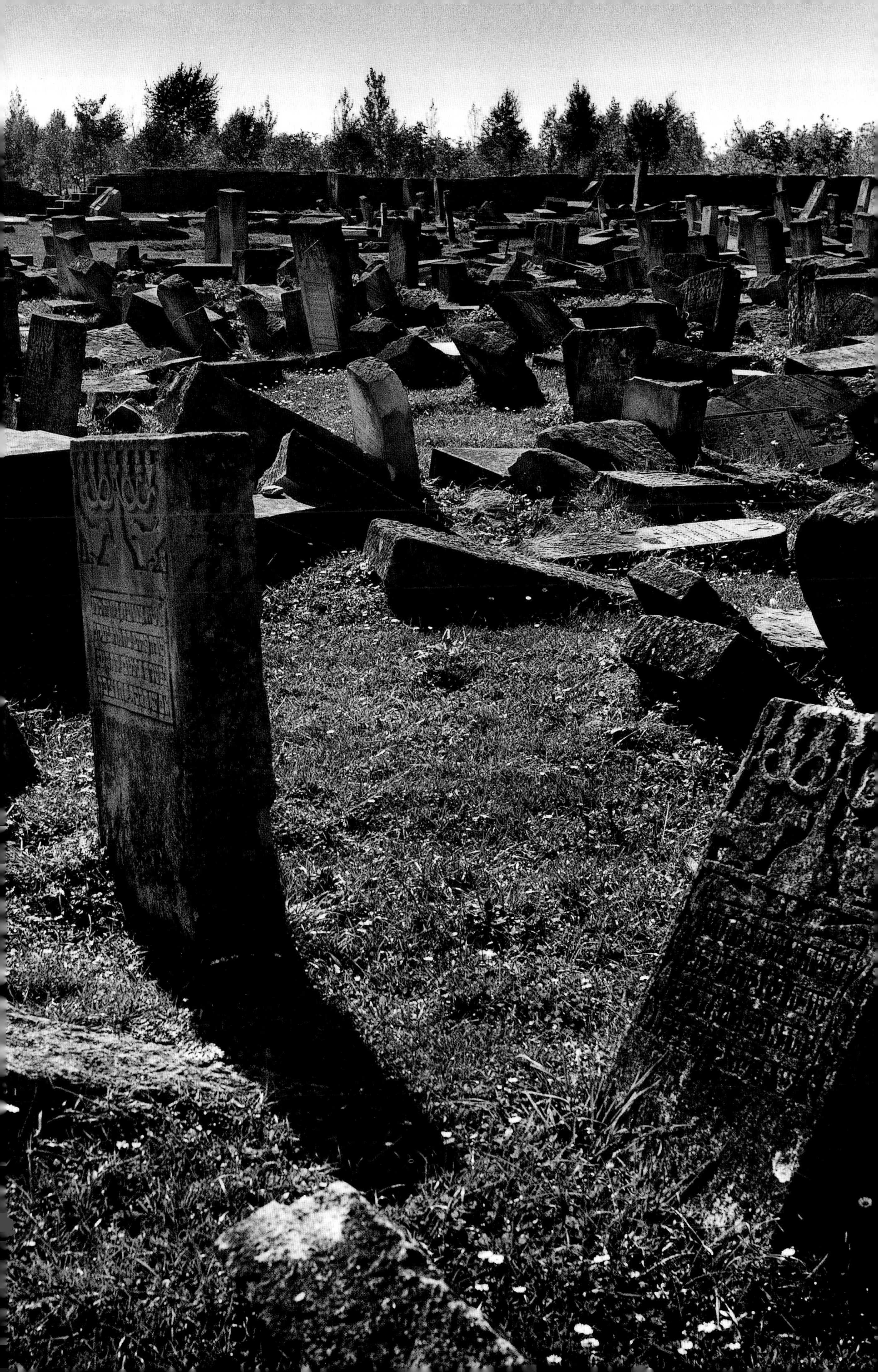

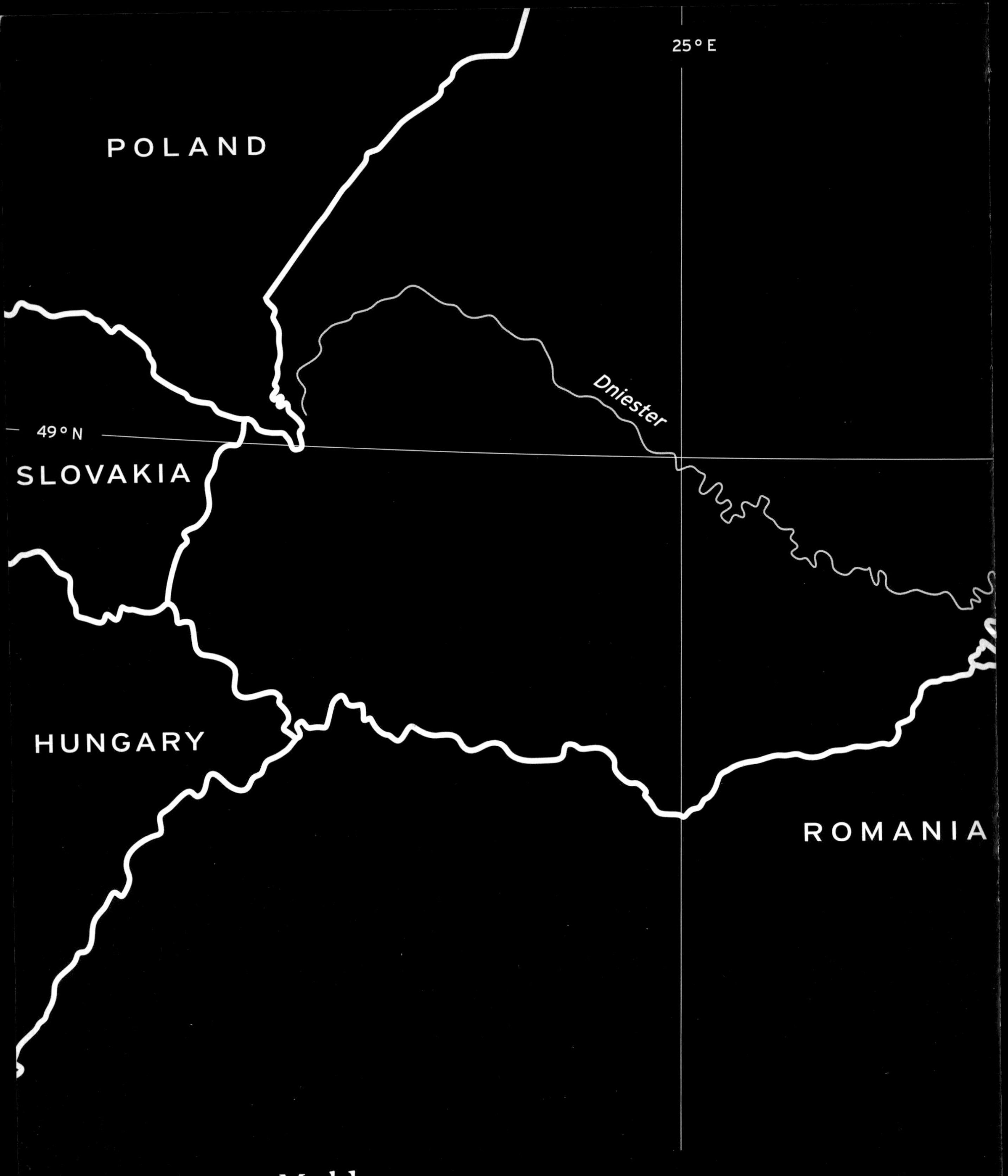

Moldova

Beltsy was settled in the beginning of the 16th century and was a center of Galician Hasidism. **Orgeyev** may have been a transit stop for Jewish merchants from Constantinople and Poland. **Kalarash**, settled by Jews during the first half of the 19th century, was home to flourishing Jewish social organizations, including a hospital founded in 1890, a Talmud Torah, and a library. Nearly half the population of **Kishinev** (now the capital of Moldova) was Jewish at the turn of the 18th century. As a cultural center of Bessarabian Jewry, it had numerous schools, including yeshivas and cultural institutions.

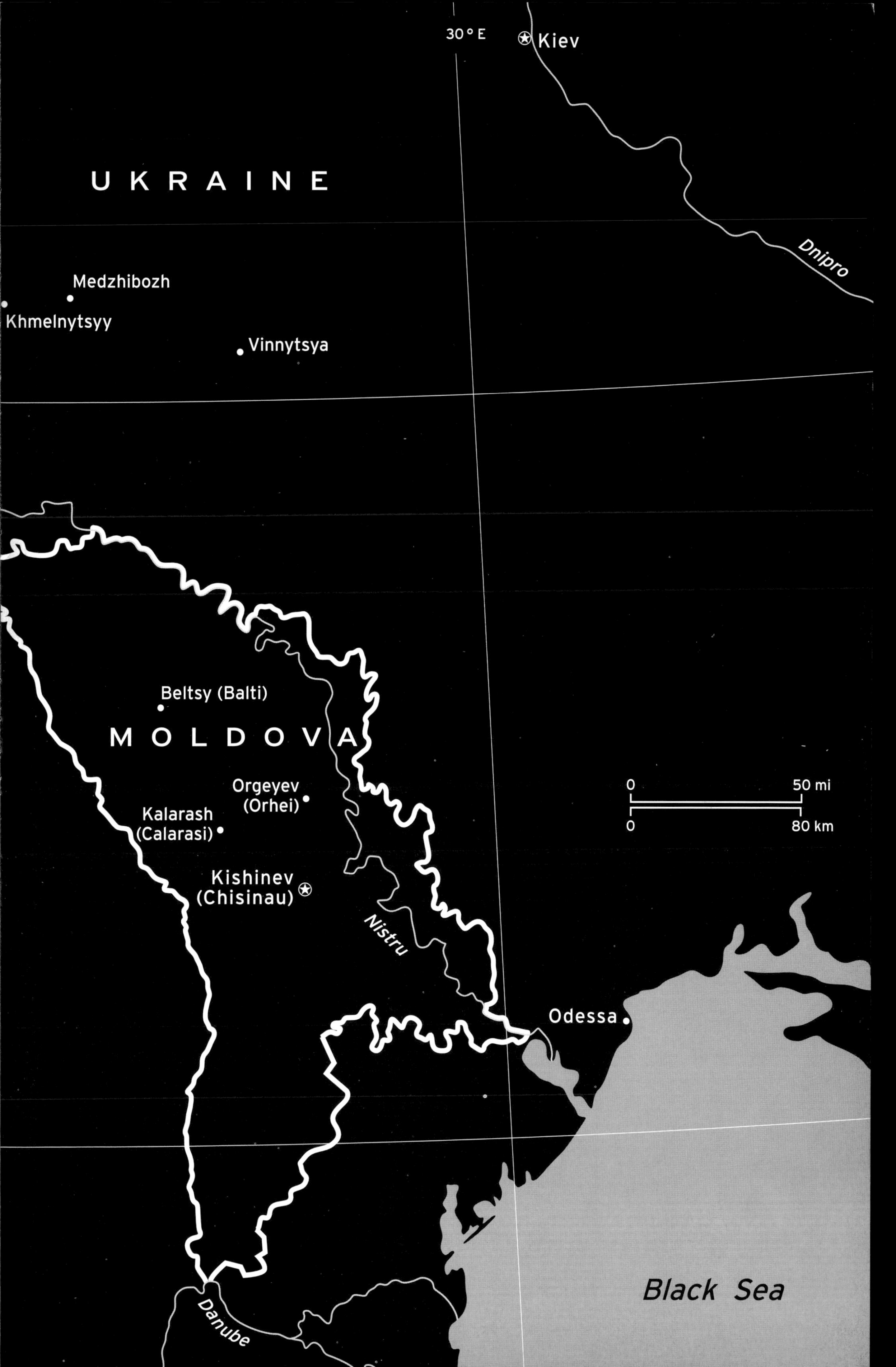
30° E
Kiev
UKRAINE
Dnipro
Medzhibozh
Khmelnytsyy
Vinnytsya
Beltsy (Balti)
MOLDOVA
Orgeyev
(Orhei)
Kalarash
(Calarasi)
Kishinev
(Chisinau)
Nistru
0
50 mi
0
80 km
Odessa
Black Sea
Danube

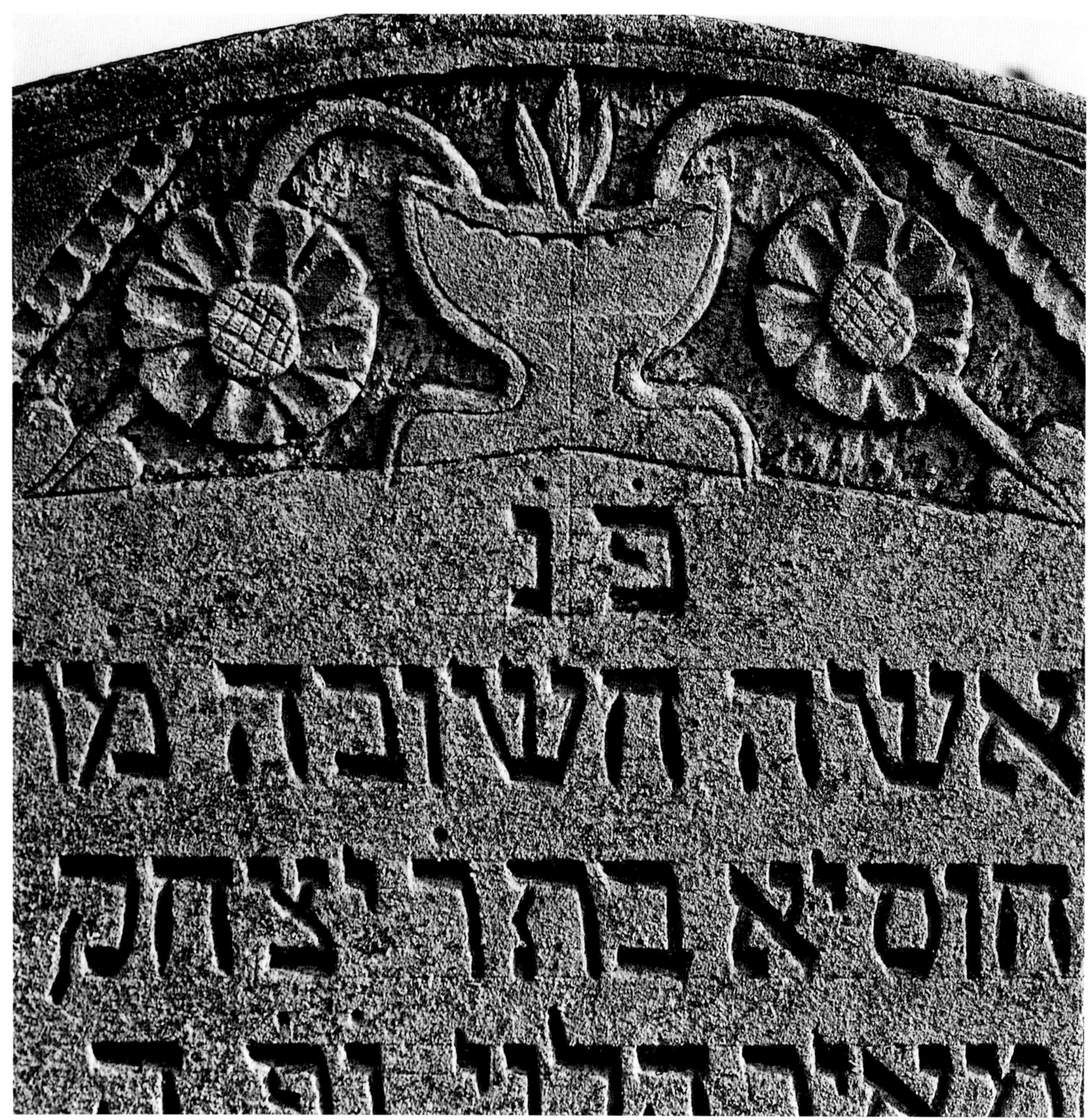

Beltsy. 1904.

Sunflowers in a vase.

Here lies an important woman, Chusya, daughter of Yitsak Meyer.

Opposite:

Beltsy. 1915.

A bird surrounded by date trees (or grape vines). Hands hold back curtains to flank the epitaph.

Here lies the important and modest woman Zeitel the daughter of Aaron Dov and the wife of Rabbi Schneur Mechler. She died on the thirteenth day of Tammuz.

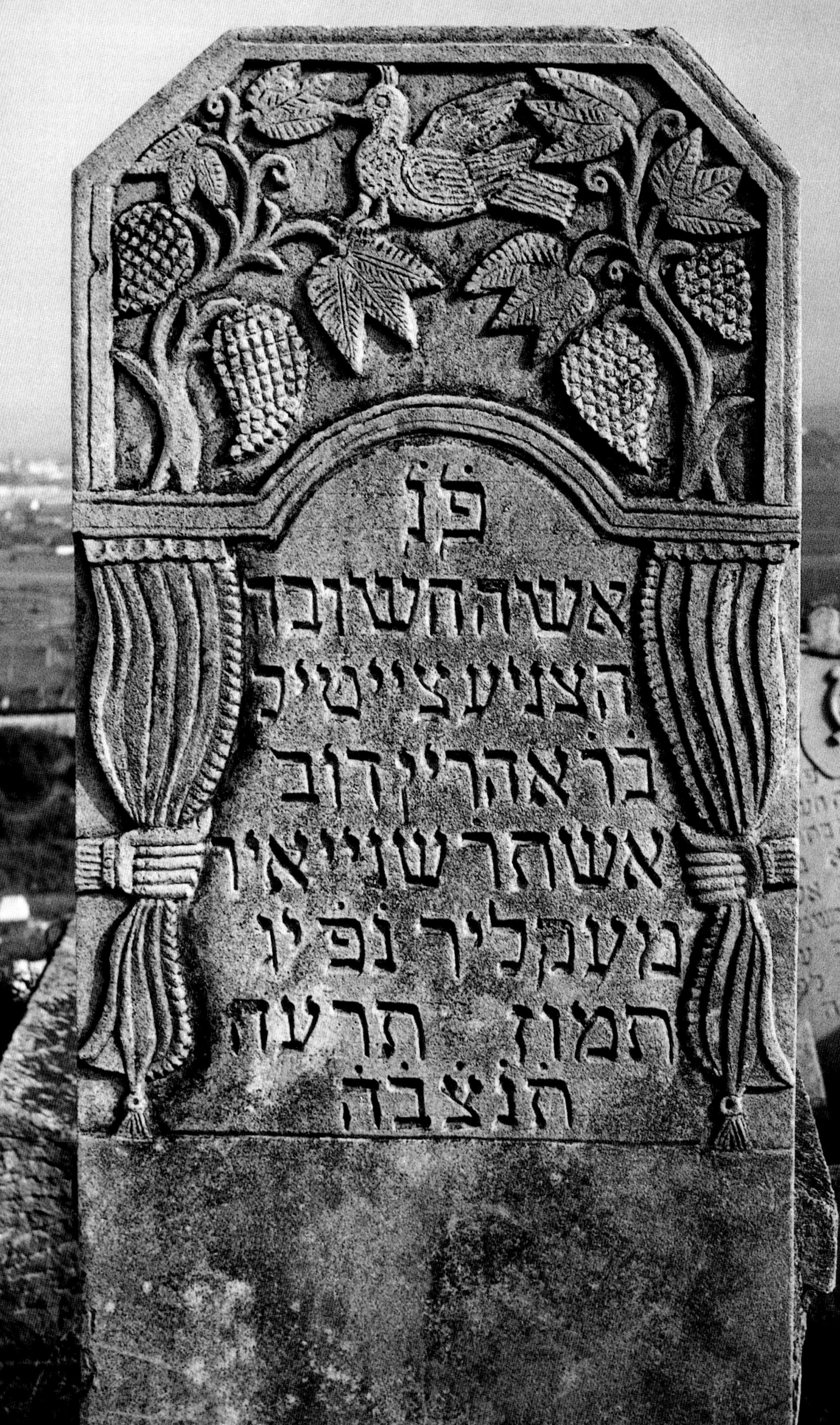
פנ
אשהחשובה
הצניעצייטיל
בראהרןזוב
אשהרשוייאר
מעקלירנפיו
תמוז תרעה
תנצבה

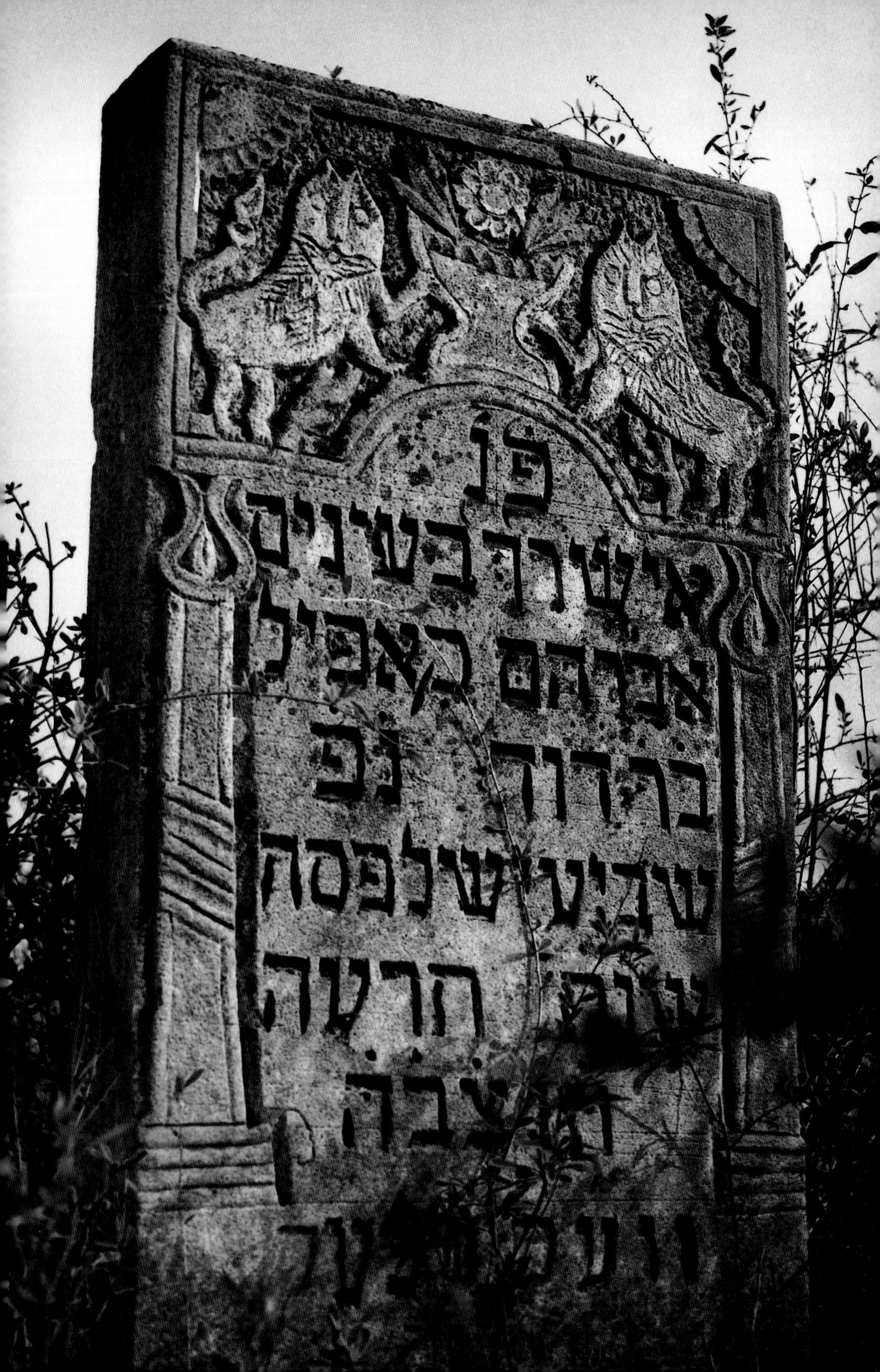
פנ
איש רך בשנים
אברהם כאפיל
בהר דוד נפ
שויע של פסח
שות הרעה
תנצבה

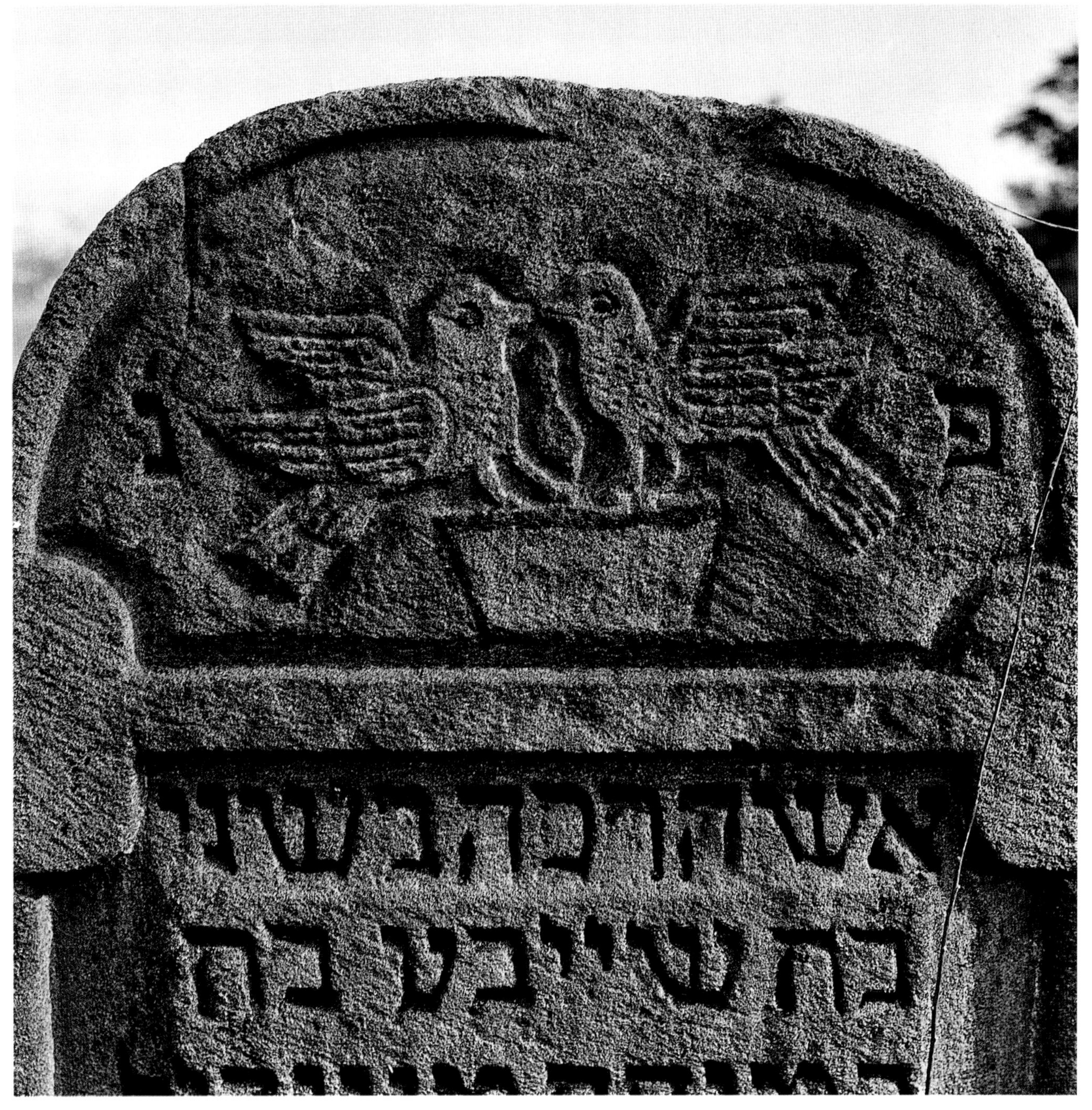

Opposite:
Beltsy. 1915.
Two catlike lions flanking a vase with flowers.
Soft in years. A young man Abraham Koppel son of David. he died on the seventh day of Passover in 5675.

Beltsy. Early 1900s.
Two birds kissing.
A young woman. Daughter of Sheybeh.

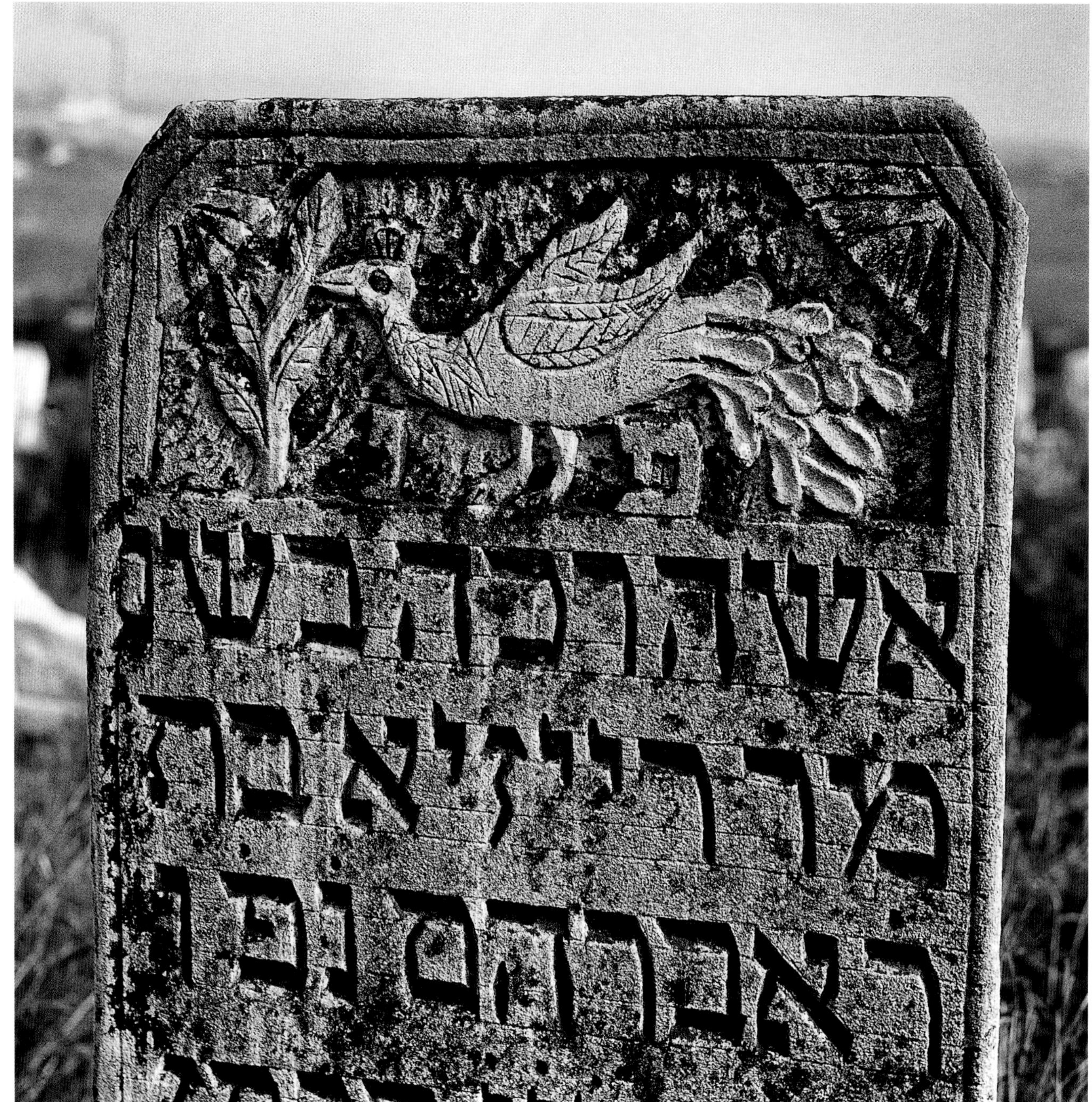

Beltsy. c. 1908.

A peacock, symbol of all that is beautiful and eternal in Paradise.

A [young] woman soft in years. Raisa, daughter of Abraham. 5668.

Opposite:

Beltsy. 1905.

A lion with a beard surrounded by four quarter-circles, which could be floral or represent radiating sunshine.

An important person, Benjamin the son of Jacob Shmuel. He died on Yom Kippur in the year 5666.

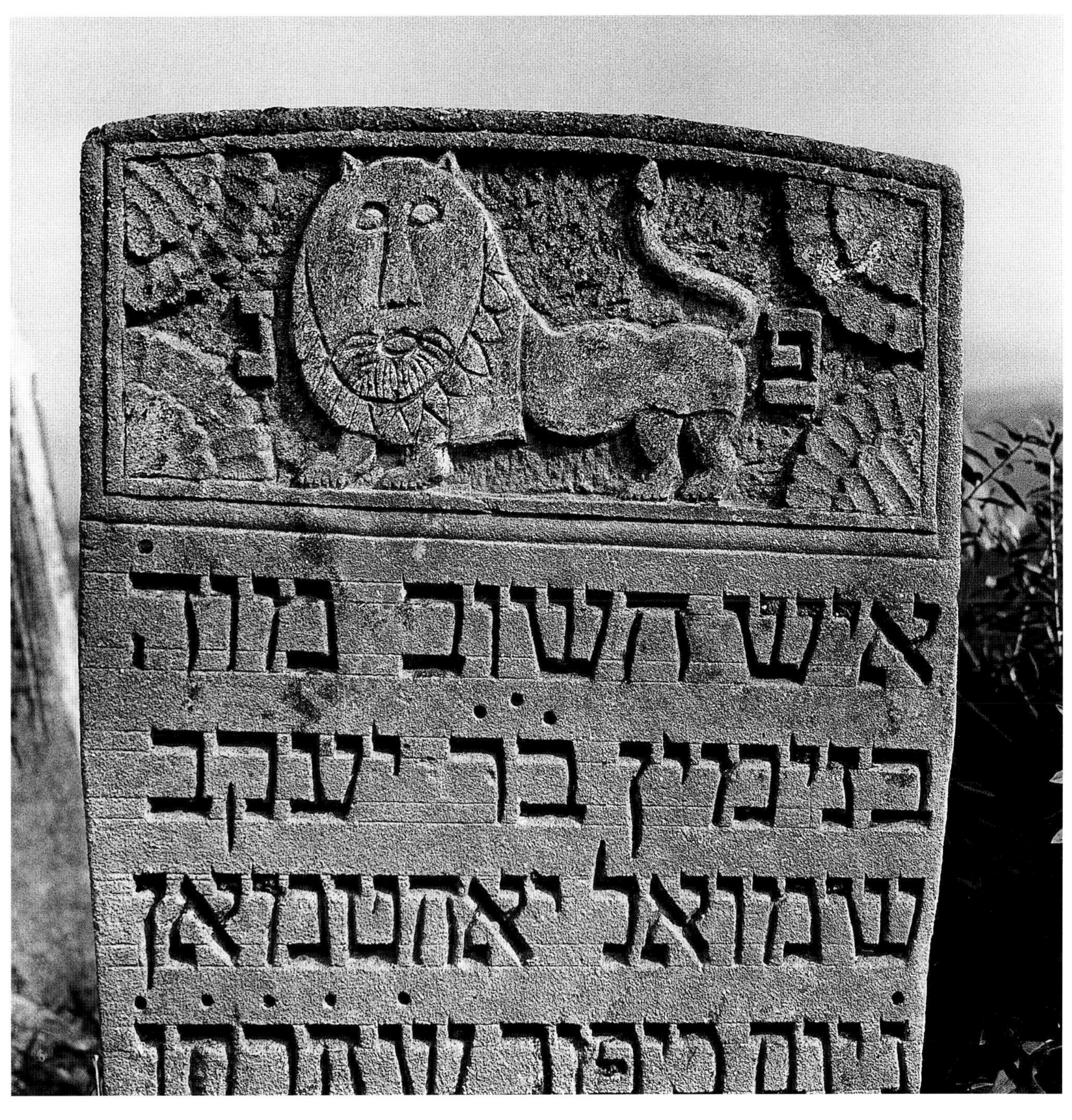
פ נ
איש השוב מוה
בנימין בר יעקב

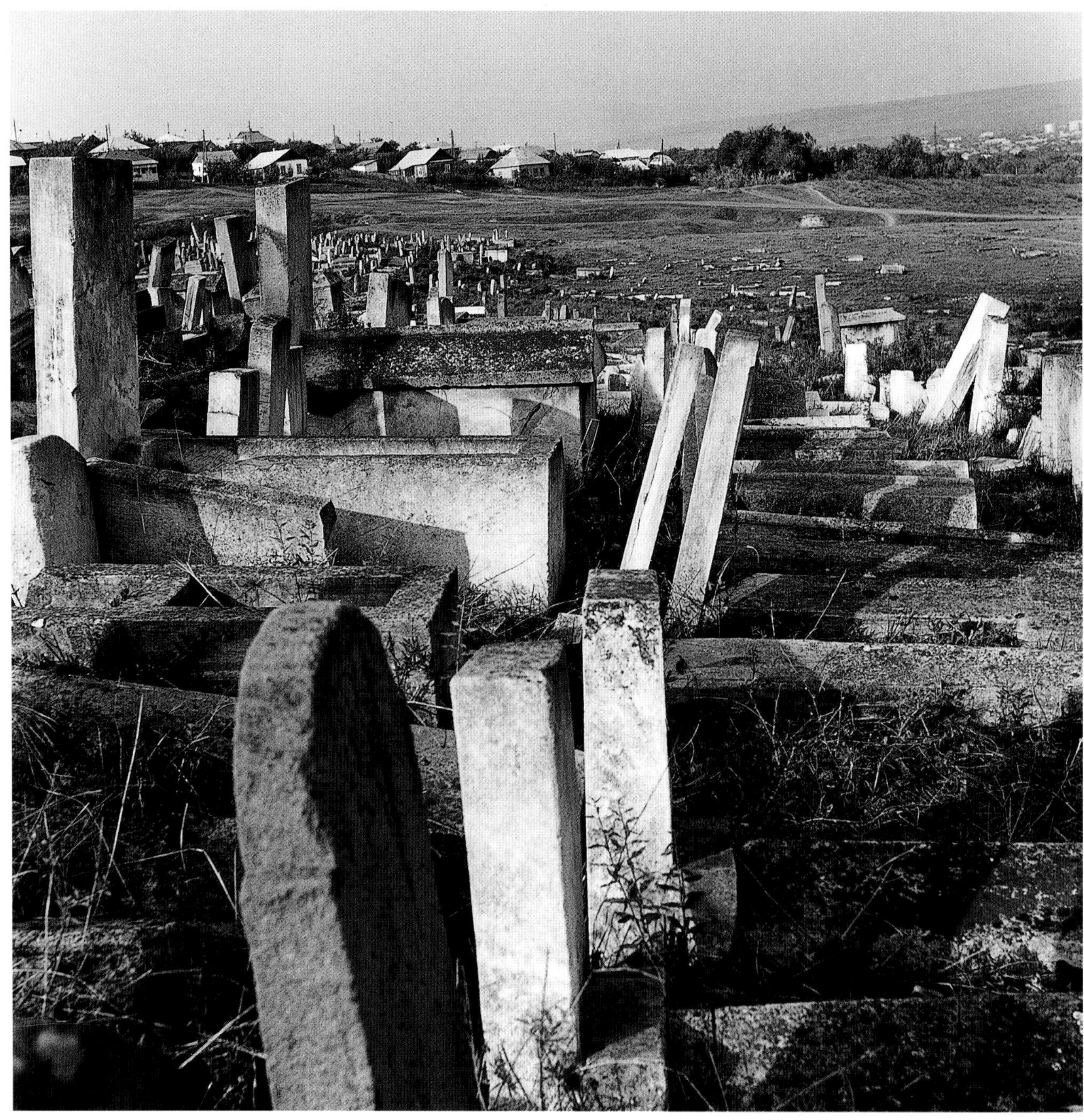

Beltsy Cemetery.

Opposite:
Beltsy. Early 1900s.
The Torah with lions opening and guarding the ark.

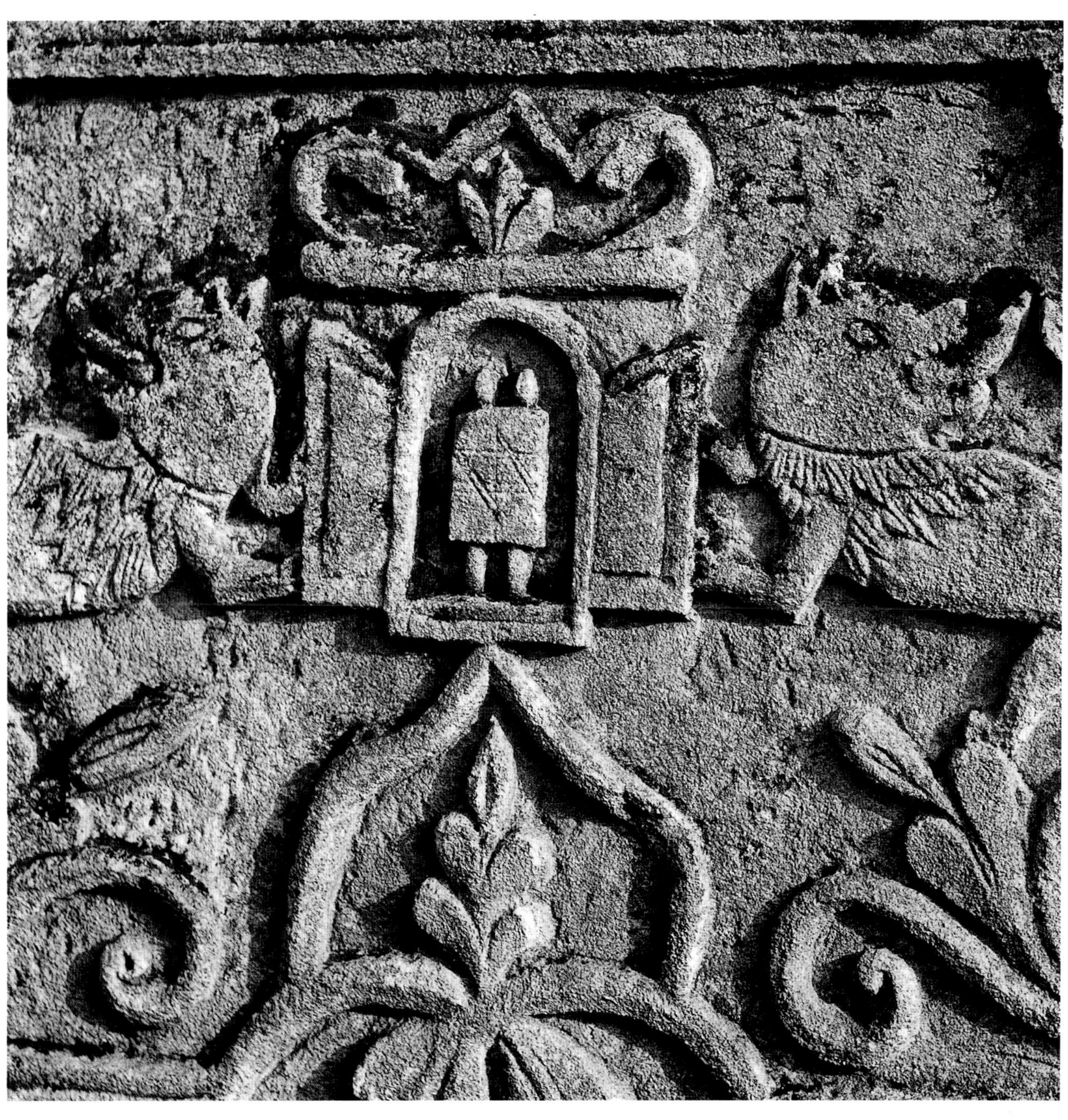

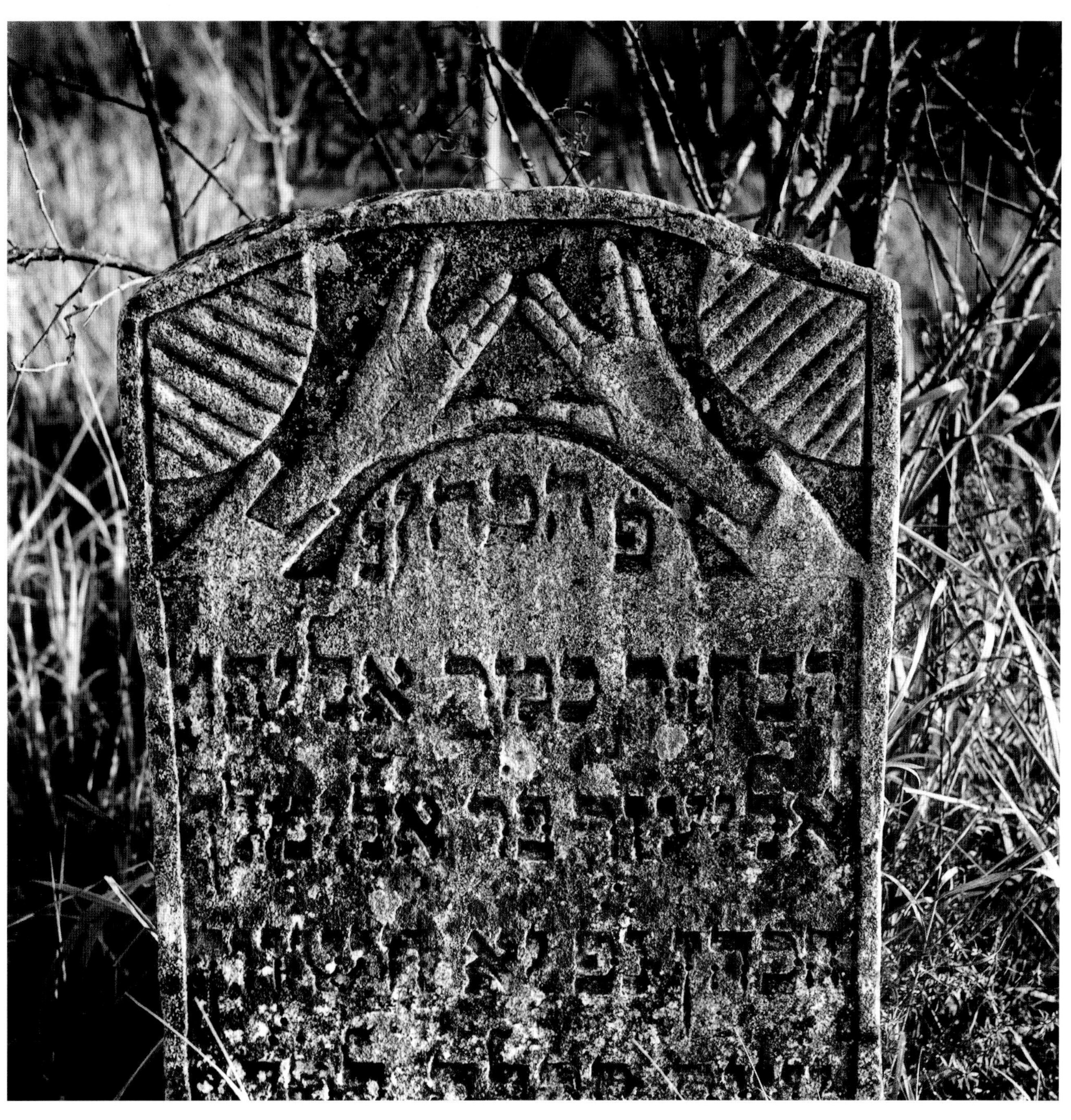

Kalarash. Between 1850 and 1900.

Hands in the ritual Cohain (priestly) benediction. The arms are dressed in a tailored shirt or robe. Semi curricular suns radiate from both corners.

Here lies a young man Eliahu Eleazar.

Opposite:

Detail.

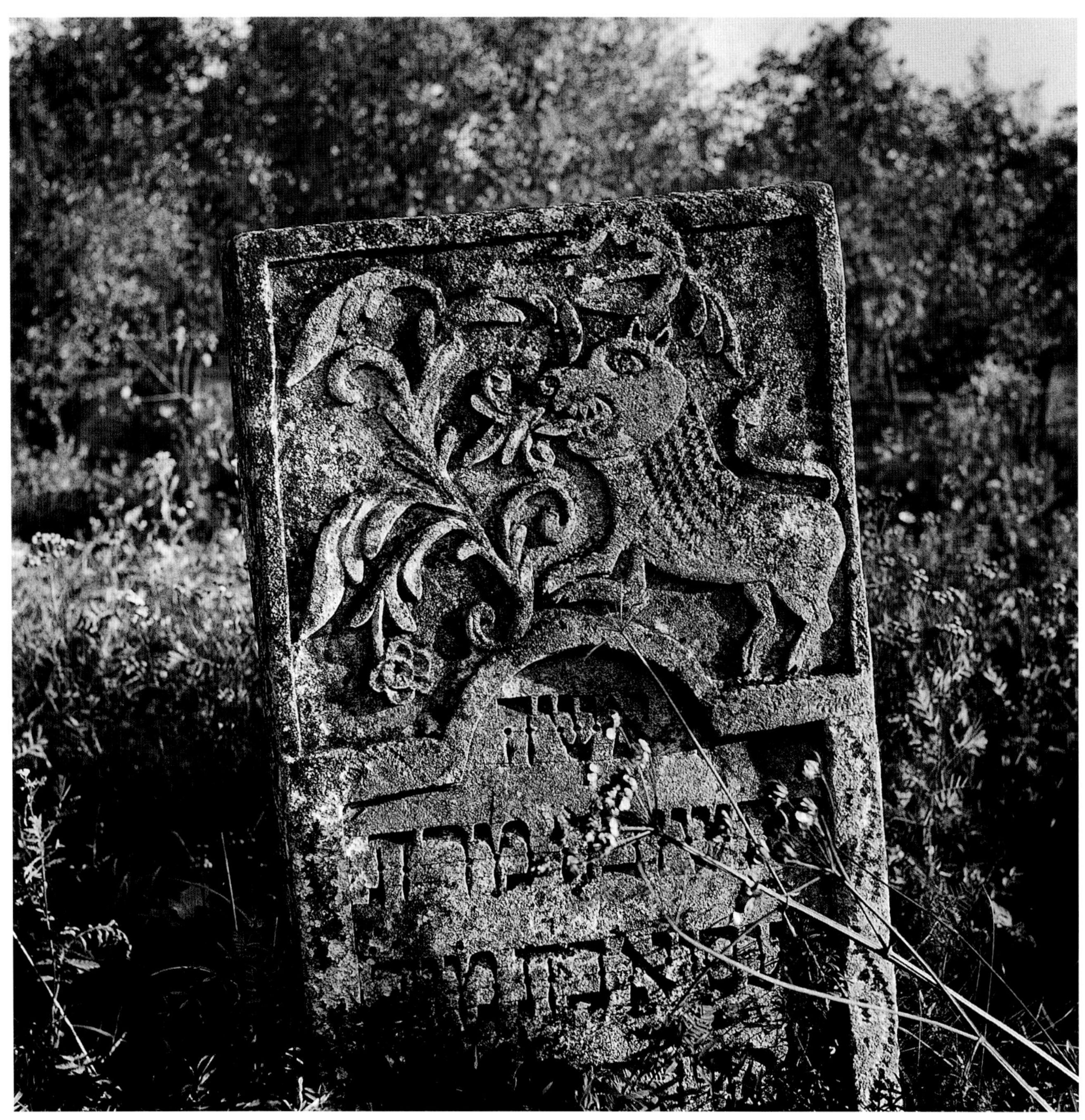

Kalarash. 1860s.

A lion catching a butterfly.

The daughter of [illegible].

Opposite:

Orgeyev. 1849.

A fallen or upside-down flower and stem in the center, flanked by upright ones.

Yehuda Leib, son of Dov. Died seven days into Teves, 5609.

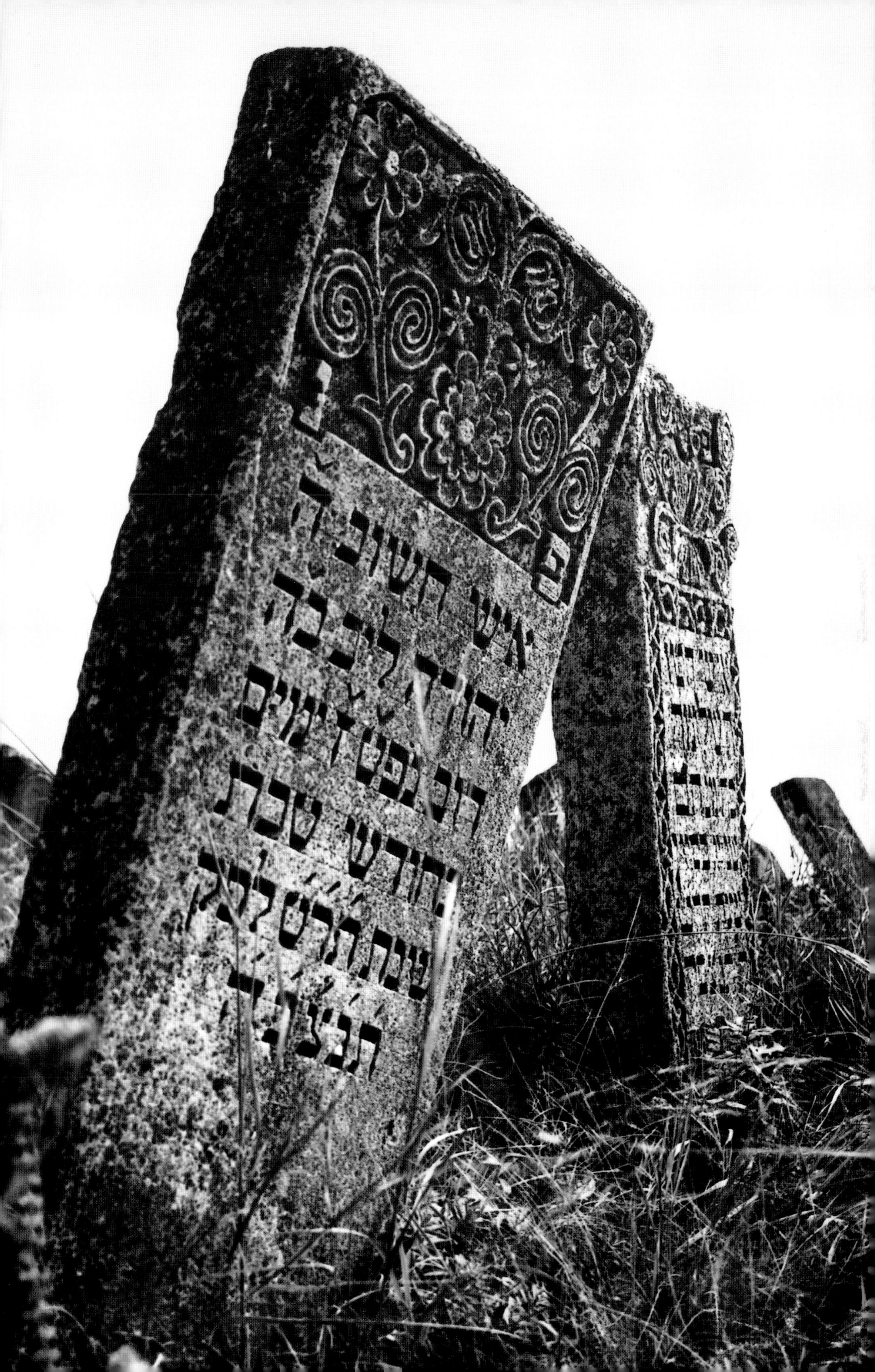
פ נ
איש חשוב
חודש שבט

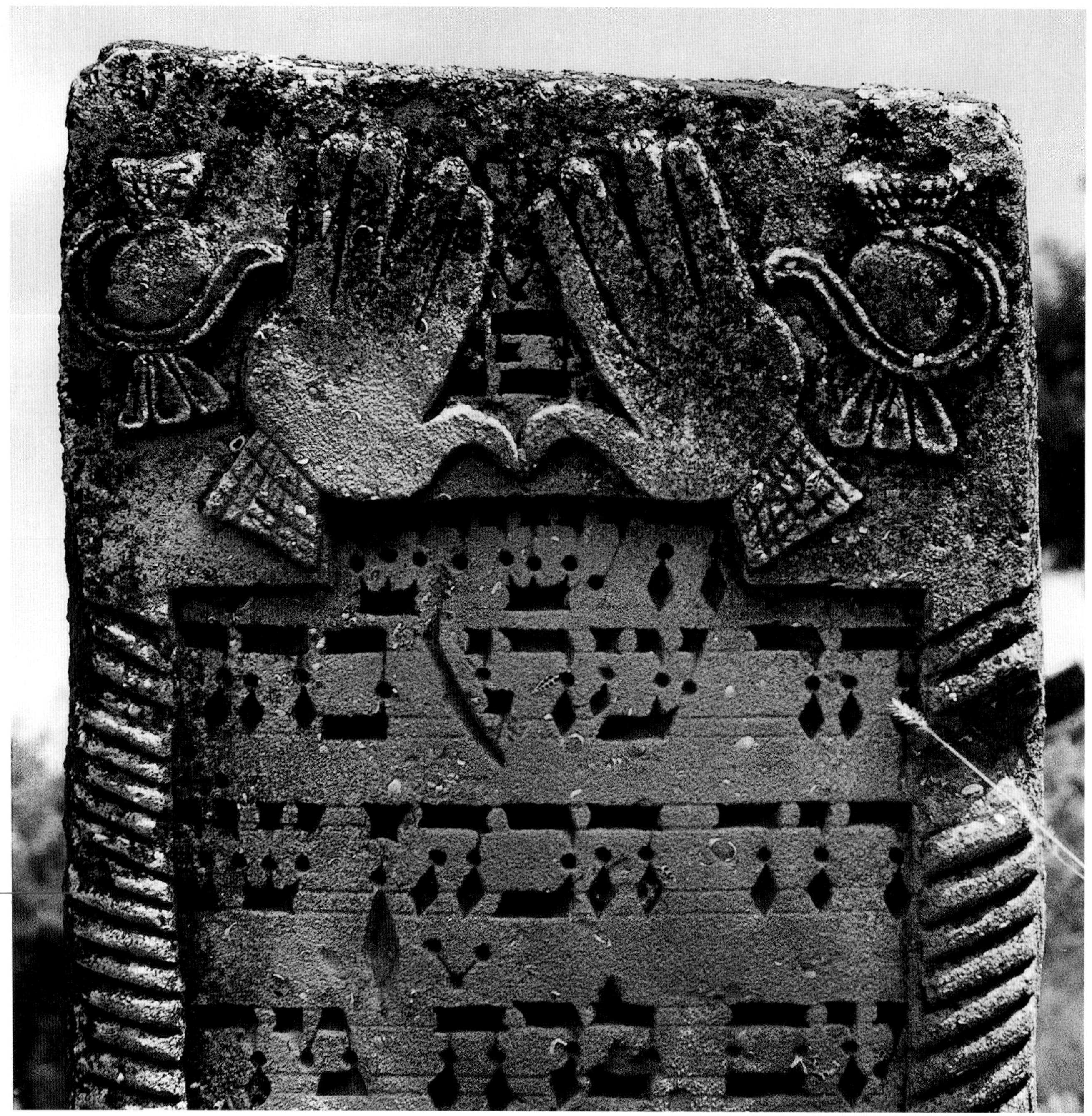

Orgeyev. 1838.

Praying Cohain hands with cuffs, flanked by pitchers.
An old man, a Cohain.
Azariel son of David. Died in Mar Cheshvan, on the first day of the year.

Opposite:

Orgeyev. 1895.

Detail of a lamb.
Eleazar Zvi, son of Avigdor Shabtai.

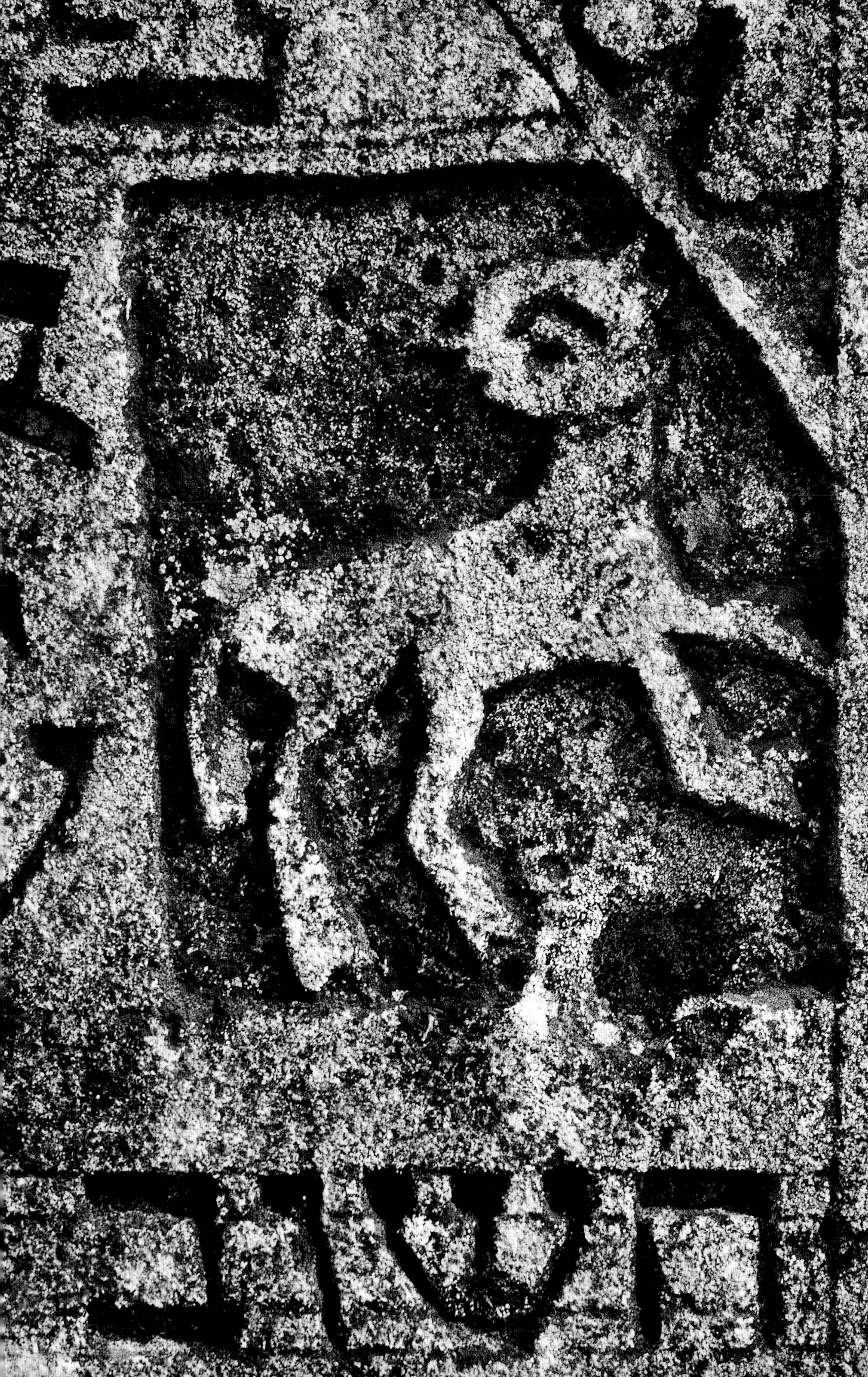

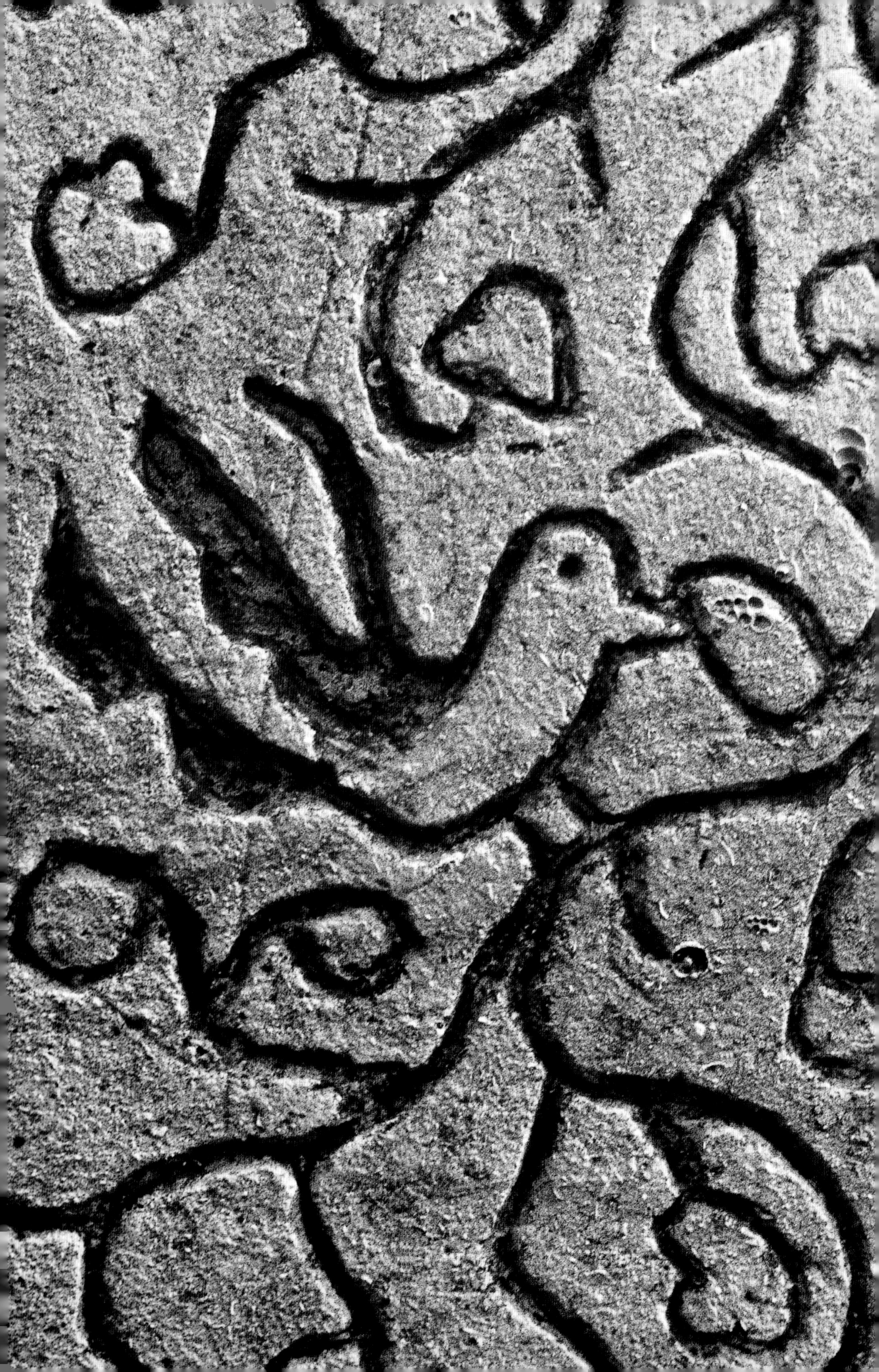

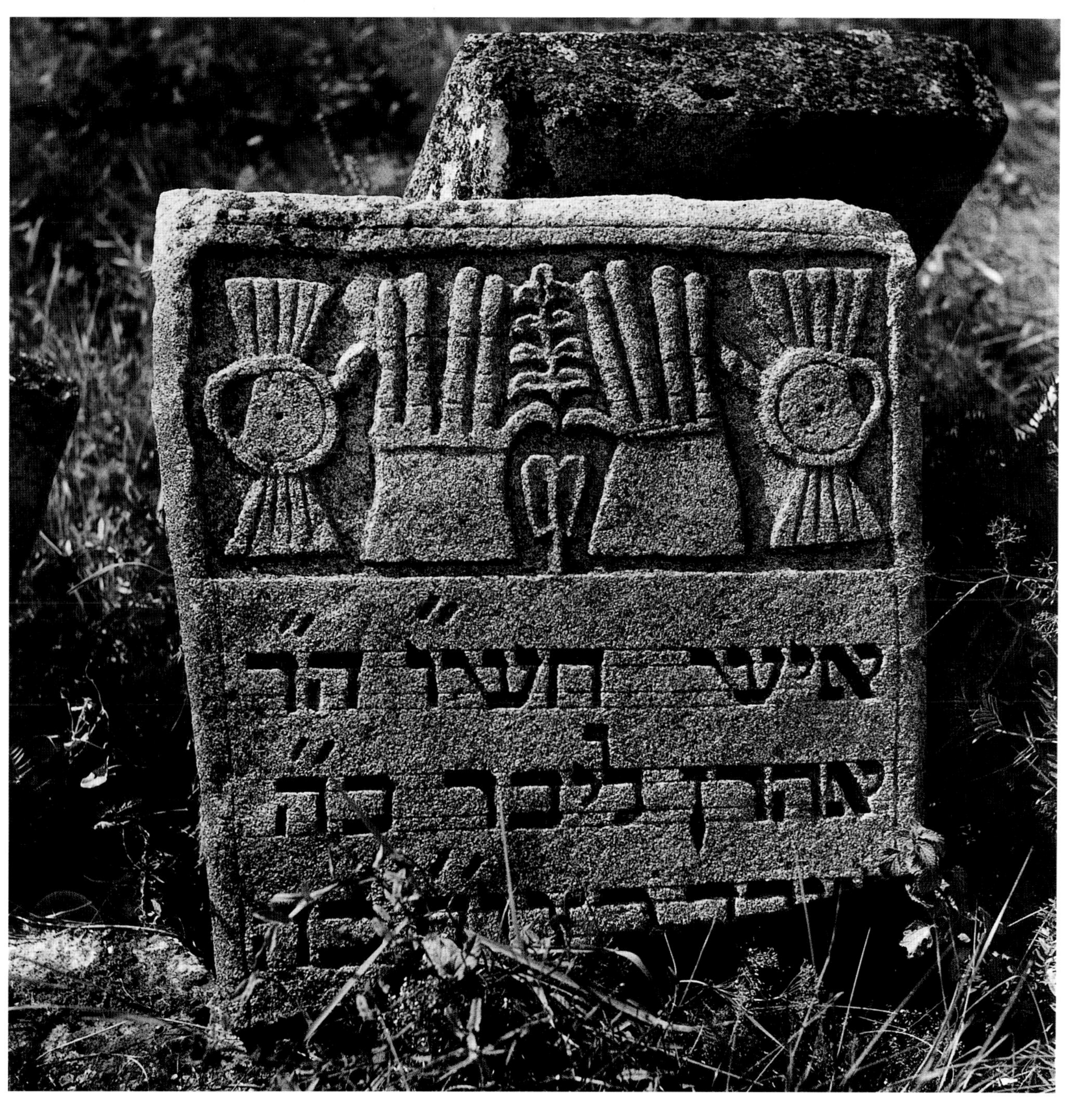

Orgeyev. 1800s.

Cohain hands in prayer surrounding the staff of Aaron and flanked by Levite pitchers.

The important man, our master Aaron Lieber.

Opposite:

Oregeyev. Late 1800s.

Bird surrounded by branches.

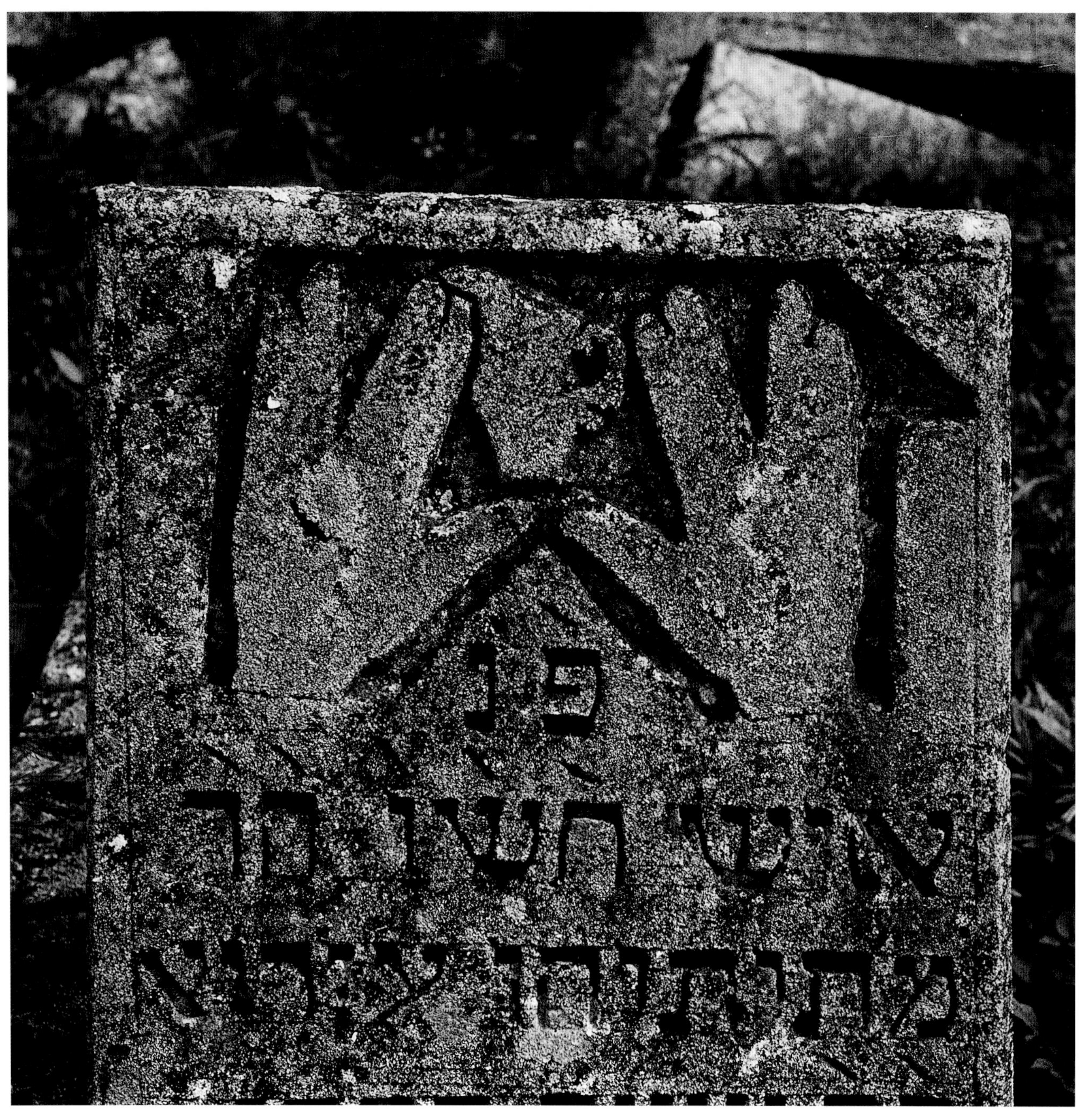

Orgeyev, 1898.

Cohain hands with a small pitcher.

An important person. Mattiyahu Ezra, a Cohain.

Opposite:

Orgeyev. 1800s.

Stylized Cohain hands in prayer surrounded by an abstract border.

Monas Moishe, son of Chaim Katz.

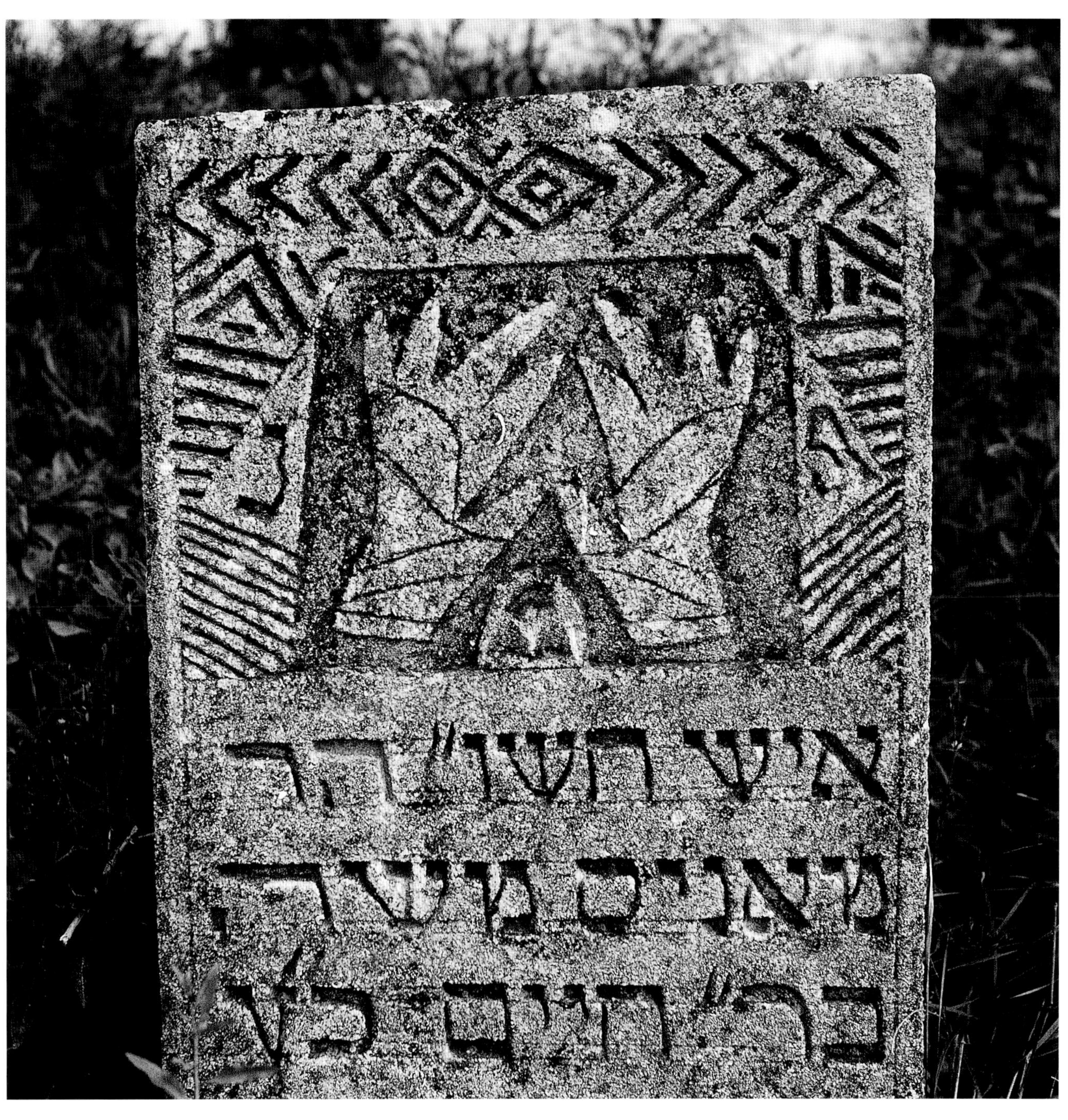

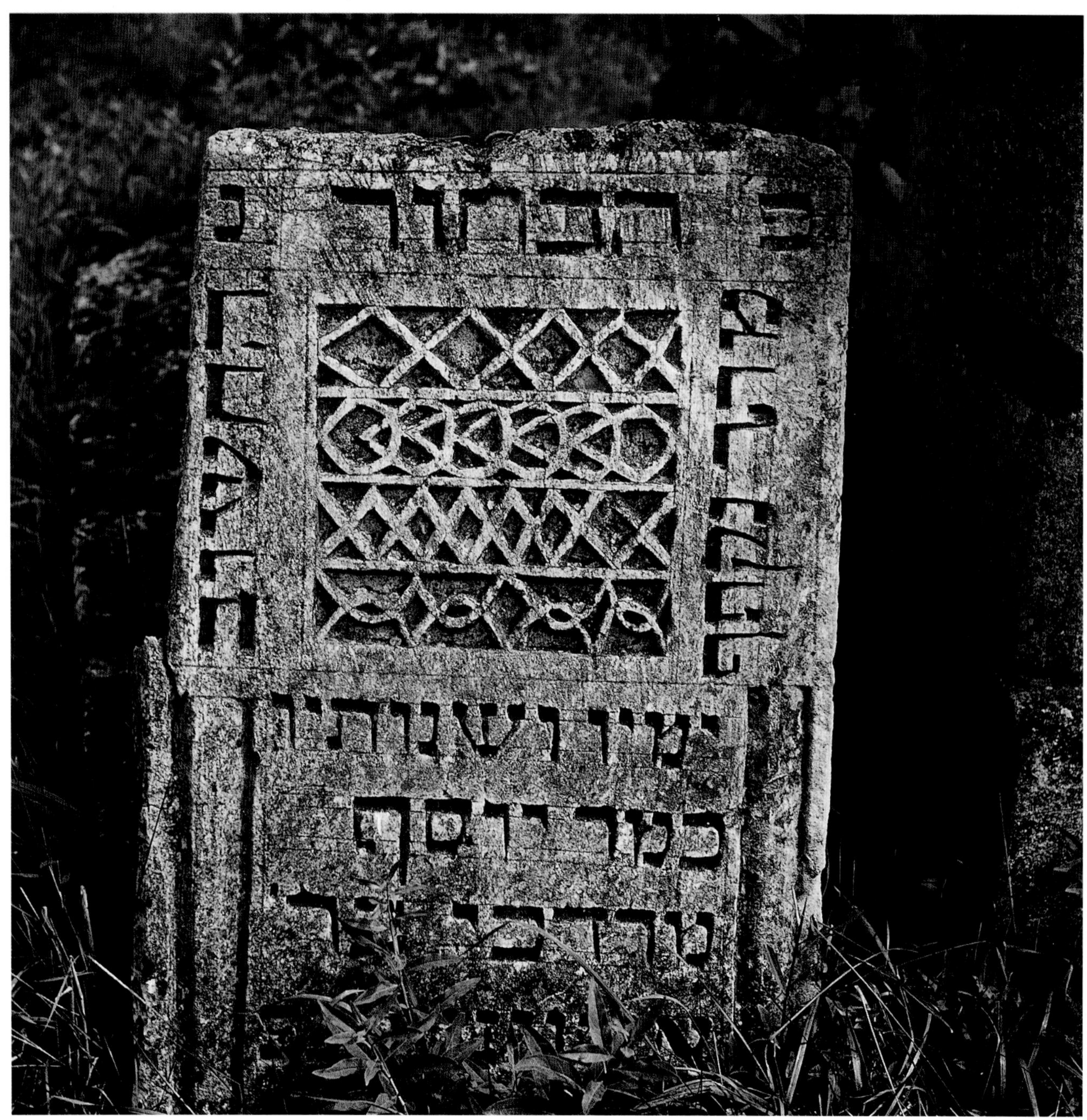

Orgeyev. Late 1800s.

A geometric design as a counterweight to the Hebrew script.

An important young man. He was cut down in his days and his years, Mr. Joseph Mordechai.

Opposite:

Orgeyev Cemetery. Late 1800s.

In the middle: *Hetta Lieber, daughter of Eleazar. Died two days into month of Siban 5654.* Stone on the left: *Hanna Bastiya, daughter of Zvi, died eighteenth day of Cheshvan, 5654.* Front right: *Pessa Mundel, daughter of Moishe Yehuda, died eigthteenth day of Tomas, 5658.*

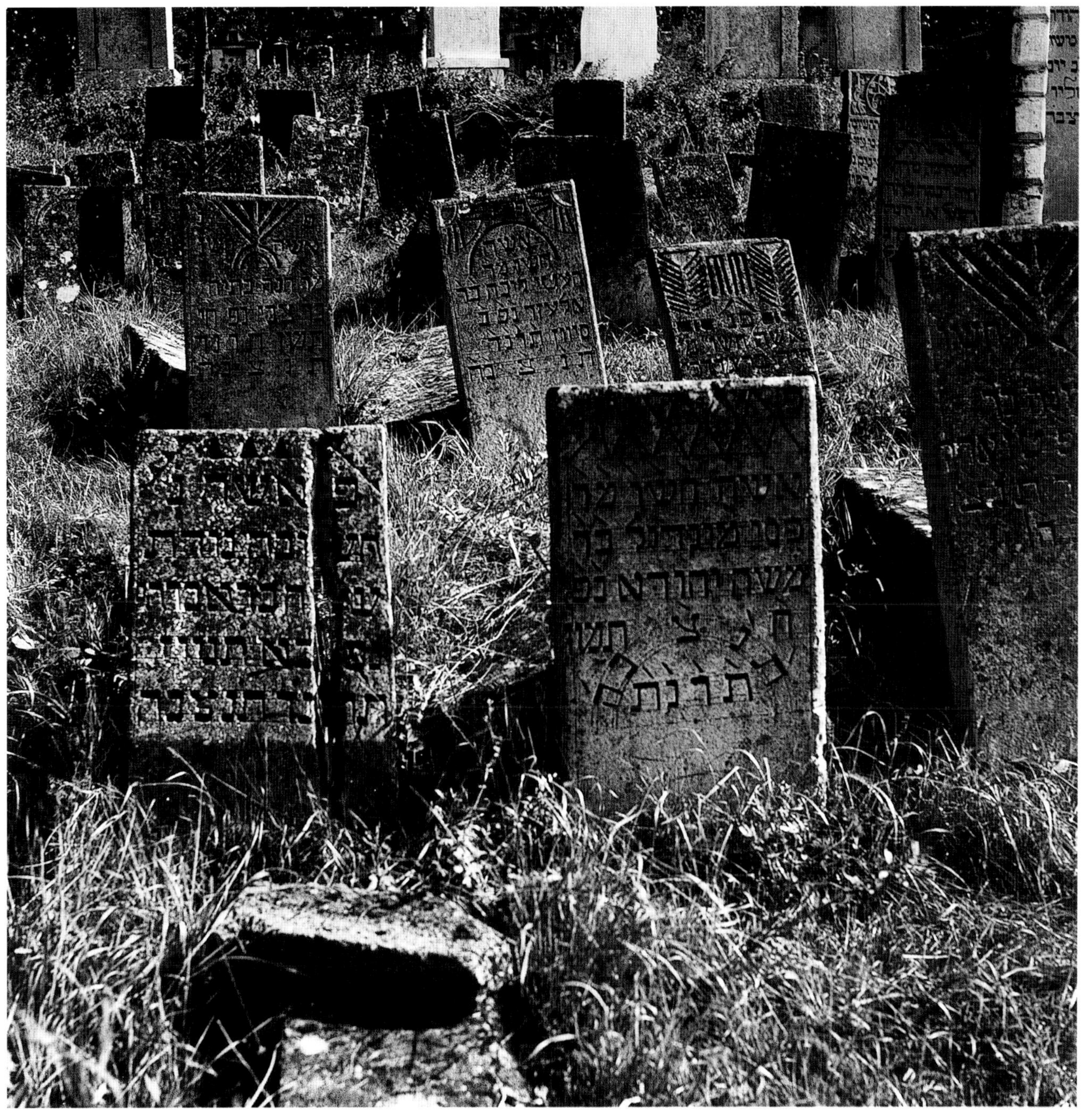

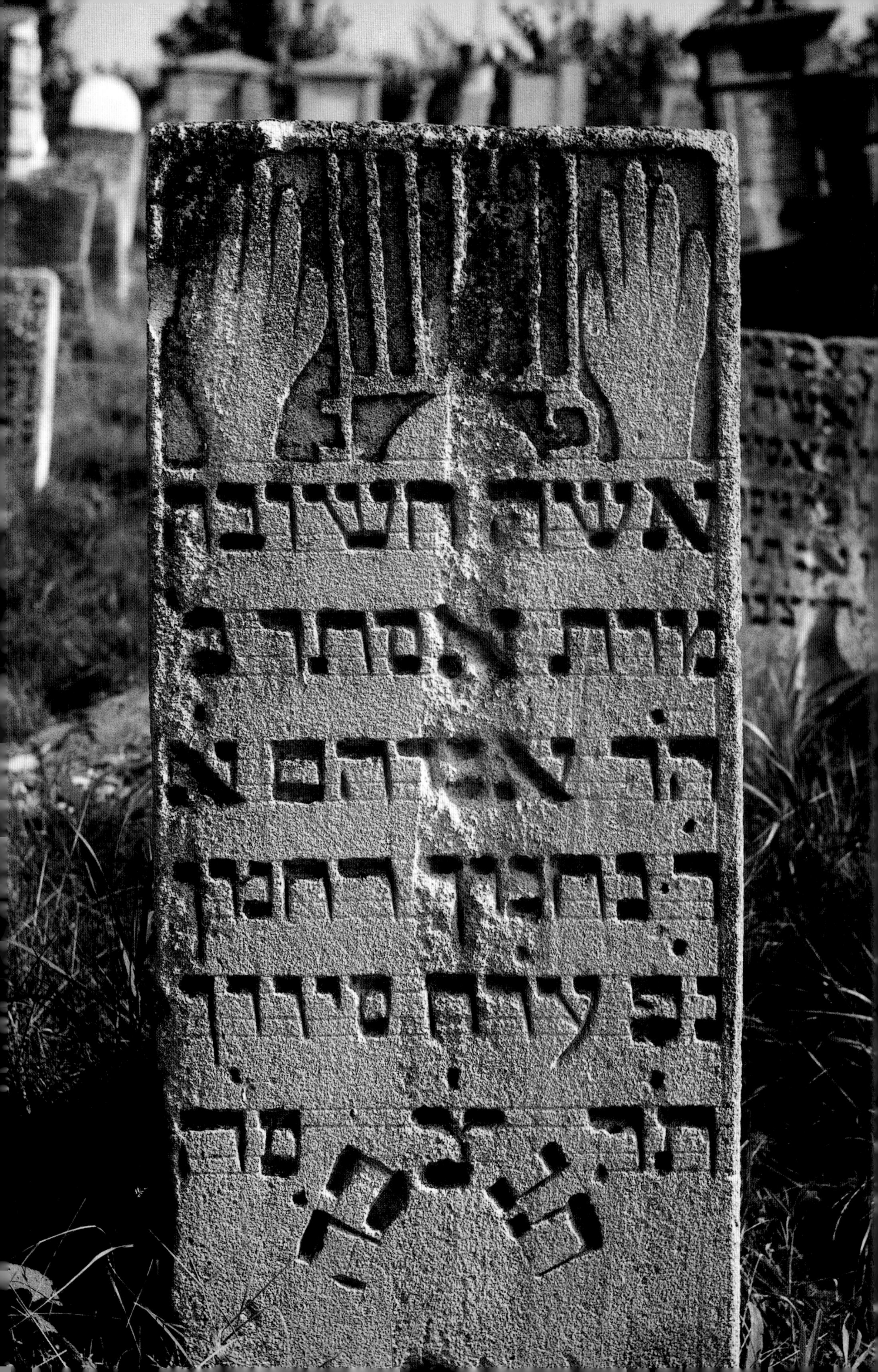
פ נ
אשה חשובה
מרת אסתר ב
נפ ערח סיון

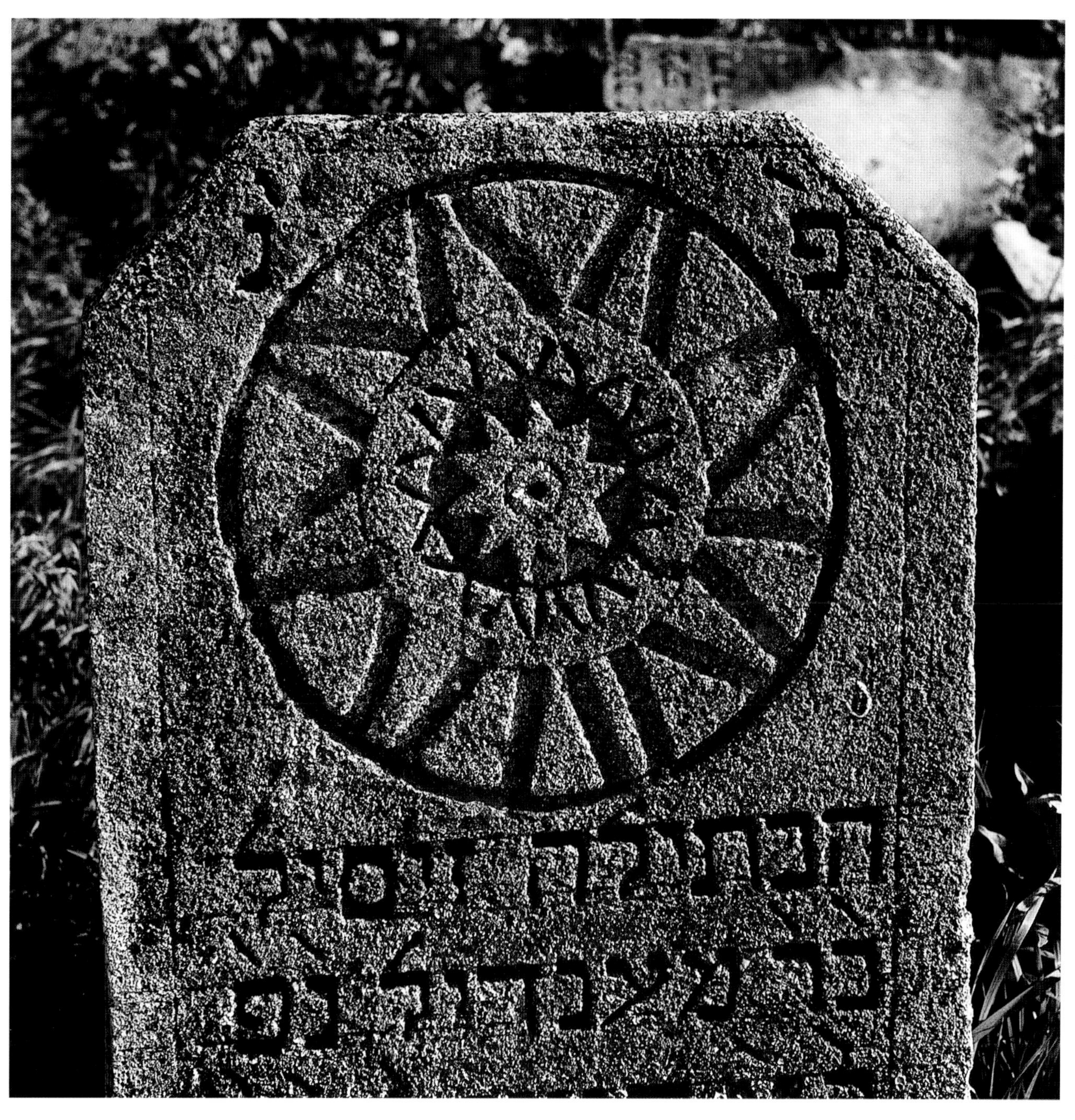

Orgeyev. Late 1800s.

Sun or flower image.

The very young woman [maiden] *Zissel* ["sweetness"], *daughter of Mendel.*

Opposite:

Orgeyev. Late 1800s.

A seven branched menorah with praying hands.

Esther, daughter of Abraham. Let her soul be embraced in the bond of life.

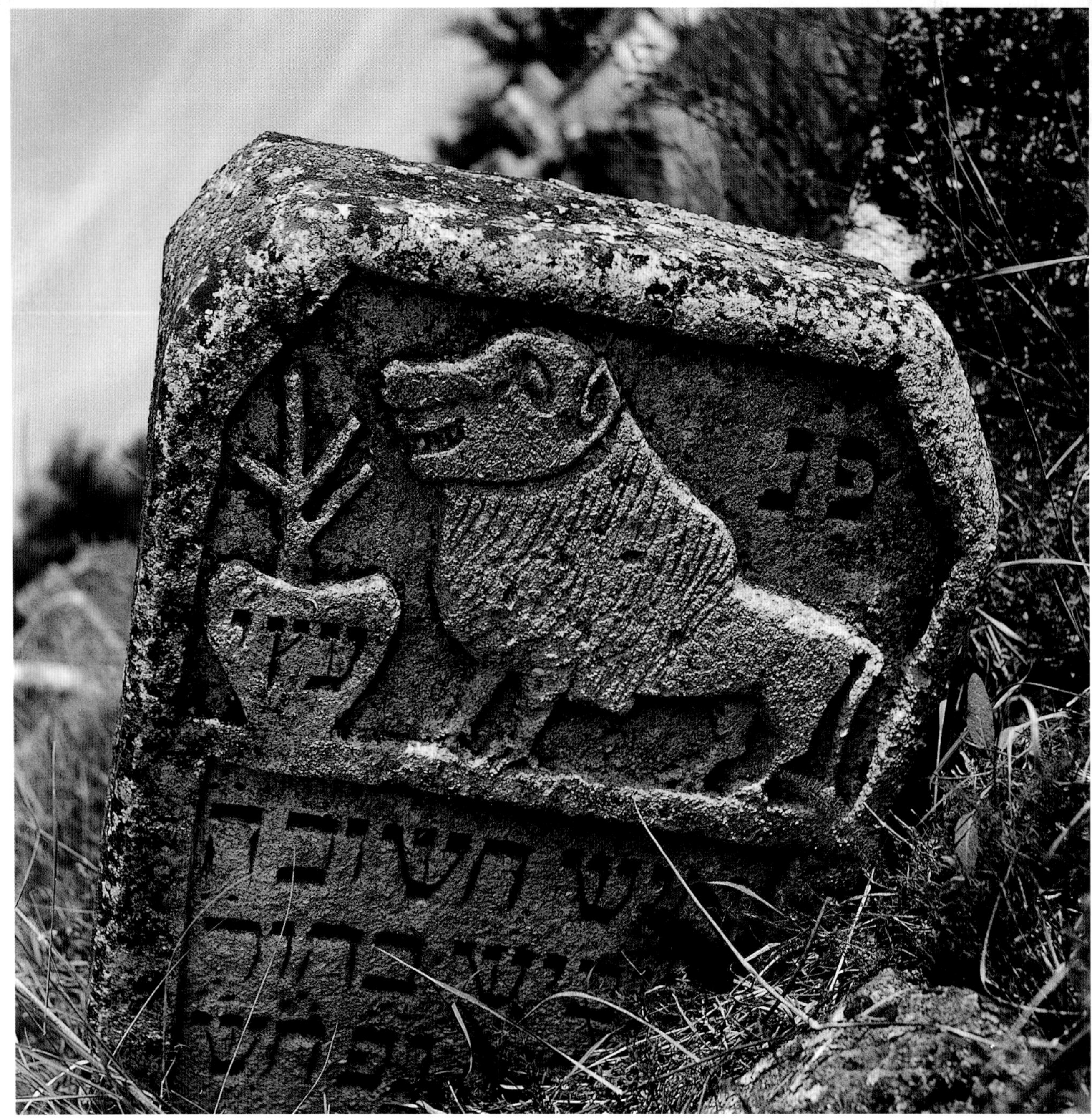

Orgeyev. Early 1800s.

A lion with a broad chest beside the Tree of Life bare of leaves, also called the Tree of God. A man's tombstone. At right, above the lion, it reads "Here lies" and under the tree is inscribed "my tree."

Opposite:

Kishinev. 1890.

The tombstone of a woman, decorated with carpenter's tools— a plane (on the left), a saw (on the right), and a carpenter's square (center, above the inscription "Here lies").

Shendel, daughter of Shimon. Died seven days into Tomas.

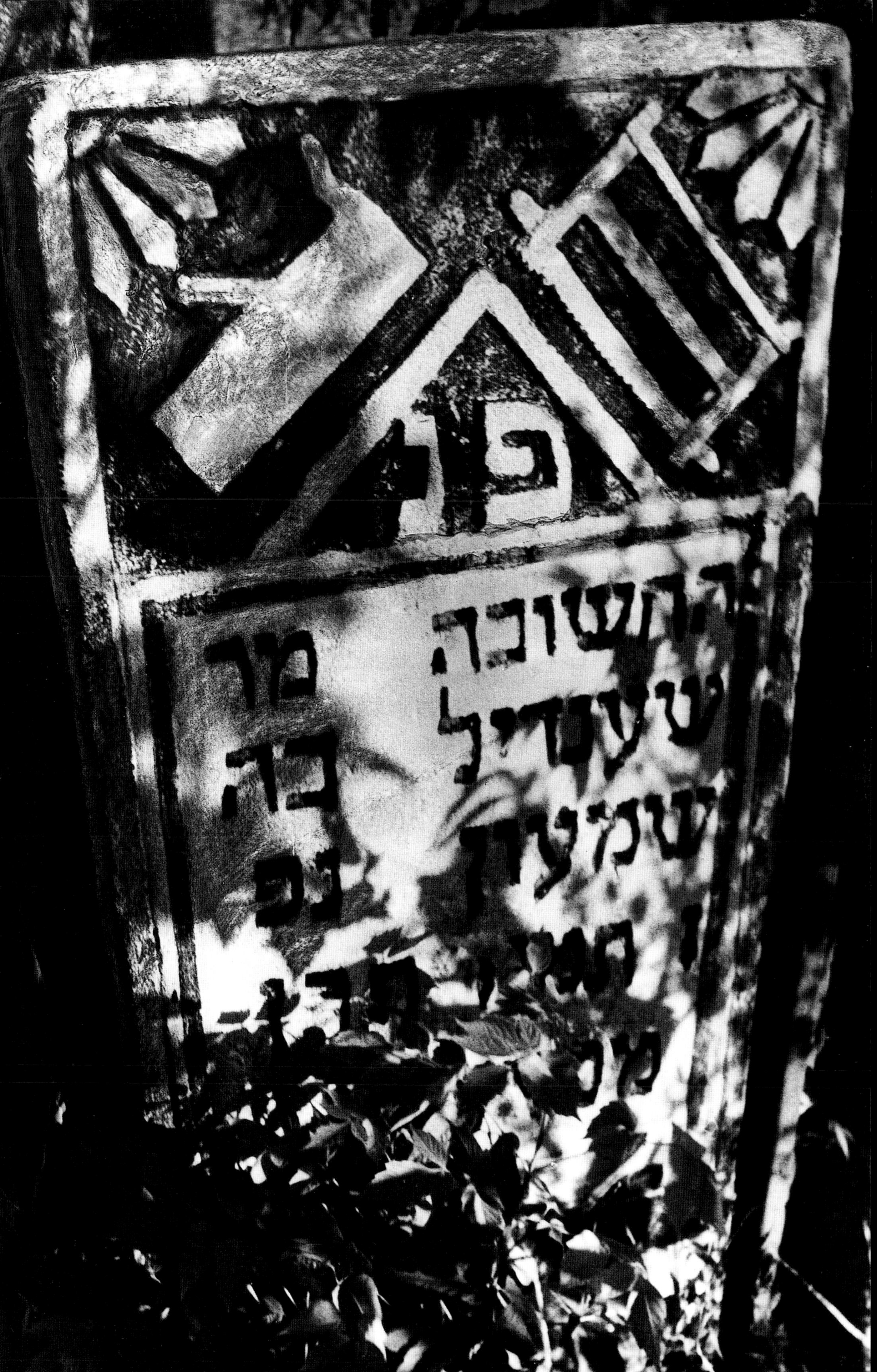

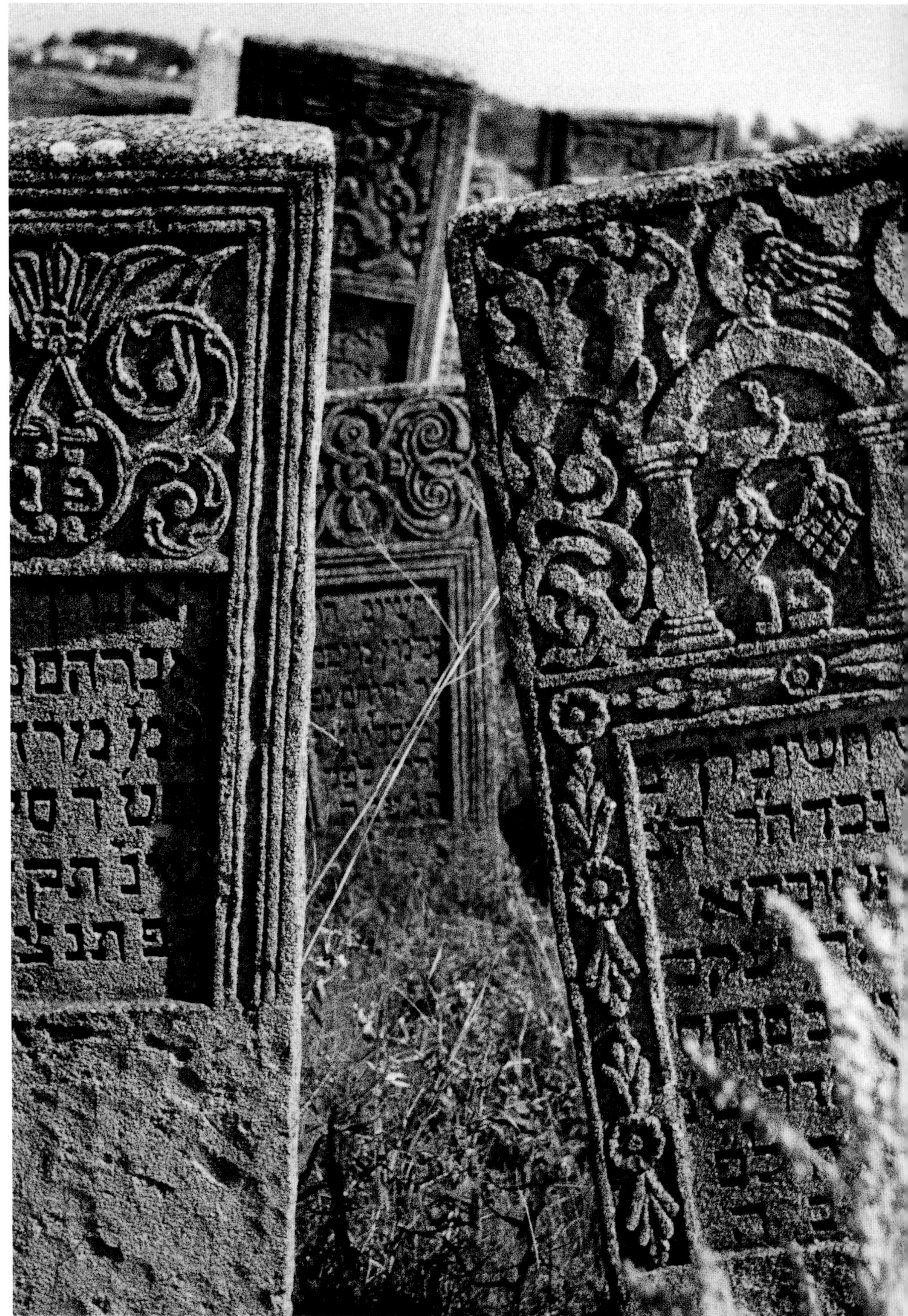

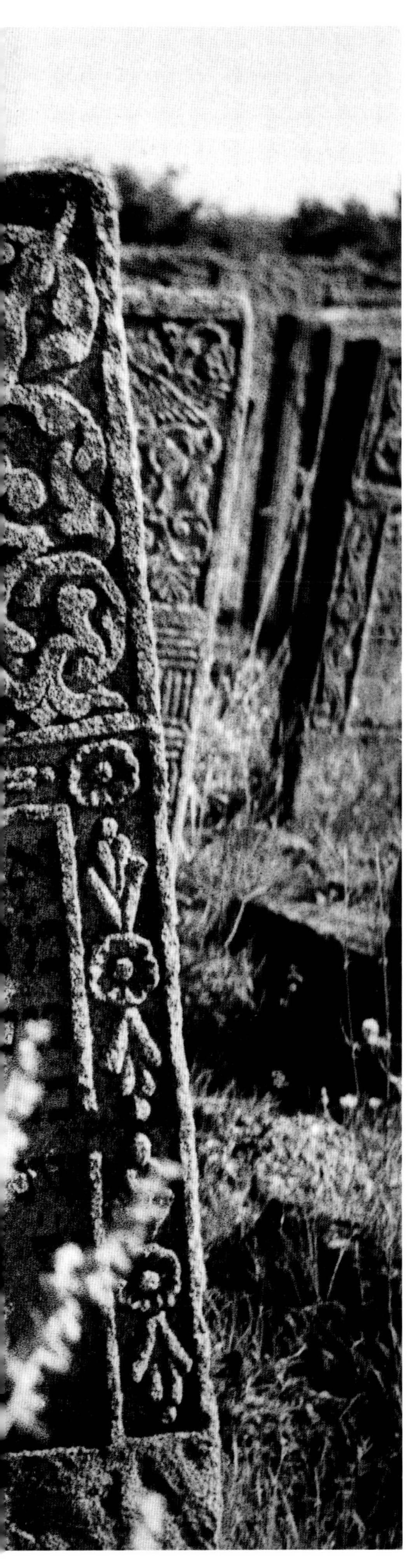

Kishinev. 1830s.

In the foreground, a staff bearing grapes under an arch. An important person, the grandson of a rabbi.

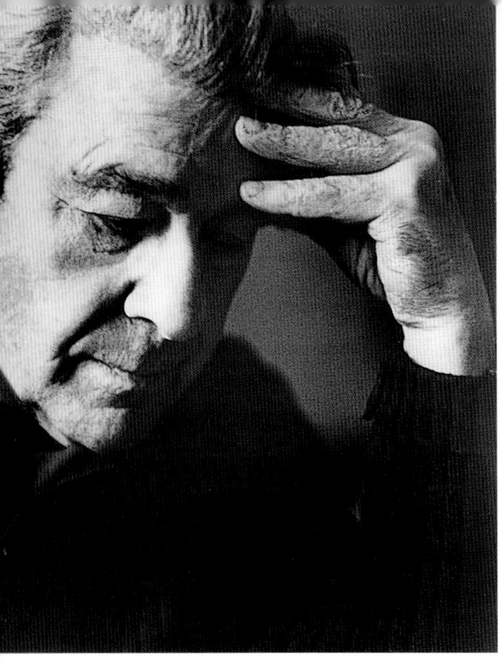

David Goberman

The photographer, artist, and art critic David Noevich Goberman, the oldest member of the St. Petersburg Union of Russian Artists, is a noted ethnographer who has published nine books dedicated to various aspects of creative folklore. He was born in Minsk in 1912 to a traditional Jewish family. His father, a musician, perished in the Minsk ghetto at the hands of the Nazis. His mother was with her son through her declining years.

Goberman's interest in Jewish tombstones began in childhood. As a young boy he passed the cemetery on his way to *cheder* (Hebrew school) and was drawn to the images carved into the stones. He showed a talent for drawing, studied at the studio of the artist Leontiev, and was sponsored by the artist and sculptor A. Brazer. In 1929, at the conclusion of secondary school, Goberman moved to St. Petersburg. There he received an artistic education at the Institute of Painting, Sculpture, and Architecture of the All Russian Academy of Art. In his fourth year of study, his coursework in the faculty of the history of art was devoted to the stones of the Jewish cemetery in Minsk.

In the postwar years Goberman focused his interest on the tombstones of Ukraine and Moldova, which had not attracted the attention of a researcher. Goberman sought to publish his documentation of the tombstones, which he gathered and organized over many years, but despite the support of prominent colleagues, it was impossible to publish this material within the ideological boundaries of that time.

This present book is one of the first attempts to study the art of stone carving in the region of Ukraine and Moldova. Of the monuments reproduced here, the greater part have disappeared in the decades since the photographs were taken, underlining the importance of these pictures as historical testimony to the genius of popular art. The Goberman Archive was established in 1998 by Anne Halliwell and Kenneth Pushkin to gain recognition for the creative legacy of David Goberman.

Acknowledgments

We wish to thank the following individuals and institutions for their part in realizing this book and the exhibition it accompanies. At the Brooklyn Museum of Art, Arnold Lehman, Director, supplied encouragement and creative vision, which gave the entire project momentum; Barbara Head Milstein, Curator of Photographs, created a superb exhibition; Ken Moser, Chief Conservator, lent his considerable expertise to preparation of the exhibition prints.

Robert Pinsky, Poet Laureate of the United States, provided for the book a beautiful introduction that reads like a poem itself; and Gershon Hundert contributed not only a fine essay but time and experience to the project as a whole. At Rizzoli International Publications we thank Christopher Lyon, Senior Editor, who championed this book from start to finish; and Laura Kleger, Editorial Assistant, who carefully moved the book through production. Kathleen Oginski conceived and executed the superb design. For help in translating and captioning the photographs, recognition and acknowledgment are due to Rabbi Philip Harris Singer, Abba Tor, and Ariel Avrech.

For their generous support of this project, we wish to express our deep thanks and appreciation to Anna M. Pearce and to UJA-Federation of New York. We also extend our gratitude to: Alexander Borovsky, Head of Contempory Art, State Russian Museum; Robert Selzer, Professor of Jewish Studies, Hunter College; Arthur Rosenblatt, National Museum Board; Jan and Warren Adelson; Jay Greenberg; Julia Korn for her help in St. Petersburg; and Barry Podgorsky of Soho Triad Fine Arts.

Finally, our gratitude and love goes to those who helped at various points in the translation, cataloging, organization, and transporting of the photographs: Naria B. A. Halliwell, Matthew Scott-Hansen, and most especially Steve Halliwell. For being there on that first afternoon in St. Petersburg, thanks to Eli B. A. Halliwell and J. J. Ramberg.

— ANNE SOMMERFELD HALLIWELL & KENNETH A. PUSHKIN

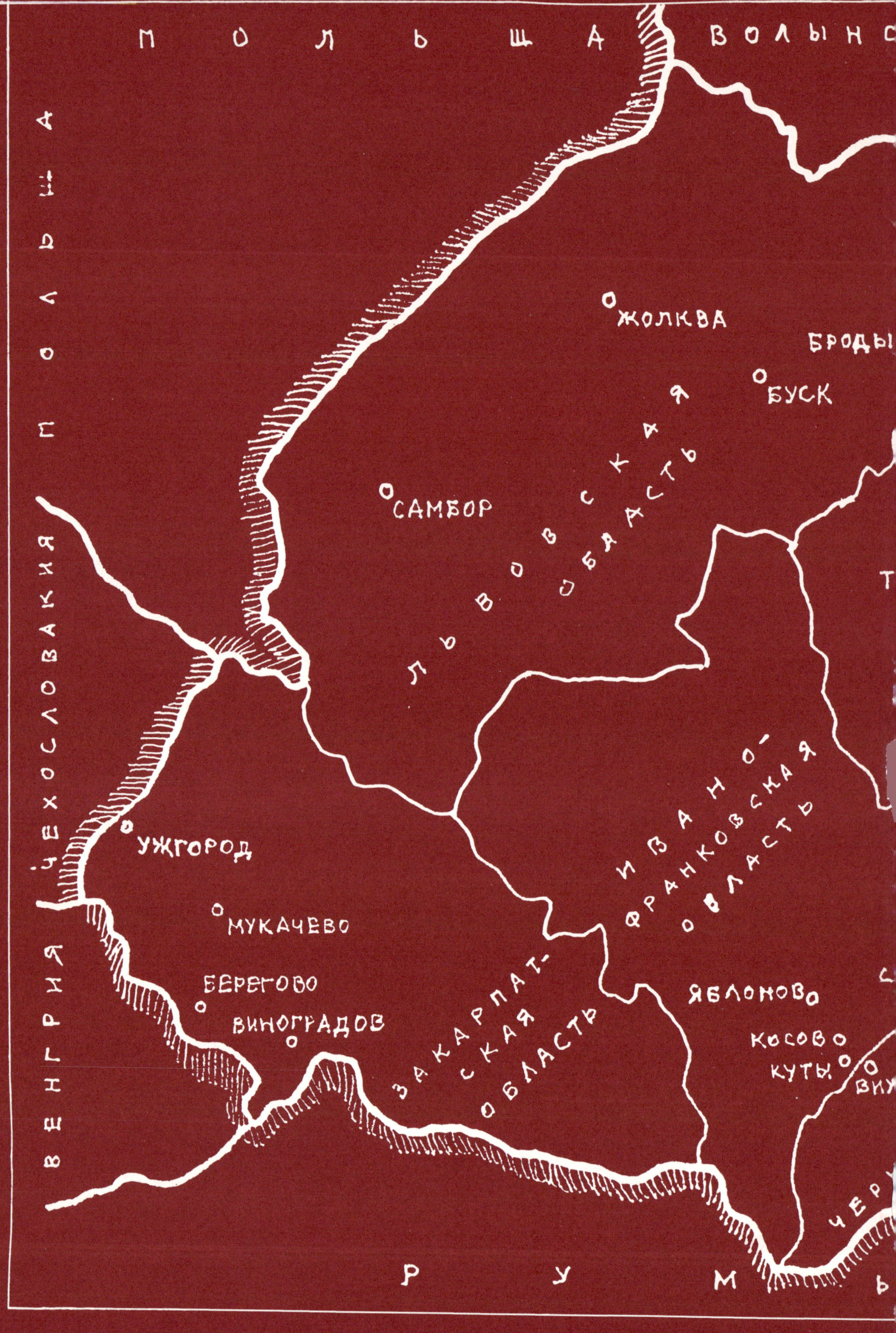
ПОЛЬЩА
ВОЛЫНС
ПОЛЬША
ЧЕХОСЛОВАКИЯ
ВЕНГРИЯ
ЖОЛКВА
БРОДЫ
БУСК
ЛЬВОВСКАЯ ОБЛАСТЬ
САМБОР
ИВАНО-ФРАНКОВСКАЯ ОБЛАСТЬ
УЖГОРОД
МУКАЧЕВО
БЕРЕГОВО
ВИНОГРАДОВ
ЗАКАРПАТСКАЯ ОБЛАСТЬ
ЯБЛОНОВО
КОСОВО
КУТЫ
ВИЖ
ЧЕР
РУМ